DESIGNING DYNAMIC ORGANIZATIONS

A Hands-On Guide
for Leaders
at All Levels

Jay Galbraith

Diane Downey

Amy Kates

American Management Association

New York • Atlanta • Brussels • Buenos Aires • Chicago • London • Mexico City • San Francisco
Shanghai • Tokyo • Toronto • Washington, D.C.

Special discounts on bulk quantities of AMACOM books are available to corporations, professional associations, and other organizations. For details, contact Special Sales Department, AMACOM, a division of American Management Association, 1601 Broadway, New York, NY 10019.
Tel.: 800-250-5308 Fax: 518-891-2372.
Web site: www.amacombooks.org

This publication is designed to provide accurate and authoritative information in regard to the subject matter covered. It is sold with the understanding that the publisher is not engaged in rendering legal, accounting, or other professional service. If legal advice or other expert assistance is required, the services of a competent professional person should be sought.

Library of Congress Cataloging-in-Publication Data

Galbraith, Jay R.
    Designing dynamic organizations : a hands-on guide for leaders at all levels / Jay Galbraith, Diane Downey, and Amy Kates.
        p.   cm.
Includes bibliographical references and index.
ISBN-10: 0-8144-7119-6
ISBN-13: 978-0-8144-7119-7
    1. Organizational change.   2. Organizational effectiveness.   I. Downey, Diane.   II. Kates, Amy.   III. Title.

HD58.8 .G344 2001
658.4'06—dc21   2001041391

Printing number

20 19 18 17 16 15 14

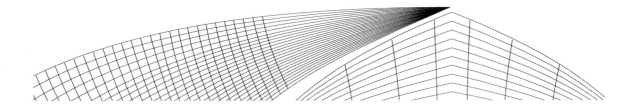

CONTENTS

Preface vii
    What Is an Organization? xi
    Who Should Read This Book xi
    Organization of the Book xii

Acknowledgments xvii

Chapter One   Getting Started 1

    Organization Design 2
    The Reconfigurable Organization 4
    Deciding When to Redesign 8
    The Design Process 9
    The Case for a Participative Process 12
    Summary 17

Chapter Two   Determining the Design Framework 22

    Translating the Strategy Into Design Criteria 25
    Clarifying Limits and Assumptions 30

Assessing the Current State   32
Summary   45

Chapter Three   Designing the Structure   58

Structural Concepts   62
Organizational Roles   81
Leadership Roles   90
Testing the Design   93
Using a Participative Process: Mapping the Structure   99
Design and Implementation Governance: Working Through
   the Details   114
Summary   120

Chapter Four   Processes and Lateral Capability   134

Lateral Capability   138
Networks   141
Lateral Processes   151
Teams   156
Integrative Roles   165
Matrix Structures   169
Building Lateral Capability   174
Summary   177

Chapter Five   Defining and Rewarding Success   189

Metrics   191
Values and Behaviors   199
Compensation   202
Rewards and Recognition   212
Summary   219

Chapter Six   People Practices   227

Staffing the New Organization   230
Assessing for Learning Aptitude   238

Performance Feedback   245
From Training to Learning   249
Summary   249

Chapter Seven   Implementation   253

Planning   254
Managing Skepticism   261
Assimilating Into the Organization   264

Conclusion   271

Glossary of Terms   272

Bibliography   276

Index   281

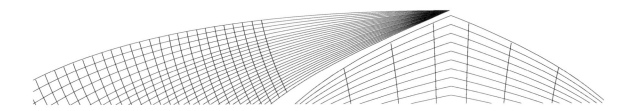

PREFACE

CASE STUDY

Gardenville had never experienced anything like the night of November 27. At 7:00 P.M. the main water line burst under Duggal Street, and the basements of many of Gardenville's shops and homes quickly began to fill with freezing water. At 9:00 P.M. a fire broke out during the second shift at the factory, which was located just on the edge of town where many of the town's Mexican immigrants worked. Most of the volunteer fire department was downtown blocking off streets and helping the utility crews when the call came in about the fire. Half the firefighters were sent over to the factory, and a call for assistance was made to neighboring towns.

Dan Roskobev was one of the first to arrive at the factory. In his twelve years on the first aid squad, he had never seen such confusion. The fire was blazing out of the upper windows on the east side of the building. People were milling about in the 20-degree temperatures, many without coats. Some people looked hurt and were bent over, crying. Others were calling out in Spanish for someone to help the workers who might still be in the factory. Everyone seemed stunned.

The leader of Gardenville's emergency services crew was away for the Thanksgiving weekend. The firefighters were preoccupied with the blaze. Dan decided somebody had to take charge. He asked one of the firefighters to break into a small restaurant that was dark and locked for the night. At least it was a place to get people inside, somewhere warm where he could begin to triage those who were hurt and needed to get to the hospital. Over the next four hours, he tended to minor burns, directed people to find blankets and supplies, and organized car pools among the onlookers to get people to the hospital. He coordinated translators to interpret when the other first aid squads arrived, and when the owner of the restaurant showed up, he convinced him to make coffee for everyone.

That week, an editorial in the county newspaper lauded Dan as "a true hero." It also called for better emergency services resources, training, and coordination, noting, "Our county is not prepared for a major disaster. We can't always count on having a hero show up at the right time."

This is not an uncommon story. When disaster strikes, people step up to the job that needs to be done. They pull together resources that are in short supply, coordinate the actions of others, and make fast decisions. We hail them as heroes. Of course, what works in a crisis is an inefficient and ineffective way to operate all the time. On a day-to-day basis, we count on organizations, not heroes, to ensure that resources are in the right place when needed, and that people have the right skills, tools, and support to carry out their jobs.

Many managers in businesses today complain that they feel as though they are "fighting fires" all the time. They are continually focused on short-term problems without a chance to pull back and think through the consequences of options and decisions. Rather than analyzing strategic opportunities, planning for business growth, or developing their people, they are caught up in day-to-day "doing."

These pressures often come from external forces. As a manager, you may not face natural disasters with lives at stake in your everyday work, but you often must react quickly to challenges. If you're in a mature company, you probably need to respond to new competitors, consolidations, mergers and acquisitions, global expansion, and e-commerce. If you are a leader of a start-up, you may be struggling with building an infrastructure that will support rapid growth while trying to avoid unnecessary bureaucracy. On top of this, you may also be faced with higher than desired turnover and a shortage of talent to draw upon in the employment marketplace.

Too often, however, it is internal forces that keep managers from attending to long-term, strategic business challenges. Issues that should be resolved at lower levels and decisions that should be made at the front line float up to the leadership level. More time is spent on smoothing internal frictions than on customers, markets, and competitors. Yet, few managers feel confident in their own ability to shape their organizations to be more effective. A survey of the 441 fastest growing U.S. businesses conducted by PriceWaterhouseCoopers in the summer of 2000 found that 32 percent of CEOs believed that their inability to manage or reorganize their business could be "an impediment to growth" during the coming year. Only 10 percent of CEOs felt that way in a similar survey conducted in 1993.[1]

As a leader, you have very few levers of change in your organization. Three key levers are setting the business strategy and vision, choosing the players on the executive team, and designing the organization. Your strategy provides the organization with direction and purpose. The quality of your executive team ensures leadership is evenly distributed and determines how well you sleep at night. The organization design defines the structure, processes, metrics and reward systems, and people practices that will ensure that individual and organizational energy is focused on those activities that support the achievement of the strategy. All levers are equally important, but organization design is frequently the lever given the least attention. If you're reading this book, you may already believe in the value of organization design. But you still may be wondering whether organization design is relevant in a world that is changing so rapidly.

The pace of change has been used as a reason for arguing, "If I hire the right people, they'll figure it out themselves." The story at the beginning of this chapter illustrates that while good people are important, they don't act in isolation. Organization design *is the means for creating a community of collective effort that yields more than the sum of each individual's efforts and results.* The organization's structures, processes, and practices channel and shape people's behavior and energy. The values and culture of the organization influence interpersonal interactions and determine which decisions get made. The form of the organization can enable or inhibit people's innate desire to do good work on a daily basis. As a leader, you have the opportunity, and the responsibility, to structure these relationships so that people find it easy to collaborate, innovate, and achieve.

Throughout the 1990s, there were numerous articles in the business and popular press on the emerging organizational forms that were destined to replace the traditional organization. A number of works came out that applied what had been learned about systems in the physical and biological world to organizational systems. The interest in the fields of complexity and chaos theory introduced concepts of organic growth and change into the study of organization design and structure. In this theory, chaos is defined as the inevitable state of a system as it moves away from order. Although there appears to be turbulence without any predictable form, chaos theory predicts that forces will come into play that will create a new order, what some have termed "order without predictability."[2]

The idea of self-organizing, self-renewing, and adaptive organizations is appealing to managers trying to create organizations that are responsive to a rapidly changing external environment. Some managers have used these new ideas to create more open, flexible organizations that have broken down hierarchical barriers to speed and innovation. Others, however, have used these ideas as an excuse to abdicate their management responsibility for designing and managing their organizations. As a result, many of these managers experienced chaos firsthand!

It is also clear that good ideas and a strong brand are not enough to compensate for the lack of a strong design. Companies that focus on growth without building an organization and without the capabilities that can leverage those good ideas (and abandon them for even better ideas when necessary) tend to fall into cycles of rapid expansion followed by retrenchment, cost cutting, and sometimes demise. For example, Cambridge Technology Partners (CTP), a corporate technology consulting firm specializing in client/server applications, recorded 61 percent compounded growth for its first seven years. Growth goals pushed the firm to pursue projects too large and complex for its capabilities, caused it to abandon a profitable pricing model, diverted attention from building its own technology and human infrastructure, and resulted in its not recognizing the potential of the Internet in the mid-1990s. With its stock price down and staff turnover of 39 percent annually, CTP was forced to pull back in the marketplace to rebuild its internal capabilities.[3]

This book makes the case that in the twenty-first century organization design is more, not less, important. A well-thought-out organization design empowers and enables employees to work in the highly interdependent, team-oriented environments that typify today's business landscape. Further, the clearer the rationale for the design, the more quickly design decisions can be reassessed and modified to respond to external forces.

A recurrent theme in this book is the need for dynamic, reconfigurable organizations that recognize and respond to rapid changes. Organizations exist to execute strategies. Yet few organizations are able to maintain their strategic advantage for long. Success formulas are quickly copied or even surpassed by high-speed competitors. Thomas Jefferson, speaking of the European laws and constitutions that had outlasted their usefulness in the changing world of the early nineteenth century, said, "We might as well require a man to wear still the coat which fitted him as a boy."[4] The same is true of organizations. When strategic advantages don't last long, neither should the organization design. "Ill-fitting coats," as much as poor strategies or the wrong people, inhibit organizations from achieving their goals.

This doesn't mean that change renders the organization design disposable. Employees in many companies feel whiplashed by the constant reorganizations implemented without apparent rhyme or reason. The need for change does mean that the leaders of successful organizations will continually assess their capabilities and purposefully realign them to execute against the opportunities that arise. More important, they will design their organizations to anticipate and accommodate change with the fewest disruptions to customers and employees.

WHAT IS AN ORGANIZATION?

The word *organization* is used frequently throughout this book. An organization for our purposes can be a whole corporation or just one part of it. It can comprise tens of thousands of people or just a few dozen. Each reader will have a different definition depending upon where he or she sits within his or her business. If you are the CEO or equivalent, then the "organization" encompasses the entire business. If you are a division director or head of a function, then your "organization" is the part of the business you have authority to change and impact. Organizations are nested inside one another. A unit of ten people within a large company is an organization both distinct from and a part of the company itself. The smaller the organization, the fewer design choices and decisions there are to make and the more those decisions will be influenced by the surrounding organization. Regardless of size, there are still tremendous opportunities for the leader to shape the organization and improve its effectiveness.

We also use the term to apply to a variety of organizational types. Although the book assumes a business environment, all of the concepts apply equally to not-for-profits and public entities.

WHO SHOULD READ THIS BOOK

The need for this book emerged out of frequent requests to Jay Galbraith and to Downey Associates International, Inc. (DAI) to provide a hands-on guide to organization design. Midlevel and senior managers, in particular, asked for a design guide to translate the concepts that apply to a whole company to their own piece of the organization. This book will enable readers to:

- Make choices about which organizational forms will best support their business strategy.

- Understand the trade-offs and impact of each design decision.

- Introduce flexibility and continuous change without losing the clarity that employees need to function effectively.

This book draws upon Jay Galbraith's written work as well as his experience consulting to clients around the world. The book also reflects the extensive experience that Diane Downey and Amy Kates of DAI have had in assisting clients to assess their organizations, make decisions, and implement new designs. The book takes a consulting rather than a theoretical or academic approach. It is built around the questions we ask our own clients, and it provides the tools to allow managers to assess options and make their own decisions.

This book is written for those who lead an organization and want to be sure that it is aligned to achieve their business strategy, including heads of companies, divisions, or business lines, and midlevel managers responsible for a product, location, or functional area.

The book is also addressed to the human resources (HR) professionals and internal and external organization development consultants who support the organization design process. All of the tools and concepts will be of use to the HR professional assisting a business leader in redesigning the organization. Corporate trainers and other executive education providers will also find the book a straightforward reference to use in their programs.

ORGANIZATION OF THE BOOK

You usually don't have a choice about whether to redesign your organization. The business changes, the strategy changes, and you are no longer positioned to deliver what needs to get done. Too often, however, redesigns are limited to reorganizing the vertical structure—i.e., what can be shown on an organization chart. This book addresses the topic of organization design holistically. The seven chapters are structured around the key decisions that will guide you through the thought process of creating a dynamic, reconfigurable organization.

Chapter One, "Getting Started," provides an overview of the design process and how to effectively involve people from the organization in that process. It answers the questions:

- What is organization design?

- What are the characteristics of dynamic, reconfigurable organizations?

- How do I know when I need to redesign?

- What are the steps in the design process?

- When and how should I involve others?

Chapter Two, "Determining the Design Framework," helps you identify the desired future state, assess the current organization, and determine priorities for change. It answers the questions:

- How does our strategy differentiate us in the market?

- What specific organizational capabilities do we need to deliver on the strategy?

- How big is the gap from where we are today to where we want to be?

Chapter Three, "Designing the Structure," provides a guide to choosing structures and defining new organizational roles. It also provides a case example of a participative process for generating design alternatives. It answers the questions:

- What are my options for organizing the work and people to best meet our strategic design criteria?

- How do we define the critical organizational and individual roles and clarify the interface among them?

- How should I structure participation for generating alternatives?

- What can I do to keep the design momentum going?

Chapter Four, "Processes and Lateral Capability," focuses on how to build strong horizontal connections through networks, processes, integrative roles, and team and matrix structures. It answers the questions:

- How can we best coordinate work across business units?

- How can we create effective integrative mechanisms?

Chapter Five, "Defining and Rewarding Success," summarizes recent thinking in the field of performance measurement, metrics, and compensation and reward practices. It answers the questions:

- How do we measure performance at an individual, team, and organizational level?

- What are the values and behaviors that should define our culture?

- How do we ensure our reward systems align everyone to our strategy?

Chapter Six, "People Practices," highlights decisions in the design of HR systems that can shape the behaviors and mind-sets that support a dynamic, reconfigurable organization. The chapter also provides a case example to illustrate an effective process for staffing the new organization. It answers the questions:

- What is an effective process for placing people into new roles?

- How can we select, manage, and support the development of people who not only have the skills we need today but can be flexible and learn new skills in the future?

Chapter Seven, "Implementation," provides guidance for the implementation process, both from a project management and from a change management standpoint. It answers the questions:

- How can I help my organization make the transition with the least amount of pain?

- What change management practices do I need to employ?

Throughout the book, we refer to a number of roles in the design process.

- *Leader.* The leader is the business head of the organization and the assumed reader of this book. A leader may be the CEO, the director of a function, or the head of a line of business. Whoever is the most senior person in the particular segment of the organization undergoing redesign is the leader.

- *Executive Team.* The executive team is the leader's direct reports. If there are a large number of direct reports, the executive team may be a subset, a "kitchen cabinet," which the leader relies on for advice and counsel.

- *Leadership Team.* We use the term *leadership team* to include a broad group of key positions in the organization beyond the leader's direct reports. In a very small organization, the executive team and leadership team may be one and the same. After the design framework has been determined, the leadership team typically undertakes the majority of the initial design work.

- *Work Groups.* These teams are charged with detailing and reality testing the organization design after initial design work has been completed by the leadership team. They usually comprise representatives from all levels and areas in the organization. An organization may have several work groups, with each focused on a single project, or each work group may have multiple projects and be organized into subgroups. The groups may work on business topics, such as developing a new marketing approach or creating a sales support function, or they might focus on organizational topics, such as communication, metrics and tracking, rewards and recognition, and training.

■ *Steering Committee.* The steering committee comprises the heads of each of the work groups. It provides a parallel governance structure to ensure that the design and change processes move forward in an integrated way and do not get derailed by daily business activities.

In addition to these roles, HR is often a central player in the organization design process. As a member of the executive or leadership team, the HR professional provides an important contribution by raising the "people" implications of the strategy, identifying current state issues, and anticipating how design and implementation options will impact the organization from a human perspective. In addition, the head of the HR function may serve as a design facilitator of the overall design process, as a coach to the leader, or he or she may help to identify skilled external design facilitators who can assist the organization through the process.

The book includes tools (located at the ends of the chapters) to allow you to apply the concepts presented to your own situation and plan your own organization design process. Although the book is organized as a set of linear steps for the sake of clarity, it is not intended to be used as a recipe book. We cannot guarantee that even if you follow the directions exactly, a perfect organization, like a perfect cake, will emerge. Rather, the book should be used as a thought-guide to instill discipline around the questions that need to be asked, the options that must be considered, and the implications that should be planned for at each phase. In many ways reaching the right answer—the right structure, the right process, the right metric—is less important than the quality and depth of the discussions that lead to those answers. To quote Bartlett and Ghoshal, "The key organizational task is not to design the most elegant structure but to capture individual capabilities and motivate the entire organization to respond cooperatively to a complicated and dynamic environment."[5] What can be depicted on a piece of paper is only the beginning. The hard work is in developing the details and negotiating the differences. We envision leadership teams using this book as a catalyst to spark deeper discussions about their own organizations, and HR professionals using it as a guide to coach, challenge, and shepherd their business partners through the design process.

NOTES

1. H. de Lesser, "More Entrepreneurs Take Help of Executive Coaches: CEOs Hope to Gain Edge as Their Businesses Burgeon Amid Sea Changes," *The Wall Street Journal*, September 5, 2000, p. B2.

2. See, for example: S. Brown and K. Eisenhardt, *Competing on the Edge: Strategy as Structured Chaos* (Boston: Harvard Business School Press, 1998); R. Lewin, *Complexity: Life at the Edge of Chaos*, 2nd ed. (Chicago: University of Chicago Press, 2000); R. D. Stacey, *Managing the Unknowable: Strategic Boundaries Between Order and Chaos in Organizations* (San Francisco: Jossey-Bass, 1992); M. Wheatley, *Leadership and the New Science: Discovering Order in a Chaotic World* (San Francisco: Berrett-Koehler, 1999).

3. J. Gordon, "Feeding the Monster: Cambridge Technology Was So Obsessed With Growth That It Forgot How to Build a Business," *Forbes,* September 4, 2000, pp. 70–1.

4. Thomas Jefferson, "Letter to Samuel Kercheval," July 12, 1816.

5. C. Bartlett and S. Ghoshal, "Matrix Management: Not a Structure, a Frame of Mind," *Harvard Business Review*, July/August 1990.

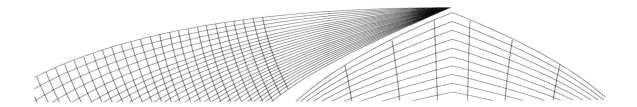

ACKNOWLEDGMENTS

This book is the result of several factors that I have experienced. The first is the reaction that some people had to *Designing Organizations: An Executive Briefing on Strategy, Structure, and Process.* Many people who like conceptual material liked the book. Others found it a "tough read." They asked if there was some way to make the book more understandable. Diane Downey and Amy Kates have been making my work, and the work others do, more understandable for many people for a long time. It seemed natural for us to collaborate on a readable version of *Designing Organizations.*

A second factor was client demand. Many of my clients had asked me if I had any tools or materials that could help them in designing their own organizations. I always had to respond in the negative because I am poor at creating these kinds of materials. As it turned out, Diane and Amy had been taking my work and creating just the kinds of tools and materials that people were asking for. Again, collaboration with them seemed the natural thing to do. But it seemed to be a better idea to pair this book with the new material that I was generating. The result was a revision of *Designing Organizations* and the creation of a useful book like this one to accompany it.

The collaboration with Diane and Amy has been a fruitful one for me. They forced me to articulate my reasoning. Before, many of my thoughts were intuitive. They made them explicit. It also took the help of Sasha Galbraith, my partner. She is good at getting me to surface my thinking. I dedicate this book to her. I want to thank all three of them for working me over.

I hope the result is a useful one for the reader. The combination of this book with its questions and tools will be a great compliment to *Designing Organizations* with its concepts.

—Jay Galbraith

We would like to thank Jay Galbraith for asking us to write this book with him. His thinking about organization design has guided our work with clients for many years. This book has provided a welcome opportunity to document and share how we have used his influential concepts in our daily consulting work to help our clients transform their organizations.

We would also like to thank our colleagues at DAI for their assistance during this project. Sheila Oh and Jenny Martel provided excellent research support. Navid Rahman and Glen Alcantara patiently created and revised all of the graphics for the book. Michael Remson provided invaluable help and encouragement. Finally, we would like to thank all of our clients, from whom we have learned so much, in particular Dave Tierno, former senior partner at Ernst & Young, who read the draft from a client's perspective and gave us honest and useful feedback.

Diane dedicates this book to her parents, Gerda and Ernest Martel. Amy dedicates this book to her husband, Muhamed Saric, and her children, Malik and Elias.

—Diane Downey and Amy Kates

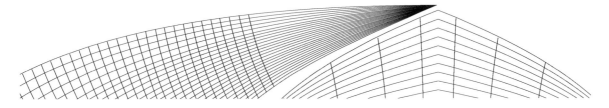

CHAPTER ONE

GETTING STARTED

A s a leader, you can actively shape your organization. It is probably the most important role you have.★

The organization can't be designed from the bottom up. Those on the front lines don't have the broad perspective necessary for making the trade-offs that will affect the whole organization, whether that organization is the entire enterprise or a particular division or department. Although they can and should be involved in the design process to help identify the problems that need to be addressed and provide insight into what customers want, organization design is the responsibility of the leader and the leadership team.

This chapter provides an overview of the design process and explains how to effectively involve people from the organization in that process. It has five sections:

★*Leader* and *manager* are used interchangeably in this book. Although some argue that there are clear differences in the roles, the differences usually depend upon perspective. The tasks of a midlevel manager in a large company would be "management" activities (e.g., focusing on short-term time frames, details, eliminating risks, keeping the organization on time and on budget) compared with those of senior executives. However, for the people who report to that manager, he is their "leader" and expected to act like one (focusing on the big picture, communicating values, motivating and inspiring people, and championing and creating change). For more on the differences between managers and leaders, see J. P. Kotter, *Force for Change: How Leadership Differs From Management* (New York: The Free Press, 1990).

1

- *Organization Design* describes the components of organization design in terms of the "star model."

- *The Reconfigurable Organization* defines the characteristics of organizations that can respond quickly and flexibly to changes in the environment.

- *Deciding When to Redesign* identifies those triggering events that are most likely to initiate a reconsideration of the organization's design.

- *The Design Process* provides an overview of the sequence of events in the design process.

- *The Case for a Participative Process* provides guidelines for involving others in the design process.

ORGANIZATION DESIGN

Organization design is the deliberate process of configuring structures, processes, reward systems, and people practices and policies to create an effective organization capable of achieving the business strategy.

Organization "design" is often used synonymously and incorrectly to mean organization "structure." The organization design process and its outcome, however, are much broader than rearranging the boxes on the organization chart. The star model (Figure 1-1) is a framework for thinking holistically

Figure 1-1. Star model.

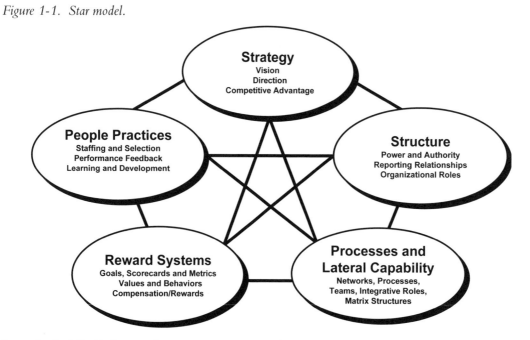

Source: Jay R. Galbraith, *Designing Organizations: An Executive Briefing on Strategy, Structure, and Process* (San Francisco: Jossey-Bass, 1995).

about the five major components of organization design. Each point on the star model represents a major component of organization design.[1] When all points are in alignment, the organization is at its most effective. The structure, processes, rewards, and people practices all support the strategy. The star model serves as the organizing framework for this book and is discussed in detail in each chapter. To provide an overview, each point on the model is briefly defined next.

STRATEGY

The strategy sets the organization's direction. The term is used broadly here to encompass the company's vision and mission as well as its short- and long-term goals. The strategy delineates which products and markets the company will pursue and, as important, those it will not pursue. The strategy specifies the source of competitive advantage for the organization and how the company will differentiate itself in the marketplace.

Strategy is the cornerstone of the organization design process. If the strategy is not clear, or not agreed upon by the leadership team, there are no criteria on which to base other design decisions. Without knowing the goal, it is impossible to make rational choices along the way.

STRUCTURE

The organizational structure determines where formal power and authority are located. It comprises the organizational components, their relationships, and hierarchy. It channels the energy of the organization and provides a "home" and identity for employees. The structure is what is shown on a typical organization chart.

Structural design presents a number of choices for grouping people together at each level of the organization. Typically, departments are formed around functions, products, markets, or regions and then configured into a hierarchy for management and decision making. As important as the structure itself are the roles within the structure. A key part of the design process is defining the responsibilities of each organizational component and clarifying how they are intended to interrelate. To use the metaphor of the human body, the structure is akin to the bones. It sets the shape of the organization and the frame around which everything else is arrayed. The organizational roles can be thought of as the organs and muscles—where the work gets done.

PROCESSES AND LATERAL CAPABILITY

Regardless of how well thought out the organization's structure, it will create some barriers to collaboration. Information and decision making must cross the borders created by the structure. These can be overcome by designing the lateral capabilities—the interpersonal and technological networks, team and matrix relationships, lateral processes, and integrative roles that serve as the "glue" that binds the organization together. To extend the human body metaphor, the lateral organization functions like the body's blood, lymph, and nerves—the connective tissues that transmit knowledge and resources to where they are needed. An organization's lateral capability is the extent to which it can utilize these mechanisms to enhance its flexibility and leverage all its resources.

The networks and processes of the lateral organization cut across department boundaries. They can be informal and reliant upon the relationships of individual managers or formalized into cross-organizational processes and team structures. They can be quickly reconfigured after a few months or they may be in place for years. Process and lateral capability allow the organization to bring together the right people, no matter where they sit in the structure, to solve problems, create opportunities, and respond to challenges.

REWARD SYSTEMS

Metrics help align individual behaviors and performance with the organizational goals. A company's scorecard and system for rewarding people communicate what the company values to employees more clearly than any written statement. The design of metrics and reward and recognition systems influences the success of all other design components.

PEOPLE PRACTICES

The people point on the star represents the collective human resources (HR) practices that create organizational capability from the many individual abilities resident in the organization. The strategy determines what types of skills, competencies, and other capabilities are required of employees and managers. Different strategies require different types of talent and different people management practices, particularly in the areas of selection, performance feedback, and learning and development.

Just as in a living organism, if any of the components of the star are not attended to in the organization design process, the result is misalignment. It means that different elements are working at cross-purposes and less than optimal performance will be achieved, as illustrated in Figure 1-2.

THE RECONFIGURABLE ORGANIZATION

The *reconfigurable organization* is able to quickly combine and recombine skills, competencies, and resources across the enterprise to respond to changes in the external environment.

Figure 1-2. *Unaligned organization design.*

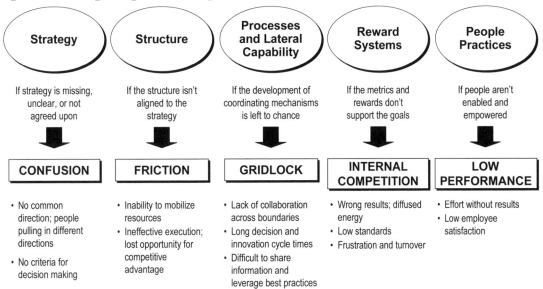

Every company needs an organization that is as dynamic as its business. If not, the "ill-fitting coats" mentioned in the preface will restrict movement and flexibility and cause you to fall behind competitors. In order to keep from falling behind, many companies are devoting enormous amounts of time and energy to "change management." This task can be made less difficult and less time-consuming if some of the change effort is focused on designing a more flexible organization from the outset. If change is constant, why not design the organization to be constantly and quickly changeable?

The reconfigurable organization is characterized by:

■ *Active Leadership.* The reconfigurable organization has a leader and leadership team that believe their organization can be a source of competitive advantage. They see their task as designing and improving the organization, choosing and rewarding people who can contribute, and enabling them to deliver excellence. Organization redesign is considered a core competence.

■ *Knowledge Management.* The reconfigurable organization is based on knowledge. Whether reconfiguring to take advantage of a new product opportunity or meet a client's demands for customization, the success of most companies today depends on their ability to quickly collect and share knowledge across organizational boundaries. Reconfigurable organizations not only use technology to allow their employees to operate virtually, they also use it to connect with suppliers, customers, and partners. They have the mechanisms and the culture that allow people to convert data into useable information and knowledge.

- *Learning.* Learning is essential for organizations that are dynamic and want to be easily reconfigurable. It starts with selecting people who have learning aptitude, who are resourceful and motivated to take on new challenges. It continues with providing them the feedback and tools that allow them to measure their performance against internal and external standards and share in the responsibility for increasing their own capabilities. The reconfigurable organization is a learning organization that rewards those who build and use knowledge.

- *Flexibility.* The reconfigurable organization is built upon the assumption that there will be change. As routine tasks are automated, more work is becoming project-based and focused around teams, deadlines, and deliverables. People may often participate on multiple teams simultaneously. Networks are actively fostered and valued to allow teams to form and reform around regions, functions, customers, products, processes, and projects. The reconfigurable organization attracts people who have a high tolerance for ambiguity, change, and unpredictability.

- *Integration.* The reconfigurable organization assumes that people will move around the organization. If they are specialists, they will be expected to apply their talents in many different arenas. If they are generalists, they will rotate through jobs and roles, learning how to operate in a variety of functions and businesses. People will understand how different parts of the organization work and they will feel a part of the whole.

- *Employee Commitment.* Much has been written on the new employee contract. In exchange for giving up job security, people want their work contribution to be recognized and rewarded appropriately. In addition, they want to be given the opportunity to learn skills that will be valued in the internal and external marketplace. They also want peers who are trained and capable of performing at high levels. The reconfigurable organization enables its employees to deliver excellence to its customers by providing the right tools, skills, and information. As a result, employees believe in the company's products and services, recommend it as a good place to work, and choose to stay longer with the company.

- *Change Readiness.* Change is difficult for everyone. Even when people acknowledge that change is necessary and that the end result will be better, the process can be demoralizing and stressful. Often, despite good intentions on the part of managers, people don't understand why change is occurring or why certain decisions have been made. It's not merely a communication problem. People are often told the reasons why a change is occurring. Usually, they're not convinced. It sometimes appears that managers are "rearranging the furniture" rather than making change for sound business reasons. In the reconfigurable organization, employees understand the design assumptions and are involved in the design process. When changes inevitably have to be made again, the mechanisms are in place to have the conversations, debate the options, and move forward with decisions. People may still experience individual negative impact, but the organization is no longer turned upside down by the change. It has developed resilience and collective competence in the process of organizational change.

Organizations have always been created to execute business strategies. The need for a reconfigurable organization arises from the decline in the sustainability of competitive advantage. Different strategies lead to different types of organizations. But when advantages do not last long, neither can the organizational forms created to execute them. In the past, managers crafted a winning business formula and erected barriers to entry that sustained this advantage. Then management created an organization—structured around functions, products/services, and markets or geographies—that was designed to deliver the success formula. After the structure was determined, the planning, information, and HR support systems would be designed and aligned with each other and with the organization's strategy and structure. The assumption was that there was plenty of time to implement these changes.

Today, in many industries, success formulas do not last very long. The advantages around which an organization is designed are quickly copied or even surpassed by alert and quick-to-react competitors. Worse, some companies find themselves cannibalizing their own advantages, setting up competitors internally to gain market share before external competitors do. By the time everything is aligned with the strategy, the strategy has changed. Therefore, you must have organizational structures and processes that are easily reconfigured and realigned to keep pace with a constantly changing strategy.

Major changes in the environment often cause panic in organizations. Managers react by "blowing up" the organization and starting all over, usually because they don't know which changes will have the desired impact. The reconfigurable organization is designed with intent. Decisions are made with awareness of the expected outcomes. Therefore, when change is necessary, a focused response to change can be made. The right lever can be pulled, whether changing the structure or roles, reconfiguring processes, or developing new skills. Changes are targeted and disruption is minimized.

The reconfigurable organization directs knowledge and information to where it is needed. It provides employees with opportunities to grow and learn. The organizations that can achieve this are those that are designed from the beginning to be quickly and easily adaptable. No longer will each redesign need to begin with a blank slate. Even a little success in designing a flexible, agile organization will go a long way toward reducing the enormous amounts of time, energy, and pain typically associated with change. Use Tool 1-1 to determine what areas in your organization need to be made more flexible and ready to respond to change.

DECIDING WHEN TO REDESIGN

Various events can trigger an organization's need to redesign.

■ *You are starting up a new company or division.* Clearly, a new business needs to be designed. Before launching Saturn, GM spent nearly three years planning the technology, systems, and organization that would be needed to launch a world class–quality small car that could compete successfully with imports. Saturn was to be not just a new car line but a whole new way of making and selling cars, with manufacturing processes, team structures, and compensation systems that are all different from those at the core GM company. Many start-up founders, however, don't think about organizational issues until the company has grown large enough to require it. Founders often wait until investors demand that they hire managers from established companies with some organizational experience before they pay any attention to creating an infrastructure.

■ *You are planning to grow.* Changes in size should trigger a reassessment of the organization. Growth can mean more employees. It can also mean greater volumes, increased sales, or an extension into new markets, new channels, or new countries. Size can change the complexity or scale of the business. Of *Fortune*'s list of the 100 fastest growing companies in 1999, about a fifth lost 60 to 90 percent of their value during the following twelve months, and almost half lost at least some value. Most suffered from not having the right infrastructure or people to support continued growth.[2]

■ *You have just assumed a new or more senior position.* New managers are often accused of changing the organization they've taken over simply to assert themselves. In order to justify the change in leadership, the old way of doing things is thrown out whether it worked or not. A new manager, however, should thoroughly appraise the current organization and make changes only if they are needed. The first few months on the job, the honeymoon period, is the best window of time to assess the landscape. If you use a structured process to understand the current organization and decide what needs to be modified, you will provide those in the existing organization with the confidence that changes are not being made arbitrarily or just for the appearance of change. As part of your assimilation process, you should assess the current organization to determine if it facilitates or hinders your strategy.[3]

■ *Your strategy has changed.* If your products or markets have changed, or you are adding a new line of business, or you are expanding into international territory, it is likely that your organization needs to change as well. For example, the Coca-Cola Company announced a reorganization in the spring of 2001 in order to allow it to focus more on marketing juice, coffee, and tea through joint ventures.

■ *The organization around you has just changed.* The organization design process can be triggered by an internal realignment. If the level above has just reorganized and key internal customers, suppliers, or partners are changing, then your organization may need to change also. For example, when Deutsche Bank bought Bankers Trust, the Bankers Trust marketing function that supported products sold to institutional customers had to begin operating on a global scale. What had been a simple organization in New York now had to collaborate with Frankfurt and London and support new products and customers. The old organization was simply no longer effective.

■ *There has been a major change in the external environment.* New competitors, new technology, and new regulations are some of the forces in the external environment that can trigger a reassessment of the organization. For example, the opportunity to automate manual processes not only reduces the number of people needed, it also impacts the skills that the remaining employees and their managers need to have. The premium that had been placed on processing accuracy and efficiency is replaced with value on complex problem-solving and exception-processing ability. On the regulatory front, when the Glass-Steagall Act, which had prohibited banks from combining with other types of financial services, was partially repealed in November 1999, it cleared the way for U.S. insurance companies and banks to acquire one another. These mergers and acquisitions have all been accompanied by organization redesigns.

■ *Your organization isn't delivering the performance expected.* Performance problems (customer complaints, loss of market share, missed financial targets, high turnover, etc.) are rarely the result of just one factor. Nor does addressing the most obvious symptom with a quick fix (training, marketing, cost cutting, compensation, etc.) usually address the underlying issues. Organization design is both a comprehensive and an integrative process that examines root causes of issues and directs organizational energy and change where it will have the most impact.

Use Tool 1-2 to confirm your need to consider a redesign of your organization.

THE DESIGN PROCESS

The star model provides a guide to the topics that are considered throughout the design process. Figure 1-3 shows how each of the points of the star

Figure 1-3. Four phases of organization design.

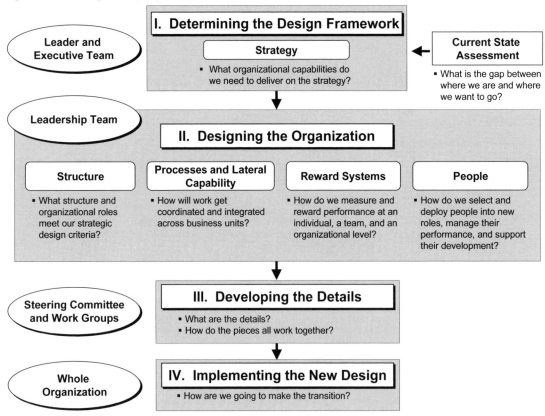

model are addressed through the design process. Each of the four phases—Design Framework, Designing the Organization, Developing the Details, and Implementing the New Design—has a series of decisions and steps within it and requires participation by different groups and levels in the organization. Given that organization design is more an art than a science, however, the order of the steps and decisions will vary depending on the nature of the organization, the issues to be addressed, and who is involved in resolving them. Each phase in the figure is outlined below and subsequent chapters are devoted to describing the process and activities in each phase.

I. DETERMINING THE DESIGN FRAMEWORK

The *Determining the Design Framework* phase is the work of translating the strategy into design criteria. The outcome of this phase allows you to clearly communicate:

- Why do we need to change?

- Where do we need to go?

- What will the end state look like?

It is your responsibility as a leader to address these issues, although you will likely involve your executive team. This phase of work focuses on what organizational capabilities need to be developed in order to achieve the goals of the strategy. Other issues that are considered when setting the framework are the goals and boundaries of the change and determining the time frame for the process. A key input to the design framework is the *Current State Assessment*, which defines the gap between where the organization is today and the desired future state. A guide for assessing the current state is provided in Chapter Two.

II. DESIGNING THE ORGANIZATION

The *Designing the Organization* phase identifies those changes in the organization that need to be made to align the organization to the strategy. The outcome of this phase will be answers to these two questions:

- What is going to change?

- How will we get there?

The work of researching best practices and generating and evaluating options is usually done by the leadership team and includes topics such as:

- Determining the new organizational structure

- Defining new organizational roles

- Identifying the key lateral processes that need to be developed to support the structure

- Determining how teams and matrix relationships are intended to function, if they are to be incorporated

- Outlining the metrics that will be used to measure performance

- Deciding what HR practices will best support the new organization

By no means will all the details be worked out in this phase, but decisions will be made that chart a clear path to the new shape of the organization. Chapters Three through Six cover the major design decisions you will have to make.

III. DEVELOPING THE DETAILS

The elements of the design are fleshed out and refined during the *Developing the Details* phase. Here is where the work groups and steering committee usually take over from the leadership team to carry the work forward. The work groups create detailed project plans to develop the design elements as well as begin implementation.

IV. IMPLEMENTING THE NEW DESIGN

During implementation, the entire organization is involved as the new design is rolled out and put into practice. The development phase may overlap with the *Implementing the New Design* phase when pilot sites are used. Chapter Seven highlights some considerations for the development and implementation phases.

Rarely is an organization designed from a clean sheet of paper. Sometimes structural decisions have to be made to accommodate existing employees and roles have to be defined around the available pool of talent. Although this may not be ideal, the desired changes can be implemented in phases over time. Seldom is the organization ready to move to the end state all at once. As with most business decisions, the commitment to execution and follow-through is as important as the design decisions themselves.

The design process always begins with reviewing the strategy. However, this process is not linear. The design process needs to be as complex and integrated as the organization itself. It is hardly ever a simple decision tree. Rather, the process often loops back on itself because a decision in one arena impacts others. For example, the design of lateral processes may point out flaws with the underlying structure and trigger a reconsideration of how work units and departments are configured. In addition, cross-functional teams can't be configured without thinking through some elements of the metrics and compensation structure. Many of the steps in the design process should be considered concurrently. The power of the reconfigurable organization is evident when its design is considered in the context of strategy. Ask the question, "How can we organize to deliver on the strategy?" Thinking this way not only accelerates the process but turns organizational change from a lagging activity to one that is an integral part of the strategy.

The focus of your design process will be determined by the biggest gaps between where your organization is today and where it needs to go. Figure 1-4 summarizes some typical gaps and which part of the design process they will lead you to consider. Where you begin impacts the scope of the design and change process. A change in strategy and structure will require some realignment in all other parts of the star. On the other hand, a determination that the current structure is fine and better developed processes and roles will address the issues will narrow the scope of change. Chapter Two provides a guide to conducting a current state assessment of the organization and determining the underlying issues and priorities for change.

THE CASE FOR A PARTICIPATIVE PROCESS

You will need to make many decisions in the organization design process. Theoretically, as a leader, you and your executive team can make all the deci-

Figure 1-4. Choosing a starting point.

Underlying Issue		Starting Point
The current strategy no longer provides a competitive advantage.	➡	Review the strategy and determine what organizational capabilities are required.
The current structure and roles inhibit, rather than facilitate, interaction with the customer, decision making, collaboration, etc.	➡	Redesign the vertical structure and clarify roles to better support the strategy.
The organization is not responsive to change or opportunities; internal friction diverts energy away from the business.	➡	Create networks, processes, roles, and structures that build lateral relationships and cooperation.
People are working at cross-purposes or in conflict.	➡	Realign the measures and rewards to focus everyone on the same goals.
The organization's people are not enabled to deliver on the strategy.	➡	Develop the organization's people and HR practices to enhance its capabilities.

sions. Usually, this is not practical or desirable for the successful implementation of those decisions. There are some good reasons to use a participative approach. By participative, we mean *involving people in the organization beyond the executive team in identifying options and making decisions.* True participation goes beyond soliciting input or informing people about decisions already made. It requires a leader to commit to accepting that a broader group will make some decisions. In many ways, participation is not a choice or "nice-to-have" option. The executive team often doesn't have enough details about the processes and jobs at the front line to make informed decisions regarding how to alter them. Participation doesn't imply that all decisions are taken out of the hands of the leader or that a broader group is involved at all points in the process. In fact, some decisions are the responsibility of the leader and shouldn't be delegated, particularly the up-front work regarding the strategy.

Nor does everyone need to have equal participation. Lower-level employees may participate either in focus groups or by communicating through representatives on work groups. Those identified as high potentials may be designated to lead work groups. Employees new to the organization may be called upon for their fresh ideas and experiences working in other environments. Employees with long tenure may be singled out to provide institutional memory to avoid repeating past mistakes.

Participation can take a number of forms in the design process:

- Identifying the current state and the gap between where the organization is today and what needs to change to achieve the strategy

- Researching and generating design options

- Evaluating and testing proposals

- Providing input and reacting to design alternatives

- Detailing and developing design decisions

- Creating implementation plans

Participation yields a number of benefits.

- *More Ideas.* The more people involved, the more ideas that are generated. In many organizations, people closest to the front lines, who deal firsthand with customers, technology, and process issues, have numerous untapped ideas. Often they can identify quick fixes that will have immediate impact.

- *Commitment to Outcomes.* People are more committed to decisions to which they feel they had input. If their suggestions and concerns have been genuinely heard and acknowledged, they will be more amenable to supporting directions with which they may not fully agree.

- *Modeling New Relationships.* Most organizational change initiatives have at least one objective focusing on building better working relationships among individuals and organizational units. If the participation process is structured to bring these groups together around the issues of design, new working relationships can be developed away from the heat of high-pressure business issues.

- *Developing High Potentials.* Work groups are ideal forums for high-potential employees to learn about other parts of the organization and gain exposure to the organization's senior leadership. The design and refinement process can be used as a development assignment for high performers who are ready to be more broadly involved in the future of the company.

Participation is not appropriate when:

- *The options are clear-cut.* Involving a lot of people requires an investment of time, money, and energy. Time spent in meetings debating options is time away from the business. While involvement up front usually eases the implementation at the back end, sometimes it does not improve the outcome. If the issues are clear and there are few options to consider, it may be best for leadership to make the decisions and involve people in implementation planning rather than analysis or evaluation.

- *The decision should remain with the executive team.* Setting the business strategy and direction are executive responsibilities and best not done by consensus. If the organization is small and there are sensitive personnel issues, a participative approach may not be appropriate. For example, if it involves asking people to eliminate their own positions and you have no alternatives for them, it's best to make the decisions yourself. People may be willing to tear down their own house and rebuild it with you; however, asking them to tear down their own house and remain homeless is cruel, not participative.

Participation is most successful when it is undertaken with clear parameters, when there is equitable representation, and when the process is structured and facilitated.

■ *Clear Parameters.* Successful participation requires the leader to be absolutely clear about the parameters for decision making, the nonnegotiables, and the rules. Many times, the leader communicates the wrong expectations. He intends only to ask for input, but he fails to make explicit that involvement doesn't mean decision making by consensus. People are then disappointed when a decision contrary to their perspective is made. Figure 1-5 illustrates the range of participation choices in decision making from making the decision alone and selling it to the group (Option 1) to fully accepting a decision that the group makes (Option 4). Note that with Options 1 through 3, the final decision still rests with the leader. In fact, only Option 4 is actually a true participative decision.

Much confusion and misunderstanding arise when leaders use Options 1, 2, or 3 and raise expectations around participation and involvement but don't clarify that final authority *still* remains with the leader. The key is to match the right style to the circumstances. If Options 1 and 2 are used too often, the leader will be perceived as autocratic. However, full participation is not always appropriate. Used too often, it may represent an abdication of the leader's decision-making responsibility. Use Tool 1-3 to assess the conditions for participation in your organization.

■ *Equitable Representation.* Most organizations are too big to involve everyone. Choosing some people and not others raises issues of equity. What is intended to be a participative process ends up creating divisiveness. For example, you want to use a work group to research and generate new reward and recognition options. By selecting the participants, you automatically create insiders. Whatever the group comes up with will be rejected by those who felt passed over. If you ask for volunteers, you may get only those with an ax to grind or those who perceive the assignment as a way to curry favor or get ahead.

One way to avoid these outcomes is to use "representatives." Announce the purpose of the work group and the general composition (e.g., ten people representing each of your five locations, four functional areas, and six levels) as well as the criteria for participation (e.g., skill level, tenure). Anyone who is interested may nominate himself or herself to be considered. The person's peers conduct a simple vote. If the results are lopsided (e.g., all women and no men)

Figure 1-5. Involvement options.

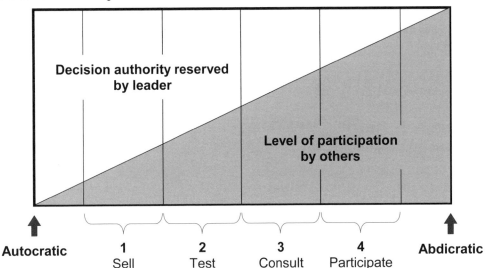

1. Sell	You announce your decision but give rationale and facts to build support for compliance.
2. Test	You present a preliminary decision and ask others to review it and provide feedback; you reevaluate it based on input and make a final decision.
3. Consult	You present the group with the problem and solicit their input; you incorporate their ideas, suggestions, and advice although you may override advice if you don't agree with it. You make the final decision.
4. Participate	You present the group with the problem along with the desired outcomes, parameters, and rules for decision making. You may participate with the group to jointly produce a final decision or rely on their consensus decision. You commit to adhere to the decision agreed to by the group as a whole.

Adapted from T. D. Christenson, *How to Decide . . .* (South Bend, Ind.: STS Publishing, 1980).

or if you want to add some particular perspectives for balance, make the adjustments before the results are announced.

Participants in this work group now speak for their level, location, or function rather than simply stating their own opinions. As representatives they should be required to reach out to others in their part of the organization to gather ideas and concerns. The recommendations of the work group are likely to be better received using this approach.

■ *Facilitated Process.* Richard Hackman notes that the effectiveness of any group is equal to its potential productivity less the inevitable process loss inherent in group interaction.[4] In other words, no matter how many good ideas the group has, they may be derailed by unresolved conflict, by group pressure to compromise rather than optimize decisions, or by a lack of process. Everyone has been in a meeting where it took longer to figure out how to proceed than to discuss the issue itself. Particularly for groups comprising people who don't know each other, haven't worked together before, or are at different levels, lack of process can get in the way of problem solving. Having a facilitator attend to the group process can improve the outcome significantly and build the group's skills in managing their own process in the future. The facilitator can be an external consultant or a skilled internal person. If internal persons are used, they should not be members of the group so that they can stay neutral and focus exclusively on managing the group dynamics and outcomes.

The UNOPS case study in Chapter Three illustrates how to use a participative design process in more detail.

SUMMARY

In this chapter we have defined organization design using the star model as a conceptual way of thinking about all of the elements to consider, how they interrelate, and how they shape the design process. You have assessed how reconfigurable your own organization is and where you need to build the characteristics of the reconfigurable organization into your design. You've also confirmed the reason you are undertaking a redesign. Finally, this chapter has made the case for a participative design approach and provided guidelines for successfully involving others.

Chapter Two will help you determine the design framework by translating the strategy into a set of design criteria and assessing the current state of the organization.

NOTES

1. J. R. Galbraith, *Designing Organizations: An Executive Briefing on Strategy, Structure, and Processes* (San Francisco: Jossey-Bass, 1995), pp. 11–17.

2. "Growth Elixirs May Be Risky," *Fortune*, September 4, 2000, p. 164.

3. D. Downey, T. March, and A. Berkman, *Assimilating New Leaders: The Key to Executive Retention* (New York: AMACOM, 2001), pp. 101–112.

4. R. J. Hackman and G. R. Oldham, *Work Redesign* (Reading, Mass.: Addison-Wesley, 1980), p. 176.

Tool 1-1. How reconfigurable is your organization?

Purpose:	Use this tool to gain a preliminary perspective on how your organization responds to change.
This tool is for:	Executive Team.
Instructions:	A reconfigurable organization is one that is characterized by active leadership, knowledge management, learning, flexibility, integration, employee commitment, and change readiness. Each of these characteristics is defined by three statements below. For each one, rate your organization by how strongly you agree ("5") or disagree ("1") with the statement. Then, total your scores.

Item	Strongly Disagree 1	2	3	4	Strongly Agree 5
Active Leadership					
The executive team believes that organization design is a source of competitive advantage.					
When strategy discussions are held, organization design is considered one of your strategic elements.					
The executive team can articulate how each of the organization's components is aligned with the strategy.					
Knowledge Management					
People have easy access to all the information they need to make decisions on behalf of customers.					
Technology and HR practices allow for rapid collection and dissemination of information.					
The organization has mechanisms in place for converting information into useable knowledge for innovation, best practices, and organizational learning.					
Learning					
People are selected for their learning aptitude.					
Performance metrics and feedback allow employees to measure their performance against internal and external standards and share in the responsibility for increasing their own capabilities.					
The organization uses a wide variety of methods in addition to training to support learning.					
Flexibility					
Employees are skilled at working in teams.					
Networks across organizational boundaries are actively fostered, not left up to individual initiative or chance.					
People expect and accept being frequently reassigned into new roles and responsibilities.					

Item	Strongly Disagree 1	2	3	4	Strongly Agree 5
Integration					
Assignments and career paths for high performers are designed to promote cross-functional skills, broaden interpersonal networks, and provide exposure to senior management.					
Specialists are available to the entire organization through either special assignment or career paths.					
Managers are moved between organizational units, not just upward in their own unit, for promotions and development.					
Employee Commitment					
Employees are provided with the opportunity to develop job-related skills and be rewarded for developing skills that increase their value to the organization.					
Employees have the tools, systems, information, and skills to deliver excellence to internal and external customers.					
Employees actively recommend the company as a good place to work.					
Change Readiness					
Employees understand the strategy and goals of the organization.					
Employees understand the rationale for the current organization design.					
Your overall organizational culture, vision, and values support organizational change and innovation.					

Now, enter your totals for each area below (your scores should all be between 3 and 15):

Active Leadership _____

Knowledge Management _____

Learning _____

Flexibility _____

Integration _____

Employee Commitment _____

Change Readiness _____

Lower numbers indicate areas of greater concern as you proceed through the organization design process. Similarly, higher numbers are strengths you can build on going forward. Continue to use this tool when questions arise as to how flexibly your organization can respond to changing strategic imperatives. Return to it to diagnose your progress as you implement change.

Tool 1-2. Reasons to redesign.

Purpose:	This tool confirms your reasons to redesign and will help you communicate the purpose of the change effort.
This tool is for:	Executive Team.
Instructions:	You have just read about the key reasons behind an organization redesign. Now, examine your own reasons for redesigning. For each item below, rate the extent to which you believe this item is a factor behind an organization redesign by how strongly you agree ("5") or disagree ("1") with the statement.

Reason to Change	Strongly Disagree 1	2	3	4	Strongly Agree 5
New company or division					
You have a start-up company or division.					
Planning to grow					
The size of the organization will increase.					
You will increase volumes, sales, or customer base.					
Assumed new/more senior position					
You have recently taken a new/more senior job.					
You have assessed your new organization and identified gaps.					
Business strategy has changed					
Your organization is considering a new focus.					
You have changed your product, market, or customer.					
Surrounding organization has changed					
Your key internal customers, suppliers, or partners are changing their organization.					
You have recently merged or acquired/been acquired.					
External environmental change					
There have been changes in your industry, market, regulatory environment, or technology.					
Organizational performance is below expectations					
The organization has not met its performance targets.					

What are your top three reasons for changing?

1. _____

2. _____

3. _____

Tool 1-3. Determining participation.

Purpose:	This tool will help you identify which participatory style is appropriate for your redesign effort.
This tool is for:	Leader.
Instructions:	You have read about the potential benefits and pitfalls of participatory approaches in implementing organization design efforts. You have also examined the four key involvement options (sell, test, consult, participate) that will dictate your participation style in an organization design effort. Refer to Figure 1-5 in the text as you complete this worksheet. Below are five dimensions that will impact the leader's extent of involvement in the design process. For each dimension, circle the rating that reflects your organizational situation.

	1	2	3	4
1. Urgency	Change needs to be made immediately.	Change can take place over time.		Change is not urgent.

	1	2	3	4
2. Executive team's understanding of the organization and the issues	Executive team has an excellent understanding.	Executive team has a good understanding.		Executive team has a limited understanding.

	1	2	3	4
3. Perspectives required	The issues are clear-cut and well-defined.	The issues are clear but the details are not well-defined.		There are conflicting perspectives on how to define the issues.

	1	2	3	4
4. Expected resistance	Little resistance to the change is expected.	Some resistance is expected.		Significant resistance is expected.

	1	2	3	4
5. Degree of change	Only limited change is required.	The change involves two or more areas that need to work together.		The redesign will involve change for all areas of the organization.

Total your ratings. Transfer your **total score** into the box at left below. Then divide your total by five and enter the result in the box at right below.

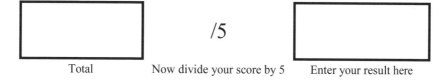

Total   /5   Now divide your score by 5   Enter your result here

Transfer your final result onto the scale below. This will help you determine the involvement option that is best for you at this time.

1	2	3	4
Sell	Test	Consult	Participate

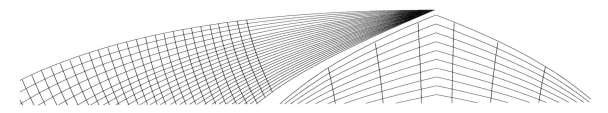

CHAPTER TWO

DETERMINING THE DESIGN FRAMEWORK

CASE STUDY

George dos Santos looked at the report on revenue projections for the next five years and grimaced. Revenues would be flat if nothing changed. "This new strategy better work," he thought to himself. As the recently hired president of Capital Bank Corp. (CBC), the New York securities division of a large diversified financial services company based in London, George felt he would have eighteen months at the most for getting the business turned around. London would be watching closely for results.

The problem was that most of CBC's business had been focused around proprietary trading and internal funds management for its parent bank. This internal focus hampered CBC's ability to grow. In addition, many of the fixed income products that had been the core of its business fell out of favor with investors looking for higher returns in the rising market of the late 1990s. CBC's risk adverse investment style and its lack of experience responding quickly to market changes was leaving it behind its competitors.

George was concerned that some of his high performers were going to begin looking elsewhere for new opportunities.

George had worked with his executive team over the past two months to develop a new strategy. The new strategic focus was based on building deep relationships with external customers and institutional investors. The goal was to have at least 50 percent of assets under management from U.S. and foreign institutional investors in three years, up from the current 20 percent. The key elements of CBC's strategy were:

From		*To*
Fixed income product focus	→	Increased focus on equities and new products
Passive response to parent client	→	Active pursuit and cultivation of new clients
Internal focus	→	External focus on outside customers
Product centered	→	Solution and service oriented
Niche player	→	Broad-based asset management
Proprietary shop	→	Institutional sales shop

As CBC moved into a broader market, staffing was expected to double from 200 to 400 employees. George's challenge would be to build a new organization that could deliver on the promises he had made to his bosses in London.

Like many leaders, George dos Santos is confident that he has a sound strategy. He is less sure that he has the organization to achieve it. Throughout our discussion of strategy, structure, and lateral capability in Chapters Two, Three, and Four, we use the case of George dos Santos and CBC, along with other examples, to illustrate the decisions that have to be made in the organization design process. The architect Mies van der Rohe's dictum that "form follows function" holds for organizations as well as for buildings. The organizational shape should be an expression of the purpose of the organization and what it is trying to achieve. Over time, like an unplanned city, many organizations become an agglomeration of parts. Functions and units are tacked on as a business need arises or to accommodate individual careers. Sometimes when a person is ready for a promotion but there are no open jobs, the company may create a new unit to provide her with the appropriate status. Rarely is anything taken away. The people in the organization seem to know that their organization doesn't operate optimally, but they are not sure how it ended up that way.

The strategy is the basis for refocusing the organization design in a logical way. The strategy sets the framework for all subsequent design decisions, thus its placement at the top of the star model (Figure 2-1). Strategy allows you to project a picture of the future—where you are going and what the organization needs to look like to get you there. The complement to this future state image is a full understanding of how the organization operates in its current state—what works well and should be preserved, and what needs to change.

As we saw in Figure 1-3, the first phase of the design process is *Determining the Design Framework*. The three activities within this phase, which may occur concurrently, are:

1. Translating the strategy into design criteria

2. Clarifying limits and assumptions

3. Assessing the current state

This chapter is structured into three sections to guide you through these activities:

Figure 2-1. Star model.

Source: Jay R. Galbraith, *Designing Organizations: An Executive Briefing on Strategy, Structure, and Process* (San Francisco: Jossey-Bass, 1995).

- *Translating the Strategy into Design Criteria* provides a guide for understanding your strategic direction and the organizational capabilities that your strategy requires. These organizational capabilities become the criteria that guide design decisions.

- *Clarifying Limits and Assumptions* guides you through the process of identifying the boundaries of the design.

- *Assessing the Current State* gives you the tools to determine the issues in the organization from multiple perspectives and identify priorities for change.

TRANSLATING THE STRATEGY INTO DESIGN CRITERIA

The *design criteria* are the organizational capabilities that the business needs to have in order to achieve its strategy. *Organizational capabilities* are the skills, processes, technologies, and human abilities that create competitive advantage.[1]

Different strategies require different organizational capabilities and therefore different organization designs. The right design choices will increase the likelihood that you will be able to build the right organizational capabilities. Each design decision can be tested against the design criteria to determine if it will result in the desired organizational capabilities.

There are three steps in translating the strategy into design criteria:

A. *Identifying Success Indicators*: What business results must the design achieve?

B. *Understanding the Value Proposition*: What are the organizational implications of our strategic focus?

C. *Determining the Design Criteria*: What are the organizational capabilities that the design must help our organization build?

IDENTIFYING SUCCESS INDICATORS

Success indicators define the desired future state in terms of the business *outcomes* to be achieved. The organization design process is a problem-solving process. When tackling any problem, you must be clear up front what success will look like and how it will be measured. This will ensure that all participants in the process are working toward the same goal as they generate and evaluate options. Each organization is unique and will have its own set of success indicators. For example, one of CBC's success indicators is "to be one of the top ten providers of investments for U.S. institutional investors based on quality of products, service, and customer relationships."

Developing success indicators is an activity for the executive team. One way of generating success indicators is to imagine the business a few years in the future and build an image of how it should look. Tool 2-1 can help determine the desired outcomes of your redesign process.

UNDERSTANDING THE VALUE PROPOSITION

In order to identify the capabilities most important for your organization, you first need to determine what type of value proposition your strategy offers. The *value proposition* is the organization's unique combination of qualities that the strategy attempts to exploit. Each organization has its own value proposition and strategy. However, if the organization that you are redesigning is one part of a larger business, its strategy will be nested within the larger business's strategy.

For example, the MetLife insurance company determined that it needed to grow its assets in order to stay competitive with other financial services companies. It developed a strategy to better leverage its many distribution channels to gain more customers, deepen relationships with its already large customer base, and operate more efficiently to increase profitability. The company is organized around its two major markets: institutional customers and individual customers. A third division, called Client Services, contains all the support functions for the company—information technology, call centers, compliance, operations, underwriting, facilities, etc. This division developed its own strategy focused on the operational excellence component of the larger company's strategy. Its value to the company lies in its ability to deliver services to internal and external customers efficiently, predictably, and at a high quality while reducing overall costs for the business. Client Services has its own strategy, yet it is fully aligned with the overall company direction.

In general, organizations try to differentiate themselves through a product, operations, or customer focus.[2] The examples below illustrate each strategic focus using some well-known companies, although the concepts are just as applicable to organizations that are parts of larger businesses.

■ *Product*: A product-focused company not only creates the best product in the industry, but creates products and services that buyers may not even know they need. Product companies focus on innovation and new product development. Their advantage is not just the products themselves, but their product development processes that allow them to get new products out to the market faster than competitors. An example is the PalmPilot. During the 1990s a variety of electronic organizers was introduced as calendars and address books. None became a must-have item or dominated the market. The first Palm, introduced in 1996, was a huge success with its elegant user interface and a character recognition system that actually worked. One million PalmPilots were sold in eighteen months, and by 1999, Palm organizers dominated the market with a 73 percent share. In less than six years, fourteen different versions of the Palm were introduced, each improving on the previous one. Examples of other product leaders are Hewlett-Packard in printers, Johnson & Johnson in disposable contact lenses, and Sony in portable electronics.

- *Operations*: Operationally excellent companies deliver a combination of quality, price, and ease of interaction that others can't match. They may not be first in the marketplace with new products and their products or services may lack some of the features of competitors. They do promise value—whether measured in cost, convenience, quality, or consistency of experience—which is seen by buyers as more important than other product or service attributes. McDonald's may not make the best hamburgers you've ever eaten, but the fact that you can count on consistent standards of quality, service, and price around the world makes it a leader among fast food chains. It is excellent at managing purchasing and suppliers and at training front-line workers.

On another front, many PC and telecommunication companies outsource their component manufacturing to Selectron, the world's largest electronics manufacturing company and winner of the national Baldrige award for quality in 1997. Selectron analyzes its client's product concepts and applies its own expertise in supply-chain management and manufacturing processes to produce high-quality, low-cost components to its customers' specifications. Companies that compete based upon the basis of their operational excellence tend to follow the innovators in the marketplace. They target a customer segment that will trade fewer features for a lower price or higher consistency of quality. Because innovation is costly, these organizations focus on standardization and products where economies of scale can be realized. Another example is Matsushita, a company that uses its Panasonic brand to follow Sony into the marketplace after Sony introduces new consumer electronics.

- *Customer*: Customer-centric companies build long-term customer relationships by tailoring the products and services they offer. They provide total solutions to customer needs rather than stand-alone services or products. The professional services industry (e.g., consulting, law, accounting) provides classic examples of customer-centric organizations. The value of Ernst & Young's accounting services to its clients increases the longer the relationship with those clients. The more the firm understands its customer, the better solutions it can provide. Further, customers don't typically buy these services based on lowest price or latest methodology, but on trust and quality of the relationship. In addition, the buyers' belief that the company is an advocate for them allows the company to serve as a portal through which an array of other products and services can be sold. For example, Amazon.com creates customized recommendations for books, music, and other products based upon what the customer has bought or searched for in the past. It also uses the information it gathers from customers to identify which other companies might provide quality products of interest to its customers. Amazon charges companies for featuring its Web-site links and therefore can increase revenue without having to sell additional products directly.

Each strategic focus implies a different culture and type of person, and different key processes and measures to execute it successfully. For example, while a product-focused company would likely have high tolerance for mistakes and experimentation to encourage innovation, an operations-focused company would have a culture of standardization and would probably reward efficiency over creativity. Figure 2-2 summarizes how each strategy results in a different type of organization.

The trend in many industries is toward customer-centric strategies. Many organizations are trying to differentiate themselves through their ideas, knowledge, experience, and ability to provide customized packages of products and services to their customers. It is becoming increasingly difficult to be a product leader. Products quickly become commodities as the latest innovation is copied by competitors. At the same time, the ability of technology to provide detailed and individualized customer data has created high customer expectations. People expect that the organizations they deal with know who they are and what they need and remember the details of the last transaction or interaction.

Hewlett-Packard, a product leader in printers, signaled a change in its strategy when it tried to purchase the consulting arm of PriceWaterhouseCoopers in the fall of 2000. According to CNN, industry observers were not surprised by the bid, considering the trends in both the information technology and the consulting industries. Many computer hardware companies have been trying to strengthen or build a services practice. An observer of the information technology industry was quoted as saying, "The constant 'mine is faster than yours' isn't what [clients] want anymore. They want a solution to their business problem, and they realize that the glue that puts together the solution is services."[3]

Understanding your organization's core strategy is fundamental to aligning the rest of the organization to support it. For example, every company believes it is customer-centric. Every bank and insurance company states how much it cares about its customers in its advertising. Yet most insurance companies are still organized around the products they create—auto, life, property, disability, dental, etc.—and have a difficult time cross-selling and creating solutions and accounts that integrate services and information in ways that customers really want. Few can provide a customer with one statement or a single 800 number for service. Few financial services companies have truly leveraged all the infor-

Figure 2-2. Implications of each strategic focus.

Strategic Focus	Implications			
	Key Processes	Culture	Measures	People
Product *How many possible uses are there for this product?* Create value through cutting-edge products, useful features, new applications.	New product development Innovation Market research	Results oriented Continually raise the bar and create the best High tolerance for mistakes and experimentation Highest reward is to work on the next most challenging product	Number of new products % of revenue from new products Market share	Creative—open to good ideas wherever they originate Specialists in research and development Adept at using technology for innovation Emphasis on brand management
Operations *How efficiently can we deliver the product?* Create value by packaging cost, quality, and convenience.	Reliable, high-speed automation of repetitive transactions Order fulfillment Logistics and supply-chain management Demand management	Standardization Rewards for efficiency No frills Team-oriented	Cost per transaction Quality and consistency Utilization	Manage volume and scale Adept at using technology for automation Can transfer success to new markets Emphasis on operations management
Customer *What combination of products and services are best for the customer?* Create value through customizing for a total solution.	Relationship management Solution development and implementation Knowledge management Life-event marketing Talent management	Decisions delegated down to those who interact with the customer Alliances with other providers to package service, support, education, advice Relationships, not transactions	Share of most valuable customers Customer satisfaction Lifetime value of a customer Customer retention	Can build long-term relationships Integrative thinkers Care about the implementation and the follow-up service Emphasis on marketing and sales

mation they collect from their customers to proactively offer them the right products at the right time in their lives. Believing that the customer is central to the strategy doesn't mean that the organization can necessarily deliver on that promise. Use Tool 2-2 to clearly state your strategic direction.

DETERMINING THE DESIGN CRITERIA

Each of the strategic directions implies not only different organizational characteristics but also different organizational capabilities. We defined organizational capability as an integrated set of skills, technologies, and human abilities that creates competitive advantage for the organization. Organizational capabilities are internal competencies, created and managed by the organization and embodied by the people who work there. They are not conferred by external sources of competitive advantage such as government regulations, patents, or physical location. These organizational capabilities are the criteria against which all design recommendations will be evaluated.

Organizational capabilities are hard for competitors to match. They may be time-consuming to build, hard to replicate or imitate, or difficult to obtain from others. This is not to say that they last forever. What may be a differentiating organizational capability today could become the baseline in the future as others catch up. Figure 2-3 lists some of the capabilities that each strategy requires.

Most organizations are not at the extremes of being product-, operations-, or customer-centric. More typically, an organization needs to maximize a number of capabilities that may span different strategic foci. Building the organizational capabilities and making design choices that meet the criteria will allow the organization to achieve its definition of success. For example, CBC is planning to grow by building customer relationships. Therefore, it will need an organizational capability that allows it to provide better, more customized solutions than its competition. As design options are generated, CBC leadership will need to test them to determine if they will help the organization build those customer relationships. Use Tool 2-3 to identify the design criteria for your organization.

CLARIFYING LIMITS AND ASSUMPTIONS

If your organization is one part of a larger organization, there are likely to be limits on what can be changed as part of the redesign. *Limits* are boundaries that determine what is included in the design process and what is not. These may be imposed from outside. For example, the customer interface for your

Figure 2-3. Organizational capabilities by strategy.

If our strategy is focused on . . .	Then our organization needs to be able to . . .
Products	▪ Create new products faster than our competitors. ▪ Build depth of expertise, particularly in research and development. ▪ Produce leading-edge products. ▪ Offer a diverse product line. ▪ Encourage innovation.
Operations	▪ Create common standards. ▪ Become a low-cost producer. ▪ Continually increase process efficiency.
Customers	▪ Build long relationships with customers and grow repeat business. ▪ Deliver high levels of customer satisfaction. ▪ Customize products at a customer's request. ▪ Cross-sell and bundle products. ▪ Create preferred sourcing relationships with customers. ▪ Exploit multiple distribution channels. ▪ Create alliances with other organizations in order to deliver comprehensive solutions.

sales area may have to look the same as in other sales areas in the company. Technology may also pose limitations on how radically work can be reorganized.

The pace of change may also become a limit. Other business initiatives, such as a new product launch, or certain times of the year, such as tax season, may place boundaries on how much can be accomplished and in what time frame.

Although limits place constraints on what can and cannot be done, they still can leave a great deal of opportunity for creativity. With clear boundaries, the executive team can explore all possibilities within the opportunity space created. However, they must be drawn carefully. If the leader specifies exactly what the design should be, subsequent design efforts become redundant. Those engaged in design work only search for options that have been sanctioned. On the other hand, without clear limits they might waste energy generating recommendations that won't be considered for implementation. Limits and boundaries can be likened to brakes on a car: Their primary function is not to slow down the car, but rather to allow it to go fast.[4] Just as brakes give a driver confidence that the car can be slowed down when required, clearly articulated design limits and boundaries empower people to make decisions and act.

You want to be careful that the limits are not based on faulty assumptions. Members of the executive team may harbor differing assumptions regarding the scope of the changes that can be considered. Before considering any options, these assumptions should be made explicit and confirmed. For example, there may be debate regarding the company policy about whether to centralize purchasing or whether to install duplicate purchasing functions locally. Until the policy is confirmed, the assumption may place artificial limits on the design. By making each assumption explicit, it can be explored and confirmed. Some limits may be truly "nonnegotiables," particularly those imposed from outside your organization.

Use Tool 2-4 to identify and confirm the boundaries of the design process.

Assessing the Current State

Having defined the design criteria and clarified limits and assumptions, you now have the strategic framework for the redesign process. You have a clear picture and agreement among your executive team of the future state and what needs to be achieved. Equally as important is shared agreement as to where the organization is today. The next step, which can also occur concurrently with the previous one, is to conduct a current state assessment.

A *current state assessment* provides a snapshot of the strengths and weaknesses of the organization at a point in time. The current state assessment provides important information on baseline conditions and helps determine what changes will have the greatest positive impact on the organization. It is a way to surface the ideas for improvement that are latent throughout the organization. The current state assessment also provides early indication of potential areas of resistance or implementation barriers. Finally, the current state assessment provides a link between the needs of the organization and the design process. The redesign is both a response to business imperatives and a response to the concerns of the workforce.

You may already have many documents on hand that can give a picture of the current effectiveness of your organization. These documents include:

- Strategy presentations
- Department planning documents listing issues and current initiatives

- Employee satisfaction and climate surveys
- Customer surveys
- Quality reports

The richest sources of data, however, will be employees themselves. This section presents a guide for gathering and analyzing employee perspectives. It is organized around five questions:

1. What are the sources of data?
2. Who should conduct the current state assessment?
3. What methodology should be used?
4. What questions should be asked?
5. How should data be analyzed?

WHAT ARE THE SOURCES OF DATA?

The current state assessment is usually gathered through a combination of interviews, focus groups, and/or surveys. This scan reflects the broader organization's perspective on what is and what is not working today and what needs to be fixed in the design process. The current state assessment allows the employees' voices to be heard early on in the process. There is good reason to include their perspective. The people who actually work day to day in the organization usually know best where there are bottlenecks, disconnects in process, areas of friction among organizational units, and problems delivering service to the customer. Assessing an organization's effectiveness as its employees and managers experience it also allows for a "root cause" analysis of issues. People may speak in terms of symptoms—what they experience personally— but when the themes are repeated consistently across levels and departments, it is possible to discern the underlying problem. There are three guidelines to consider when choosing which employees should participate in the current state assessment.

1. *Representative Sampling.* A representative sample should be chosen from all levels and from all areas (functions, locations, business lines, etc.). This ensures that all viewpoints are heard and one level or department doesn't skew the findings. Not every level has to be represented at every location or every function represented at every level. Choose population segments based on your hypotheses regarding which groups may have differing perspectives.

The table in Figure 2-4 illustrates an example of criteria used for capturing various population perspectives. In this case the organization is a call center operation for a large telecommunications company. As part of the current state

Figure 2-4. Target population matrix.

Location		Comparison Dimensions		
		Level	**Function**	**Tenure**
	St. Louis	Nonexempt Exempt	Information Technology Administration	At least half of group with less than three years
	Chicago	All nonexempt	Staff groups (HR, finance, legal) Product development	N/A
	New York	All exempt	Sales Administration	At least half of group with less than three years
	Wichita	Nonexempt Exempt	Operations	N/A
	Dallas	All exempt	Call center	N/A

assessment, the call center leadership determined that five locations, two levels, and seven functions should be sampled. Some earlier employee surveys had indicated that employee satisfaction levels were quite different at different sites and among different functional areas. In addition, it was important to sort the data by tenure in some locations, because there were many long-tenured employees who had never worked anywhere else. The head of human resources (HR) suggested selecting some newer employees for the groups to hear how they contrasted the company's practices, policies, and work environment with those of other companies where they had worked.

2. *Large Enough Numbers.* Enough people should participate to allow trends to emerge and to ensure the data are not distorted by the opinions of a few people. There is a cost to including more people in terms of time to complete the assessment, the cost of people's time away from the job, and the time to process all of the information. However, the assessment can also be used to introduce the goals of the redesign and the decision-making process. It will increase commitment to the ultimate recommendations. This up-front involvement pays for itself in easing implementation at the back end.

3. *Knowledgeable Participants.* Participants should be high performers who have knowledge about the organization and are not afraid to express their opinions. Choose people who:

- Are familiar with the organization (don't choose a disproportionate number of recent hires).

- Work across organizational lines and have experience dealing with other departments within the organization.

- Have at least some customer contact, either internal or external.

In addition to employees, you may want to gather perspectives from those internal partners who depend on your area for services, external customers, internal or external suppliers, and other key people outside your immediate organization. These groups will identify the issues that they find most important and can help validate the employees' assessment of what needs to change.

WHO SHOULD CONDUCT THE CURRENT STATE ASSESSMENT?

We recommend that an external consultant conduct the current state assessment (Figure 2-5). It will be faster and more objective than if done by an internal team. Whoever gathers the information should not render their own judgments about the effectiveness of the organization but report the data accurately and organize it in such a way that decisions can be made by the executive team.

Figure 2-5. Who should conduct the current state assessment.

Internal Team Advantages	External Consultant Advantages
Benefits from hearing the information firsthand Can best understand the nuances of issues and how different parts of the organization fit together	Can usually complete the assessment faster than internal staff, who must attend to their regular work as well Can ensure confidentiality to individuals—participants are more likely to be candid Is usually more neutral when hearing issues—is unbiased by organizational politics or past events Will generally elicit more honesty and be able to raise sensitive issues that cross organizational boundaries

WHAT METHODOLOGY SHOULD BE USED?

The assessment can be carried out using a combination of interviews, focus groups, and surveys. Each is discussed next:

1. *Interviews* allow for in-depth questioning and ensure that each person's view is heard. However, they are time intensive and expensive to conduct. Choices have to be made regarding whom to interview and how many interviews to conduct.

- The senior managers in the organization should be interviewed. At whatever level you define "senior manager," all the people at that level and above should be invited to participate in an interview. Implementing change at the end of the design process depends on this group's support. Hearing the group's ideas and concerns in detail will allow the executive team to anticipate sources of resistance down the road. In addition, the senior managers can help provide the framework for the questions asked during focus groups or in a survey. They should be interviewed first, so that any differences in viewpoint can be probed during focus groups with lower-level employees.

- Other people to interview might include key customers, senior executives in other parts of the company who would have a broad view of the organization, and employees in the organization who have extensive knowledge or history of the company and can contribute unique insights.

2. *Focus Groups* permit a larger number of people to be involved in the assessment than individual interviews. A focus group essentially allows for a group of people to be interviewed all at the same time. Although some people may not say as much in a group as they would in a one-on-one interview, hearing others' comments can actually help people to stimulate their own thinking. The discussion can crystallize issues and help everyone focus on those that have the highest impact. The design of the focus group and the skill of the facilitator affect the quality of the output. Some general guidelines include the following:

- Eight to ten people are an ideal number of participants—large enough to break into subgroups and to ensure there will be a range of opinions in the room. With more than ten people, the intimacy of the group is lost and some people will feel too intimidated to actively participate. Invite ten to twelve people, because a few always fail to show up.

- Use a comfortable, private room where people will feel free to speak openly.

- Assure participants of their individual confidentiality. The findings will need to identify differences in viewpoint by group (function, location, or level), but they should be reported in such a way that none of the comments can be traced back to an individual source.

- Ideally, two people should conduct the session. One serves as a facilitator, who asks the questions, manages the discussion, uses a flip chart to record key points, and focuses the group. The second person takes detailed notes in a notebook or on a laptop. In cases where only one person is available, you can use a tape recorder, although it tends to inhibit candor and transcriptions can be expensive.

- People from different departments and areas can be in the same focus group. However, if you believe that they may have different viewpoints on the some topics, divide them into small groups by department within the focus group and have them report their conclusions separately. Don't include more than three different population dimensions in a focus group.

- Don't mix levels or have people who report to each other within a given group. Mixing junior and senior people may dissuade lower-level people from speaking candidly.

3. *Surveys* allow you to gather data from a large number of people, particularly when they are in multiple locations. *Quantitative* surveys (e.g., asking people to rate a series of statements about the organization on a scale of 1 to 5) are the least useful tool in an organization assessment. You may get a superficial sense of what works but will miss the detail and complexity regarding how one issue impacts another. In addition, without knowing the issues, it is difficult to formulate the right questions. Once you have identified the issues, however, you might use a quantitative survey to determine how pervasive they are.

A *qualitative* survey, however, which asks for written responses to open-ended questions, can provide more valuable information. Focus groups can be used after the survey to clarify issues or gain additional detail.

WHAT QUESTIONS SHOULD BE ASKED?

Regardless of the method, the quality of the questions will determine the depth of information that the assessment will provide. Begin by reviewing past assessments and relevant reports and documents to build a base of knowledge. Then craft a set of open-ended questions that allow respondents to paint a picture of the organization's current effectiveness and the factors that shape it from their viewpoint.

Figure 2-6 provides a series of questions that can be customized as an interview or focus group protocol or as a qualitative survey. The topics followed by an asterisk (★) indicate core topics from which you'll probably want to include at least some questions. Other questions and detail can be added or deleted depending on the time available, types of issues anticipated, and the level of participants. For each topic, the purpose of the questions and some suggested "listen-fors" are provided. These will help you recognize themes that emerge from the data.

After an introduction, the protocol begins with eliciting peoples' views of the key business challenges and desired future state to ground them in a business context. They are then asked to assess the current state, including strengths. The questions follow the star model and ask people to consider the full range of design dimensions. For each topic area, ideas for improvement are solicited. To determine the highest impact changes, at the end of the interview, focus group, or survey each person is asked to identify the top three to five change priorities that they believe would most help the organization achieve its strategy.

Use Tool 2-5 to determine who should participate in the current state assessment and to select questions from Figure 2-6 for your protocol.

(text continues on page 43)

Figure 2-6. Generic current state assessment protocol.

Topic and Questions	Purpose of Topic/"Listen-Fors"
Introduction Explain purpose of interview/focus group. ▪ What is your role in the organization? ▪ How long have you been here? ▪ Where did you work before coming here?	Explain the purpose of the interview/focus group and how it will be structured. Asking for a little bit of background on each person alerts you to his or her perspective, any biases hhe or she might have, and useful experiences or insights from other companies he or she may be able to contribute.
Business Challenges* ▪ What are the key business challenges facing our organization today? ▪ What do you believe are the three major goals the business must achieve in the coming eighteen months?	The business challenges ground the participants' later assessment of the organization in a broader context. They can be referred to if the discussion becomes too personal or narrowly focused. Listen for: ▪ Do people agree on the business challenges and the business goals? ▪ What are the dynamics of the business and what external forces are driving change?

Future State
 	
▪ Imagine our organization is on the cover of *Fortune* magazine eighteen months from now. The article is about the success we've achieved.
 	
  – What would you like the article to say?
 	
  – What would make us an industry leader, a benchmark for other organizations like ours?
	The future state provides another anchor for participants as they assess the current organization. It also surfaces whether people have a shared picture of where the organization needs to go.
	
	Listen for:
	
	▪ Do people have a clear idea of what the best-in-class in their industry would look like?
	
	▪ Is there agreement on a future state?

Topic and Questions	Purpose of Topic/"Listen-Fors"

Organization Assessment Overview*
 	
■ Rating
   – On a scale of 1 to 10, how would you rate us overall against this picture of the desired future? (1 = not there at all, totally broken to 10 = already there, a leader in the industry)
■ What factors went into your rating?
■ Strengths
   – What works well?
   – Why didn't you rate it lower?
■ Gaps
   – What isn't working well?
   – Why didn't you rate it higher?
■ How do you think your clients would rate the organization?
   – Why?
	Asking people to rate the organization's strengths gives a basis for what to preserve. The question about gaps is deliberately left open-ended and vague. It allows the person to choose what he or she believes is most important to report. What people choose to focus on at this point gives a quick sense of the magnitude of the change required.
	
	The questions for each of the topics below are intended to uncover the gap between the current and the future state.
	
	Listen for:
	
	■ Where do the strengths lie? Are they a strong base to build upon (e.g., "we have a great business proposition") or more superficial (e.g. "the people here are really nice")?
	■ What gaps does the person immediately identify?
	■ Is there a difference in how the customer might perceive the organization than the employees?

Strategy
■ How would you describe the organization's strategy?
■ What is our primary source of advantage over our competitors?
	The question on strategy gives the leadership team important information on how well and consistently they have communicated.
	
	Listen for:
	
	■ Do people have a common understanding of the strategy?
	■ If there is not a common definition of the strategy, is it an issue of the strategy:
	   – Not existing?
	   – Not being clearly articulated or translated into terms that lower-level people can relate to? or
	   – Being defined differently by different members of the leadership team?

(continues)

Figure 2-6. (Continued).

Topic and Questions	Purpose of Topic/"Listen-Fors"

Structure
 	
▪ Who are your (your team's) immediate clients? Who needs the work you produce?
 	
▪ From whom do you require input so you can do your work? What work products do you hand off to others?
 	
▪ What are the most common points of friction between areas? Where are the bottlenecks?
 	
   – To what do you attribute the bottlenecks and friction?
 	
▪ What are your major points of interface within and outside the organization?
 	
   – How would you describe the quality of these relationships?
 	
   – What gets in the way?
 	
▪ If you could move another department or group into your department, which would it be? Why?
 	
▪ What changes in the structure have you thought about, if any, that might improve the effectiveness of the organization?
	Most people aren't used to thinking in terms of "organizational structure." These questions are designed to determine if people are working around the structure to get their jobs done or if the structure facilitates the work.
	
	You may want to have people draw the structure for you as they talk about how the parts interrelate.
	
	Listen for:
	
	▪ Do people have to work with others outside their own department but find it difficult to cross organizational boundaries?
	
	▪ Does the structure create barriers to working with people outside the organization (e.g., internal and external customers, key suppliers, business partners)?
	
	▪ Are there groups that should be combined into new departments?
	
	▪ Is there a logic and a rationale for each of the pieces (departments, units) or have they just grown organically (or represent past political decisions)?
	
	▪ Are there overlaps between the roles of the departments or units?

Topic and Questions	Purpose of Topic/"Listen-Fors"

Processes
 	
• What type of collaboration occurs across departmental units?
  – Does it happen informally or are there formal teams set up?
  – What type of collaboration needs to occur that isn't happening?
• How are differences and conflicts between areas resolved?
• How are priorities set? How is it decided what you are *not* going to do?
• How do you typically receive communication about the organization?
• How are business plans made?
  – If there needs to be a change during the year, how is it done?
• How are decisions made?
  – What additional decisions should be pushed down to your level? Where do you need more authority (e.g., hiring, budget, decisions that serve the end customer)
• How could these processes be structured or supported more effectively?
	These questions determine how effective the current processes are in "gluing" together the organization.
	
	Listen for:
	
	• Where are there issues of speed? What do people identify as happening too slowly?
	• Does everything happen vertically—up and down the chain of command—or are there also effective lateral processes built into the organization?
	• What kinds of collaboration need to happen or occur more effectively?
	• Is there meaningful involvement in processes at every level or must all decisions go up to a certain management level?

Management/Leadership • What do your managers need to do more of to support you? • What do they need to stop doing or do less of? • What skills do they need to develop? • What do you believe gets in the way of them being better managers?	A person's assessment of his or her organization is closely tied to his or her assessment of the quality of his or her management. Listen for: • What kind of culture and climate has the leadership style created? • Are managers spending their time on high-value activities? • Are management gaps an issue of mind-set or lack of skills?

(continues)

Figure 2-6. (Continued).

Topic and Questions	Purpose of Topic/"Listen-Fors"
Metrics and Rewards ■ How are goals set for you and your group? ■ How are you measured? – How do you know if you are succeeding? – What feedback do you get? ■ What metrics tell you about potential problems or successes (leading indicators) versus how well you did in the past (lagging indicators)? ■ What additional or different measures would you suggest? ■ What nonmonetary rewards and recognition are given in addition to compensation?	As important as any other factor in harnessing the energy of an organization is the alignment of team and individual goals to the organizational goals. These questions uncover if the measures and rewards are communicating the messages that senior leadership intend them to convey. Listen for: ■ Do people understand their goals? ■ Do the measures drive the right behaviors and results? ■ Do they get timely and specific feedback? ■ Do they feel adequately and equitably rewarded for their effort and results?
People Management and Development ■ How would you assess the quality of people in this organization? – Do we have the right people to move us to the future state you envision? – What do people need to have/be able to do to be successful here? ■ What needs to be improved in the areas of recruiting and selection? ■ Are there gaps in orientation, job training, and development that need to be addressed? ■ What career opportunities are available? How much internal mobility do you perceive? ■ How well does your immediate manager support your development and career?	The organization's HR policies and practices are only as good as people perceive them to be. Listen for: ■ What are the criteria that people are selected against? Is there a clear success profile? ■ If people are dissatisfied with development or career opportunities, what are the root causes: – Wrong people in the jobs? – Lack of skills and training? – Lack of development and opportunity? – Lack of systemic support or lack of front-line manager support?
Tools ■ What additional tools and resources do you need, if any (e.g., technology, systems, information, people)?	People can't deliver excellence if they don't have the tools. Listen for: ■ What else do people need to do their work well?
Priorities* ■ Given all we discussed, what are the three priority issues that if addressed would have the greatest impact on the organization overall?	The questions in the protocol are purposefully leading to ensure all topics are covered. One danger is that people may come up with issues to please the interviewer or focus group facilitator. Asking them to review their responses and choose just a few sorts the "nice to have" changes from those that are critical.

HOW SHOULD THE DATA BE ANALYZED?

The data from the assessment are organized into a findings report that highlights the most important issues. This report is presented to the executive team.

A findings report has five basic sections:

1. *Introduction*: The purpose of the current state assessment, methodology, and who participated.

2. *Strengths*: Organizational strengths to preserve and build upon.

3. *Key Issues Overview*: Summary of the dominant themes that emerged and the specific issues within each theme. There are typically five to seven themes under which multiple issues can be grouped.

4. *Detailed Findings*: Description of each issue. This is a good place to use quotes from the interviews and focus groups that capture the feelings of a majority of participants or a particular viewpoint. Only use quotes that protect the confidentiality of individual sources (you may need to modify them slightly to do so). If a survey was used, detailed analysis of the data would go in this section.

5. *Recommendations*: This can be a summary of next steps or a set of proposed recommendations.

To be useful, the report should be as direct and detailed about the issues as possible. In cases where there are concerns that the report may be too sensitive to share beyond the executive team, or that it exposes too much "dirty laundry," or that it could be demoralizing if circulated without a context to the rest of the organization, the report should be shared in its full form with only the executive team. Even then, you may want to remove any personal references to individual members of the executive team.

A high-level summary of the findings should be shared with the whole organization or at least with those who participated in the assessment process. Nothing is more frustrating to people than a lack of feedback after they've honestly shared their viewpoints in interviews, focus groups, or surveys.

When you've completed the current state assessment, use Tool 2-6 to summarize the findings and determine next steps.

Our CBC case illustrates how a current state assessment is used with a strategy review to identify priorities for change.

CASE STUDY

While he and his executive team were developing a new strategic direction for CBC, George dos Santos engaged an external consultant to undertake a current state assessment of the organization. Interviews and focus groups were conducted with 30 percent of the employees in the organization. The assessment found a number of strengths to build upon:

- CBC has a strong reputation in the marketplace.

- The technical and intellectual quality of the employees and managers is highly regarded.

- The company is perceived as having significant opportunities as a small firm backed by a large, financially sound parent company.

However, a number of challenges were also uncovered, focusing particularly on barriers created by the current structure and poor cross-business collaboration and cooperation. Issues regarding the management team's lack of alignment and management skills were also surfaced. The overview of the key issues from the findings report are shown in Figure 2-7.

Figure 2-7. CBC current state assessment: key issues overview.

1. Strategy and Direction	2. Structural Alignment	3. Cross-Business Collaboration and Cooperation	4. Infrastructure and HR Systems	5. Management Style and Skills
■ There is a need to develop new products and shift emphasis to equity markets. ■ People do not believe CBC is ready to compete in a broader market. ■ Risk levels are perceived as being set too low. ■ CBC needs an e-commerce strategy.	■ Too many small groups with their own support functions encourages duplication. ■ There is no "one face" to the customer. ■ There is no management team—all decisions go through the president. ■ Departments set their own, often conflicting, priorities. ■ Trading, marketing, and credit skills need to be better leveraged and shared.	■ Lack of collaboration is seen as deliberate to preserve centralized power. ■ Open interpersonal conflicts among senior managers inhibit cross-functional collaboration. ■ Managers have a blaming rather than a problem-solving orientation. ■ The support functions are perceived as fragmented and not equally available to all groups. ■ Operations/execution time is slower than industry standards.	■ The computer system, which requires multiple manual entries, is outdated, error prone, and cannot accommodate growth. ■ Employees perceive few long-term opportunities within CBC. ■ There is little formal or informal training and development. ■ The compensation system is not linked to clear measures.	■ Managers place little value on supporting and managing their people. ■ Decision making is highly centralized and employees feel their input is not valued. ■ Senior managers tend to micromanage rather than focus on larger, strategic issues. ■ Middle managers are given little authority and don't feel trusted. ■ People are afraid of making mistakes; they don't know the criteria on which they're being assessed.

George dos Santos brought together his executive team to review the new strategy and the results of the current state assessment and to identify the priority issues to address. As an outcome of the meeting, the team determined that their organization needed to develop the following capabilities in order to achieve their strategic goals. The design criteria for CBC were:

- Leading-edge customer service and customer orientation

- Ability to customize products for the U.S. market

- Decreased cycle time for new product launches

- Formation of long-term, in-depth relationships with institutional clients

- Ability to coordinate service for customers with multiple relationships at CBC

After comparing these design criteria to the results of the current state assessment, the team also agreed on four priorities for change:

- Revisit the current organizational structure.

- Create new processes for developing products and servicing customers.

- Build better synergy among marketing, product development, and support areas.

- Develop communication and client relationship skills.

These priorities became the focus for CBC's change efforts. The team's immediate next step was to examine the current structure.

SUMMARY

This chapter has presented a framework for thinking about organization design. You have identified the design criteria based upon the strategy and the organizational capabilities you will need to develop to achieve the strategy. In addition, you have clarified the boundaries for what will be included and what will be off the table in the design process. The chapter has also helped you structure and conduct a current state assessment to gather the data to determine priorities for change.

The remainder of this book builds on this discussion of strategy, organizational capabilities, and the current state assessment to make informed decisions about designing new structures, defining new roles and integrative mechanisms, and aligning metrics and people practices. For each section, we guide you through a process to determine:

- How well your current design enables the organization to achieve its goals—is it helping or hindering you from building the organizational capabilities that you need to execute your strategy?

- What are the (re)design options?

- Which option provides the most advantages and the least drawbacks?

- What do you need to consider and what questions should you be asking?

NOTES

1. For a complete discussion of organizational capabilities and competencies, see G. Hamel and C. K. Prahalad, *Competing for the Future* (Boston: Harvard Business School Press, 1994).

2. M. Treacy and F. Wiersema, *Discipline of Market Leaders: Choose Your Customers, Narrow Your Focus, Dominate Your Market* (Reading, Mass.: Addison-Wesley, 1995).

3. "HP Confirms Price Talks," www.cnnfn.com, September 11, 2000.

4. R. Simons, *Levers of Control* (Boston: Harvard Business School Press, 1995).

Tool 2-1. Developing success indicators.

Purpose:	Use this tool to create a picture of the desired future state.
This tool is for:	Executive Team.
Instructions:	Success indicators define your organization's desired future state in terms of the outcomes to be achieved. Use your output from Tool 1-2, *Reasons to Redesign*, to focus the group on why change is necessary. If your organization has separate components, it might be helpful to first focus on each major area and then combine your results to develop success indicators for the organization as a whole.

Individual Activity

Imagine you are reading *Business Week* eighteen months from now. Your organization is featured as a success in your field or industry. The article praises not only how well you are doing but also how far you have come in the last year and a half. You are now a benchmark for other organizations in your industry.

1. What does the article say you are successful at doing? Be as specific as possible and quantify where you are able.

   _____

   _____

   _____

2. Why are you successful? What is it about your organization that works so well?

   _____

   _____

   _____

3. What has changed?

   _____

   _____

   _____

4. What is the value you provide to your customers and employees? How would they describe your organization?

   _____

   _____

   _____

(continues)

Tool 2-1.   (Continued).

Executive Team Activity

Share your responses to the questions above. Go around the table and have each person answer one question before proceeding to the next one. Agree on those outcomes that would indicate organizational success. If possible, quantify the indicator. Then, translate those outcomes into a list that states the outcomes in the most quantifiable terms possible (an example is provided).

Success Indicator	Quantifier
Become the preeminent provider of wealth management services in the markets we serve	*35% market share in markets served*

This tool is the first step to aligning the executive team around shared goals and creating a platform for the redesign. Use the output from this tool as a basis for completing Tool 2-3, *Determining Design Criteria.*

Tool 2-2. Confirming your strategic focus.

Purpose:	You have read about the three ways that organizations typically differentiate themselves (product, operations, customer focus). Use this tool to help you confirm the strategic direction of the organization.
This tool is for:	Executive Team.

Individual Activity

1. What is our current strategic focus?

   - Are we primarily product-, operations-, or customer-centric?

   _____

   _____

   _____

   - Why? What is the rationale?

   _____

   _____

   _____

2. What are our existing strengths?

   - Refer to Figure 2-2, *Implications of Each Strategic Focus*, and list the items that best describe existing strengths that you want to protect and grow in the "current state" column in the table on the following page.

3. What has changed in the environment?

   - What challenges are we facing because of changes in our markets, customers, or competitors?

   _____

   _____

   _____

4. What are our priorities?

   - What opportunities do we need to pursue and what changes in the marketplace do we need to respond to?

   _____

   _____

   _____

(continues)

Tool 2-2. (Continued).

Executive Team Activity

Referring again to Figure 2-2, list the organizational characteristics you believe you need to have to achieve your success indicators in the "future state" column.

Current State (must maintain)	Future State (want to build)
Key Processes	
Culture	
Measures	
People	

This tool highlights the organization changes required by the shift in strategic direction. Use the output from this tool as a basis for completing Tool 2-3, *Determining Design Criteria.*

Tool 2-3. Determining design criteria.

Purpose:	Use this tool to create common agreement on the design criteria.
This tool is for:	Executive Team.
Instructions:	The design criteria will be used throughout the design process. Use this tool in a group setting. Reproduce the table as a wall chart for everyone to work on.

Individual Activity

1. **Review the capabilities:** Individually review the list of organizational capabilities in the table on the next page. Add any that you believe are missing. Use the output from Tools 2-1 and 2-2 to think about your business strategy and identify what is missing in the current organization. Change it into a positive and add it to the list if it is not there.

2. **Identify priorities:** Divide the list into three equal groups by checking the appropriate box next to each capability:

   A. Highly important in our strategy.

   B. Nice to have in order to meet our strategy.

   C. Not as important to our strategy as the others.

As an Executive Team—On the Wall Chart

3. **Compare priorities as a group:** Compile your results with the others on the wall chart by placing a check mark with a marker or stick-on dot on the wall chart for all your "A" category capabilities.

4. **Agree on most important capabilities:** Discuss areas of difference in the "A" category until a list of five organizational capabilities are agreed upon.

5. **Identify** the key organizational capabilities. Transfer the five highest priority organizational capabilities as identified and agreed upon by the executive team. For each one, capture the rationale and key points of the discussion.

1. _____

2. _____

3. _____

4. _____

5. _____

The output of this tool is the design criteria against which you will evaluate all design decisions. Return to this information after completing the current state assessment and when you are ready to use Tool 2-6, *Determining High-Priority Issues*, to help you understand the gap between where you are now and where you want to be.

(continues)

Tool 2-3. (Continued).

Organizational Capability	A. Highly Important	B. Nice to Have	C. Not as Important
Product			
Create new products faster than our competitors.			
Build depth of expertise, particularly in research and development.			
Produce leading-edge products.			
Offer a diverse product line.			
Encourage innovation.			
Operations			
Create common standards.			
Become low-cost producer.			
Continually increase process efficiency.			
Customer			
Build long relationships with customers and grow repeat business.			
Deliver high levels of customer satisfaction.			
Customize products at customer's request.			
Cross-sell and bundle products.			
Create preferred relationships with customers.			
Exploit multiple distribution channels.			
Create alliances with other organizations in order to deliver comprehensive solutions.			

Tool 2-4. Limits and assumptions.

Purpose:	Having identified the design criteria, the next step is to determine the constraints that may exist—both internally and externally in the design process. Use this tool to identify limits and confirm assumptions regarding the design.
This tool is for:	Executive Team.

1. **Identify the limits for the design:** What are the nonnegotiables or other boundaries to the redesign, including:

   - Existing elements of the structure
   - Interface points with other parts of the larger organization or key customers
   - Roles and functions that must be maintained
   - Constraints posed by the larger organizational structure
   - Systems and processes that must remain
   - Organizational culture

   _____

   _____

   _____

   _____

   _____

   _____

   _____

   _____

2. **Identify the limits for the process:** What are the limits to the design process, including:

   - Timing
   - Stakeholders outside the organization that must participate or be consulted
   - Other organizational initiatives that must be integrated and accounted for
   - Funding

   _____

   _____

   _____

   _____

   _____

   _____

   _____

(continues)

Tool 2-4. (Continued).

3. **Identify your assumptions:** As a group, examine the list you have generated. List the key nonnegotiable items in the left-hand column of the chart. In the right-hand column, you and your team should identify the assumptions upon which these judgments are based.

Nonnegotiables	Assumption(s)

4. **Play Devil's Advocate:** Have members of the executive team play "devil's advocate" to test and challenge your assumptions. Ensure that the team is not creating any artificial boundaries to the redesign effort. The goal is to create as few boundaries as possible.

5. **Confirm the boundaries:** Check each limit to ensure that all agree it should be in place. Identify those that you may want to test with others in the organization.

Use the output of this tool to communicate the boundaries of the design and focus the executive and leadership team's design work. You may also want to test some of the assumptions in the current state assessment.

Tool 2-5. Planning the current state assessment.

Purpose:	Use this tool to help you identify and define what questions you will ask to assess your organization's current state as well as who should be involved in the assessment.
This tool is for:	Executive Team.

1. Refer to Figure 2-6, *Generic Current State Assessment Protocol.* What are the key questions you want answered by your current state assessment?

   _____

   _____

2. Who needs to be interviewed in the assessment?
   - Senior manager: _____
   - Other key employees: _____
   - Customers: _____
   - Partners, suppliers: _____

3. What groups in the organization are likely to have different perspectives? Use the table to identify the dimensions of the organization you want to sample through focus groups (e.g., department, tenure, gender)?

Comparison Dimensions

Locations					

4. What documents can you draw upon to augment the employee feedback?

   _____

   _____

Tool 2-6. Determining high-priority issues.

Purpose:	Use this tool to identify the gap between your current state and the organization you need to build.
This tool is for:	Executive Team.
Instructions:	Complete the individual portion of the exercise first and then share your results with the executive team.

Individual Activity

- In the left-hand column below, list your five design criteria for the new organization from Tool 2-3.

- Review the key issues and ideas that were raised as part of your current state assessment. Consider each issue or idea individually. Place that issue/idea in the middle column aligned to the design criteria that it is most related to.

- List issues not specifically related to any of the design criteria in the space provided at the bottom.

- Identify the changes that will close the gap.

- An example from the CBC case is filled in.

Design Criteria	**Current State Issue/Idea**	**Changes to Address the Gap**
▪ Formation of long-term, in-depth relationships with institutional clients.	▪ There is no "one face" to the customer. ▪ Too many small groups with their own support functions encourages duplication.	▪ Revisit the current organizational structure.
1.		
2.		
3.		
4.		
5.		
Other current state issues not directly related to your design criteria:		

As a group

- Share your assessment of the issues, how the design criteria will address them, and the type of change required. Where is there agreement? Where is there divergence?

- As a group, agree on your five most important priorities:

1. _____

_____

2. _____

_____

3. _____

_____

4. _____

_____

5. _____

_____

Use this tool to ensure that you and your executive team are in agreement over the issues to be addressed. If any of the priority issues that emerged is a strategy issue, ***do not proceed any further in the design process***. Consider the following:

If the issue is . . .		Then you need to . . .
People don't agree with the strategy or don't believe the strategy provides competitive advantage.	➡	Consider undertaking some strategic-planning work. Include the people who had the most concerns on a task force to reexamine the assumptions of the strategy, to better understand the market, and to assess the competition.
People don't know what the strategy is or have different interpretations of it.	➡	Translate the strategy into concrete terms that link it to the day-to-day realities of the organization's staff. Inconsistent interpretations may also reflect that the senior team is not aligned in their thinking about the strategy. Meet at the senior level to clarify it and then develop a communications plan to engage the rest of the organization in understanding the strategy, direction, and goals.

CHAPTER THREE

DESIGNING THE STRUCTURE

CASE STUDY

As we have seen in Chapter Two, George dos Santos and his executive team at Capital Bank Corp. (CBC) were in agreement that the current organization structure would need to be reevaluated. CBC's strategy required it to build deep relationships with new institutional clients while improving the speed of development and quality of the products the firm offered. The new strategy required CBC to transform itself. Where it now focused on selling a few niche products to the captive in-house market of its much larger British parent, CBC had to focus on developing relationships with U.S. and other institutional investors.

The current organization, however, was structured along historical distinctions of public and private markets that did not reflect the current trends (Figure 3-1). Nor did the structure create an easy interface for those clients who bought more than one product from CBC. Each of the six product divisions had its own sales officers. There was little coordinated marketing or feedback from clients. Further, credit and trading specialists were scattered throughout the product units, but none had the necessary depth of skill. Some people performed both credit and trading roles, sitting on the

Figure 3-1. Current CBC structure.

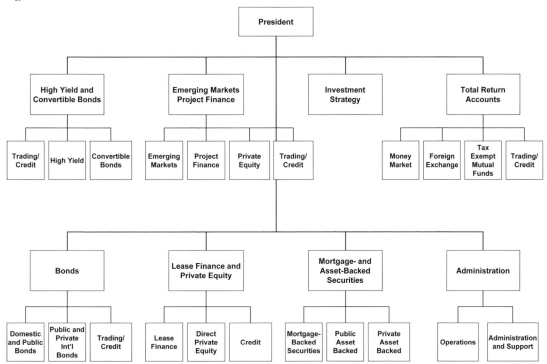

trading desk two days a week and analyzing credit the other three days. The current state assessment had shown the structure to be neither effective nor logical. Employees and managers at all levels and in all areas noted the duplication of effort, how the business lines didn't work together, and the inability to flexibly move resources to where they were needed.

Knowing it could not compete on volume and price with the major U.S. players, CBC planned to capitalize on its good reputation for strong analytics by offering customized and value-added features on its products. CBC would need to double in size from 200 to 400 employees in the next three years in order to build the talent and capacity to deliver to a demanding new client base. CBC also needed a new organization that could develop, market, and service these products competitively. George and his team recognized that some of the issues raised in the current state assessment were process, skill, and behavior issues. But it was also clear that the structure exacerbated these problems. With the new strategy, they would only become worse.

George wondered what his options were. What structural changes would get his organization focused in the right direction?

The *structure* of an organization refers to the formal way in which people and work are grouped into defined units. Any organization with more than two dozen people or so will need to begin to group people together in order to manage the work effectively. Grouping activities and positions into organizational units establishes common focus by creating standard processes, access to information, and a common chain of authority. It allows for efficient use of organizational resources and provides employees with an identifiable "home" within the larger organization.

The structure sets out the basic power relationships in the organization—how limited resources such as people and funds are allocated and coordinated. The structure defines which organizational components and roles are most central for execution of the strategy and how the business's profit centers are configured.

No one structure is best for every organization. The best structure is the one that helps the organization achieve its strategy. There are multiple ways to structure the organization to achieve its goals. As with every design choice, each involves trade-offs and compromises. The objective in choosing a structure is to maximize as many of the strategic design criteria as possible, while minimizing negative impacts.

In this chapter, we move into the *Design* phase of the organization design process (Figure 3-2). At this point the broader leadership team usually joins the executive team to explore options and make design decisions. Whereas the tools in Chapter Two were for use by the executive team, the tools in this and the following chapters are targeted to the leadership team.

Structure is usually the first issue addressed in this phase although it may overlap with consideration of the other design components in the star model (Figure 3-3). The steps in determining the structure are:

Step 1. Selecting a structure that is most likely to support development of required organizational capabilities

Step 2. Defining the new organizational roles in the structure and clarifying the points of interface among them

Step 3. Reality testing the design

Step 4. Determining a process to involve others in mapping the design

Step 5. Setting up a governance structure to move the design process forward

The five sections of this chapter guide you through these steps:

1. *Structural Concepts* outlines the basic ways to structure the organization and provides tools for choosing among those structures.

Figure 3-2. Four phases of organization design.

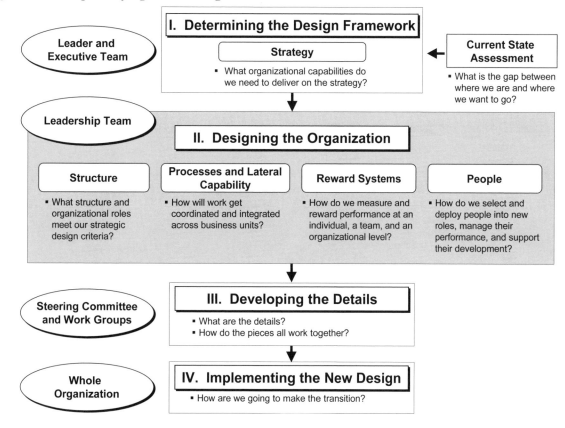

Figure 3-3. Star model.

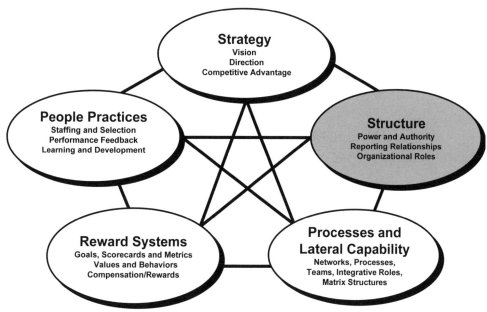

Source: Jay R. Galbraith, *Designing Organizations: An Executive Briefing on Strategy, Structure, and Process* (San Francisco: Jossey-Bass, 1995).

2. *Organizational Roles* provides tools for defining individual and unit roles and responsibilities, and clarifying the gray areas where they intersect.

3. *Testing the Design* provides lenses through which to examine design options and identify any pitfalls.

4. *Using a Participative Process: Mapping the Structure* is a process guide for involving the leadership team in creating a new structure for your organization.

5. *Design and Implementation Governance* defines a mechanism for moving the design, development, and implementation process forward.

STRUCTURAL CONCEPTS

An organization can be structured in five primary ways:

1. Function

2. Geography

3. Product

4. Customer

5. Front-back hybrid

In addition, there are overlay structures (teams, matrix) that complement these primary forms. These are discussed in Chapter Four. More than one structure can align with each of the core strategies (product, operations, and customer) discussed in Chapter Two. Although some of the words may be the same, a *customer*-centric strategy doesn't automatically imply that a *customer* structure is the best choice. Choosing the right structure depends on the particular focus of the strategy, complexity of the business, and size of the organization. It also depends on the organizational level that is being designed. When we defined *organization* in the preface, we noted that organizations are nested inside one another. Each of these nested organizations represents a *level*. Different choices can be made at different levels. For example, the overall structure of the company may be functional with all of the information technology (IT) people grouped into one department in order to gain the advantages of a functional structure. As the head of the IT department, however, you may choose to organize your function by customer in order to build relationships with the various internal clients your organization supports.

This section provides the conceptual framework for understanding the various structural options. For each option, an example is provided to illustrate how a particular structure supports that company's business strategy. Many of the examples look at structure from a corporate level in order to provide familiar and identifiable illustrations of the different options. The concepts apply, however, at all levels.

1. FUNCTIONAL STRUCTURE

A *functional structure* is organized around major activity groups such as operations, research and development, marketing, finance, and human resources (HR). The functional structure is best for companies that:

- Have a single line of business.

- Are small.

- Require common standards.

- Have a core capability that requires depth of expertise in one or more functional areas.

- Don't have a diverse line of products.

- Don't compete in the marketplace based on speed of product development cycle times.

An example of a company that uses a functional structure is Amazon.com. Amazon bills itself as providing "Earth's Largest Selection." It not only offers books, videos, music, toys, home improvement products, and electronics directly through its on-line "stores," but also beauty products, sporting goods, groceries, pet supplies, jewelry, and almost anything else in "z-shops" formed through partnerships with other Internet companies. Although there are many portal sites that sell products or link to other companies, Amazon has set the standard in selection, searching, and ease of ordering. All the z-shops use Amazon's familiar payment interface that automatically recalls the customer's preferred shipping address and payment method.

Amazon's strategy is to be both customer-centric and operationally excellent. It wants to create a place where consumers can find anything they want in one place and count on superior customer service. By carefully choosing the companies with which it partners and through on-line product reviews, Amazon has positioned itself as an advocate for the consumer. The message conveyed is, "We're giving you as much information as we can so that you can make the best choice."

Amazon's goal—"to get big fast"—has been criticized by those who note that it failed to turn a profit in its first seven years in business. However, rapid growth allowed Amazon to gain a competitive edge by creating communities of users that come to Amazon to find others with similar interests, and for Amazon to collect information on these customers and engage in highly customized marketing. The bet is that by offering customers more than just selection and easy ordering, they are less likely to go elsewhere.

Although Amazon sells many products, it does not produce any. It only has one line of business—providing access to those products. As a retail operation, Amazon's structure needs to provide IT, operations, customer service, and logistics capabilities along with the flexibility to continually add new products and stores.

Figure 3-4, which illustrates Amazon's structure during its start-up phase, shows how people are grouped together into functions. The day-to-day activities take place in customer service, operations, product development, and IT. The customer service unit answers e-mails and phone calls. Some "stores" require more service and may get a dedicated group. Operations runs the fulfillment function and the distribution centers. Product development consists of all the stores. In each store there are buyers, marketing people, and content providers (e.g., editors for books). IT supports the overall site as well as any unique needs of the various stores or auction sites.

Additional functions include HR (called "strategic growth" by Amazon to reflect the importance of recruiting, training, and development to its strat-

Figure 3-4. Functional structure.

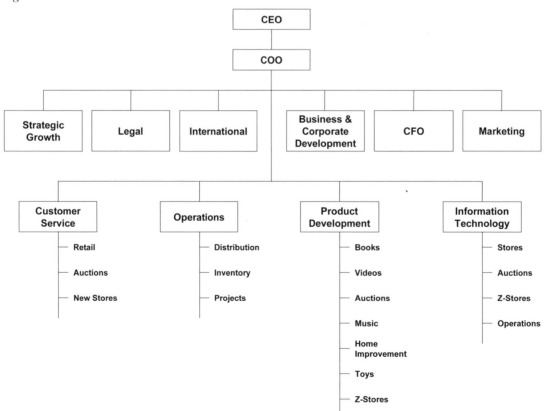

egy), legal, chief financial officer, and marketing. One particularly important function is business and corporate development, which focuses on the acquisitions, partnerships, and new stores that provide the engines for Amazon's growth.

The functional structure provides a number of advantages for Amazon and other single line of business companies:

+ *Knowledge Sharing*. Grouping employees together, especially those with specialized knowledge, promotes success transfer. As part of the same department, people have frequent contact with one another and can easily share ideas and confer with one another. People in a functional unit are part of a well-defined community and have strong identity with their "professional" group.

+ *Specialization*. A functional structure allows for specialization in particular areas of expertise. Creating a department of lawyers allows them to specialize in different areas, such as contract law or labor law, and build a depth of knowledge that is available to the entire organization. If they are dispersed among the business units, then each will tend to be a generalist, needing to know a little about everything but without the opportunity to develop true expertise in any one area.

+ *Leverage with Vendors*. A functional department that has common needs can present one face to the vendor. Its coordinated buying power can allow it to negotiate better contracts and prices.

+ *Economies of Scale*. Particularly in manufacturing, where equipment can be extremely expensive, grouping people into functions can provide economies of scale. For example, if all testing is performed in one department, a single piece of equipment can be shared across product lines.

+ *Standardization*. A functional structure reduces duplication and divergence in systems and procedures. For example, a central IT function sets documentation standards, which are then used for development projects throughout the organization. If IT is not grouped together as a function (or coordinated through strong lateral processes, teams, or policies, as discussed in Chapter Four), each business unit may set its own policies. When systems need to be shared or developed across business lines, the lack of common standards can become a source of conflict.

Amazon is a fast-growing start-up that expanded to more than 6,000 employees in its first six years. As it increases the complexity of its business, it may encounter the two significant disadvantages that functional structures create:

— *Managing Diverse Products or Services.* A functional structure is most effective for managing a single product or service line. Once the company branches into multiple, distinct product or service lines, a functional structure doesn't allow the attention that each requires. For example, Sony produces both televisions and portable CD players. In order to be a leader in each product line, Sony needs to marshal its resources around these products.

— *Cross-Functional Processes.* A functional structure tends to create barriers between different functional areas. The very strength of a specialized focus becomes a source of tension when areas must collaborate. Each area develops a unique, and often inward-focused, perspective. The classic example is the conflict between sales areas, which want to push ahead with new products, and operations areas, which are concerned about their ability to deliver on the promises made to customers. Although both areas have valid points of view, the result can be gridlock rather than collaboration. Decisions continually get pushed up to more senior executives for mediation, thereby creating bottlenecks and delays in decision making.

If the organization has a single product or service that does not often change, it can afford the long cycle times that occur while functional units negotiate across these boundaries. If speed is required to enable cross-functional business processes, such as new product development, conflicts can render the functional structure ineffective.

Functional organizations work best for small companies and for companies that have little diversity in the products they produce or the markets they serve. Since speed to market and product diversity are important in many industries, a straight functional structure provides few advantages for most organizations as they begin to grow.

Some writers use the term *functional structure* as a synonym for outmoded, traditional, or hierarchical organizations. The staid, functional structure is frequently contrasted with images of fluid, flexible organizations populated by empowered employees. Although the functional structure does have limitations, it is no more hierarchical than any other structure. Hierarchy is a result of the number and nature of management levels, distribution of power, strength of integrative processes across organizational boundaries, and overall organizational culture. The functional structure shouldn't be dismissed out of hand simply because it doesn't feel new. At some level in the organization, it can be expected to be a preferred design option.

Use the following checklist for a functional structure to determine which criteria your organization meets:

☑ Single line of business.

☑ Small.

☑ Core capability requires depth of expertise in one or more functional areas.

☑ Product diversity or fast product development cycles not critical.

☑ Common standards important.

2. GEOGRAPHIC STRUCTURE

A *geographic structure* is organized around physical locations such as states, countries, or regions. The geographic structure is best for companies that:

- Have a high cost of transport.

- Deliver service on-site.

- Need to be physically close to customers for delivery or support.

- Need to create a perception that the organization is "local."

The suitability of a geographic structure is highly dependent on whether you need to be close to the source of your products or to your customers. Cement companies have high transportation costs for their products and tend to organize geographically near quarries. Chains of hair stylists and restaurants require their customers to physically come to them, so they need to be located close to those customers.

A national pizza chain provides a good example of a geographic structure. The company shown in Figure 3-5 is organized into northern, central, and southern regions. Each region is large enough to support its own functional organization at the next level. However, two functions—purchasing and real estate—are centralized and shared by all the regions. The reason for this is that the staples of the pizza business—flour, cheese, and tomato sauce—can be purchased more efficiently when prices are negotiated with national vendors. Maintaining consistency while ensuring freshness makes a streamlined, efficient distribution supply chain a core organizational capability for the company. In addition, site selection, leasing, and management of real estate requires specialized expertise. It makes more sense for these specialists to work together than to have their knowledge diluted across the regions.

The geographic structure provides one clear advantage:

+ *Local Focus.* A geographic structure is important when culture, language, or political factors influence buying patterns and differ significantly by region. For example, Citigroup is organized by market

Figure 3-5. Geographic structure.

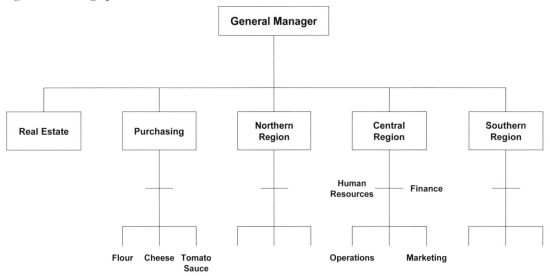

segment at a high level: consumer or corporate. However, each country in which the company operates has a senior executive who coordinates operations for that country, particularly in the areas of government relations and customizing products and services for the local marketplace.

The geographic structure often poses one distinct disadvantage:

— *Mobilizing and Sharing Resources.* The geographic structure gives power to the regional or country manager. As soon as a customer needs a "global" solution requiring talent from multiple regions, the geographic structure slows down response time. Consider a large enterprise-technology consulting firm organized by country. A Spanish bank announces that it will be outsourcing the management of its IT around the world. It puts out a request for bids. The managing partner of the consulting firm located in Spain begins what he calls the "begging process" of asking other country managers to free up people and send them to Madrid to work on the proposal. During the two weeks it takes to mobilize this team, a competitor, with profit centers organized around customer segments, such as banking, has already completed its bid. When a company is organized by country or regional profit centers, the power to allocate a limited resource (in this case, talent) resides with the geographic manager.

Advances in technology reduce the importance of location for geographically based businesses. For example, networks of automobile dealerships have traditionally been organized by region. The "Tri-State" dealers are defined by their local market (e.g., New York, New Jersey, and Connecticut). The growing practice of selling new cars over the Internet may change this. Whereas the need will remain for service centers to be located close to car owners, the importance of car dealerships in the sales process may diminish. Being "local" may no longer provide an advantage. On other fronts, Internet-based learning programs have expanded the reach of colleges to new customers. On-line banking allows banks to decrease the cost of building and maintaining branches. If the company's product can be easily and quickly transported or delivered, geography does not necessarily provide an advantage. Semiconductor plants need to be located where there is skilled labor, not necessarily close to raw material suppliers or clients. Credit-card call centers can be located anywhere as long as the employee shifts cover a range of time zones.

Use the following checklist for a geographic structure to determine what criteria your organization meets:

☑ High cost of transport

☑ Service delivery on-site

☑ Proximity to customer for delivery or support

☑ Perception of the organization as "local"

3. PRODUCT STRUCTURE

The *product structure* is organized into product divisions. Each division has its own functional structure to support its product(s). The product structure is best for companies that:

- Compete on the basis of product features or being first in the market.

- Produce multiple products for separate market segments.

- Produce products with short life cycles; speed in product development time is an advantage.

- Have a large enough organization to achieve the minimum efficient scale required to duplicate functions across the organization.

A product structure often evolves from a functional structure when a company diversifies its product or service lines and each line is large enough to support its own production. As the company grows, it continually subdivides divisions. As each division becomes large enough to support multiple product lines, it is subdivided further.

Figure 3-6 is an example of a medical equipment company. The company has three divisions: electronic instruments, medical instruments, and handheld computers. The medical instruments division is divided into imaging, measurement devices, and therapeutic devices. Each of these is further subdivided by

Figure 3-6. Product structure.

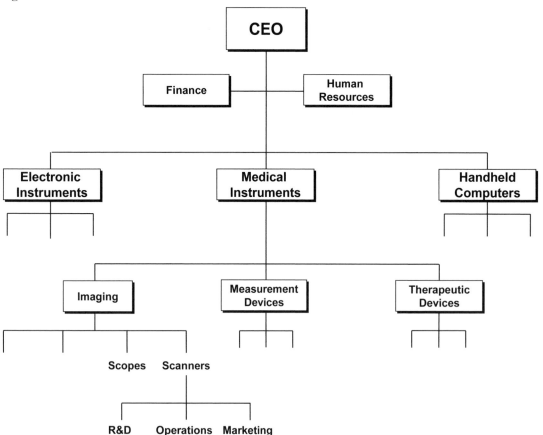

product. Each product line has its own research and development (R&D), operations, and marketing functions. The company's electronic instruments and handheld computers divisions are spin-offs from the main division of medical instruments that allow the company to leverage its experience with small computing and electronic devices to create equipment aimed at the medical market. Structuring by product line allows a clear focus on developing new product features and variations. Since each product line has access to its own support, it can focus on R&D and compress its new product cycle time without regard to what else is occurring in the organization.

The product structure has two primary advantages over the functional structure:

+ *Product Development Cycle.* By having each division focused on a single product or service line, the ability to design or redesign products end to end is compressed, an important benefit in markets where buyers expect new products or significant enhancements to be continually introduced. The personal computer industry is the best example of a product that competes based on rapid product development cycles.

+ *Product Excellence.* Structuring by product line also allows an organization to focus on innovation and product improvement. Each R&D division is narrowly focused on its line of products.

+ *Broad Operating Freedom.* The divisions in product companies usually have a high degree of autonomy. The head of each division is a general manager with complete responsibility for everything that goes on in that division. This freedom allows each division to pursue opportunities or new directions without the constraint of coordinating with other divisions.

The product structure introduces some challenges, as well:

— *Divergence.* In a product structure, each division manager is essentially running his or her own business and may even see himself or herself as being in competition with other division managers. In the example given, the imaging equipment product line developed a new scanning technology. At the same time, the handheld computer division was looking for scanning features to incorporate into its computer products. However, since the research departments work independently, the managers in handheld computers didn't find out about the scanning technology until it was released into the market. They lost valuable months of R&D time.

— *Duplication.* Each functional area is duplicated across the company and is more strongly aligned to the division it supports than the broader functional community. Standards, policies, and procedures diverge and efforts may be duplicated. Without strong lateral processes to re-create the benefits of the functional structure, a lot of energy can be wasted.

— *Lost Economies of Scale.* By dividing functions across product or service lines, economies of scale are lost. One solution is to create a hybrid structure where multiple product lines share a centralized function. Sometimes also called a "shared service," the shared function allows for greater depth of expertise and efficiency. This was illustrated in the example of the shared purchasing function for the national pizza chain discussed earlier.

— *Multiple Customer Points of Contact.* The product structure can create multiple points of contact for customers who buy more than one product from the company. Most large banking and insurance companies, whose separate product lines are largely a reflection of past regulatory restrictions, are still unsuccessful in their efforts to build front-end systems that allow the customer to access all products through one portal.

Use the following checklist for a product structure to determine what criteria your organization meets:

☑ Product features or being first in the market is important.

☑ Multiple products are produced for separate market segments.

☑ Short product development time is an advantage; products have short life cycles.

☑ The organization is large enough to achieve the minimum efficient scale required to duplicate functions.

4. CUSTOMER STRUCTURE

The *customer structure* is organized around major market segments such as client groups, industries, or population groups. The customer structure is best for companies that:

■ Compete in market segments where buyers have strength and influence over the market.

■ Can use customer knowledge to provide an advantage.

■ Compete based on rapid customer service and product cycle times.

■ Have a large enough organization to achieve the minimum efficient scale required to duplicate functions.

While functional and product organizations have internal advantages, they don't necessarily provide an easy interface to the customer. What is a simple and rational structure for managers is cumbersome and complex for clients. For example, AT&T is broken into separate businesses around its products of wireless cell phone services, local service, long distance, and Internet access. A customer might believe that buying all of these services through AT&T would confer some benefits—perhaps simplified billing or discounts. In fact, there is no way today that a customer service representative or salesperson working in one AT&T business is able to provide information about other products across the company, much less access billing records or resolve problems.

Organization structures based on customer, market, or industry segments make it easy for the buyer to do business with the organization. For service businesses that must intimately know the preferences of their clients in order to stay competitive, organizing by market segment makes sense. While Marriott International is a large, multifaceted company, it is also a good example of an organization that has chosen to primarily organize itself around distinct market segments, such as lodging, ownership resorts, and senior living. Figure 3-7 shows how within its lodging business Marriott has further segmented the mar-

Figure 3-7. Customer structure.

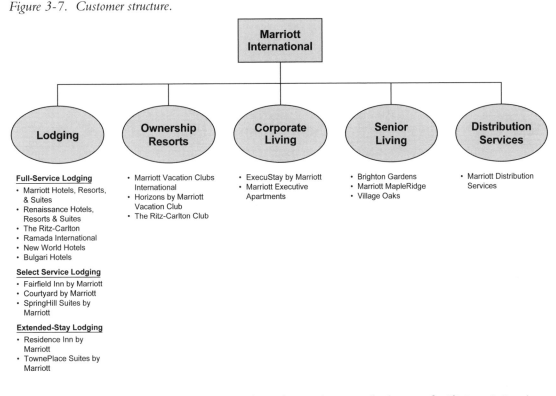

ket into full-service hotels, budget hotels, and extended-stay facilities. Marriott collects extensive information regarding its customers' preferences, so that on return stays, a visit can be customized down to the type of pillows on the bed.

The customer structure meets a number of growing needs for organizations, particularly those in service businesses:

+ *Customization.* Buyers have begun to demand customized products and services in exchange for their business. With the trend toward preferred providers, outsourcing, and contracting out, buyers are realizing the power they have to influence their suppliers. In addition, technology is allowing for more "mass customization" in both products and services. For example, Johnson Controls makes car seats for both Toyota and DaimlerChrysler. Rather than trying to sell essentially the same product to both companies with only cosmetic differences (which would make sense from a product perspective), each client gets seats tailored to its exact specifications.

+ *Relationships.* If long relationships and repeat business are important, customer structures provide an advantage. For example, a bank's customer service call center takes calls from a variety of bank customers. Although the call center ultimately supports the buyers of the bank's products, the call center exists to meet the needs of its internal customers—the managers who run the bank's divisions. Therefore, the call center's managers customize their services for their internal customers (e.g., scripts, wait time, follow-up service). Knowledge of the customer and responsiveness can keep an internal activity from being outsourced. It can also keep an external supplier as a preferred vendor.

+ *Solutions*. More and more organizations are finding that their customers want solutions, not just individual products. They want products bundled with services, such as consulting, advice, training, or follow-up technical support. Gathering together these capabilities in the organization and presenting them to customers in an integrated, attractively priced package is a challenge if they are located in a variety of divisions. The customer organization puts information and power in the hands of those employees who interact with and understand the unique needs of each customer or market segment.

The customer structure poses the same challenges as the product structure:

— *Divergence*. Knowledge and standards don't get shared across customer segments.

— *Duplication*. Development efforts may be duplicated.

— *Scale*. Opportunities for leveraging scale are lost.

These challenges can be addressed through strong lateral connections and by centralizing some common functions or services. A computer manufacturer that uses the same part across product and customer lines will benefit from a shared purchasing function that can pool purchases or negotiate the best prices with suppliers.

Use the following checklist for a customer structure to determine what criteria your organization meets:

☑ Important market segments where buyers have strength.

☑ Customer knowledge provides an advantage.

☑ Rapid customer service and product cycle times are required.

The organization is large enough to achieve the minimum efficient scale required to duplicate functions.

5. FRONT-BACK HYBRID STRUCTURE

The *front-back hybrid* structure combines elements of both the product and customer structures in order to provide the benefits of both. It allows for product excellence at the back end while increasing customer satisfaction at the front end. The front-back hybrid structure is best for organizations that:

- Are large and have multiple product lines and market segments.

- Serve global customers and must have cross-border coordination.

- Need to maximize both customer and product excellence.

- Have managers skilled in managing complexity.

The front-back structure bears special discussion because it addresses many of the disadvantages posed by other structures. It also introduces complexity into the design. Both the front-end customer organization and the back-end product organizations are multifunction profit centers. This is what distinguishes it from the other types of structures in which the profit centers are either geographically, product, or market oriented.

Figure 3-8 is an example of a global commercial bank, where the front-back structure allows the company to focus on global customers across borders. The "front end" is segmented by industry and then by client. Local account managers are assigned to countries where the client has a major presence. Local account managers build local relationships and deal with local delivery issues. The global account managers coordinate the overall delivery of service to the client.

Each industry group has its own profit-and-loss (P&L) accountability and includes functions such as sales, service, and local marketing. Each group sells

Figure 3-8. Front-back structure.

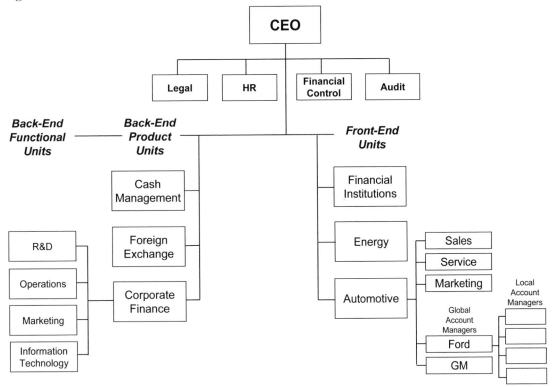

the company's products in ways tailored to its unique purchasing needs. They also use the knowledge gained by having an industry focus to feed back new product ideas to the product organization.

The front-end organizations draw upon the resources of the back-end organizations. As "buyers" of the product, they can ask for customization to meet the unique needs of their customers.

The "back end" is segmented by product line—cash management, foreign exchange, and corporate finance—each with profit-and-loss responsibility as well. In this example, each product is large enough to have dedicated functional support (operations, IT, marketing, etc.). If the organization didn't have such scale, these functions could be shared across product lines.

The front-back structure meets a number of needs that organizations have today:

+ *Single Point of Interface for Customers.* This is when customers are buyers of multiple products but want a single point of interface and one account. Although complex on the inside, the front-back structure creates a simple and clear interface with the customer. They have one account for all their products and no matter what distribution channel they choose, all information is available.

+ *Cross-Selling.* New customer acquisition is expensive. It is more profitable to sell more and different products to existing customers and develop long-term relationships with them than to find new ones. A front-back organization allows the sales channels to cross-sell and bundle products because databases and technology allow them to access complete information about existing customers.

+ *Value-Added Systems and Solutions.* A customer that plans to build a trading room needs someone who will sell him more than excellent computers. He is in the market for consulting advice, implementation support, and service contracts as well as equipment. These are all front-end services that can add considerable value to commoditized products.

+ *Product Focus.* The front-back structure preserves the product divisions that allow for innovation, product excellence, and sustained product development that characterize a product-structured company. In the bank example, the cash management, foreign exchange, and corporate finance divisions have the support and focus that allow them to compete with top rivals in the industry.

+ *Multiple Distribution Channels.* Almost every company today is developing an Internet strategy to allow it to sell products directly over the

Internet. Companies already organized around customers find it easier to move to e-commerce than those organized by product. Rather than completely shift focus, the front-back model allows the product-focused company to present a new, integrated face to the customer.

The front-back structure also introduces complexity into the design that, if not managed, can overwhelm the organization:

— *Contention Over Resources.* If the front-end unit is a small geographic or market segment, it may not be able to get attention from the back-end unit (e.g., adjustment in production schedules, customization of product features, pursuit of a new customer opportunity). Conversely, back-end units may be frustrated when trying to get front-end units to promote products or address functional priorities (e.g., resources for launching new systems or cost-saving changes).

— *Disagreements Over Prices and Customer Needs.* Front-end units are likely to push for price concessions to win new business or they may ask for highly expensive customization to meet a preferred customer's need. The back-end units will be focused on maintaining prices and margins. They may try to push products out to customers whether they are appropriate or not to maintain product profitability. These conflicts will require clear processes for resolution as well as managers skilled enough to negotiate solutions that are for the good of the company, rather than for just their own unit.

— *Determining the Placement of Marketing.* In a front-back hybrid structure, it may be difficult to figure out where marketing belongs, and it is often split into two parts. In the bank example, product marketing (e.g., cash management) would be placed in the back end. Segment marketing (e.g., automotive) would go in the front end. Coordinating the efforts of these marketing groups and avoiding having anything "sit in the middle" becomes another challenge.

— *Conflicting Metrics.* Front-end units will measure success in terms of speed, agility, and ability to customize solutions, while the back-end units will focus on scale, uniformity, integration, and efficiency. These conflicts will drive different behaviors within each part of the company, which will need to be recognized and managed.

— *Information and Accounting Complexity.* This structure is heavily dependent on shared information and accounting systems to ensure that both ends have the same access to data. The multiple and sometimes overlapping P&Ls require transaction and accounting systems that credit income, allocate expenses, and generate MIS (management information system) reports from multiple perspectives.

One company that is experimenting with a front-back structure is Hewlett-Packard (HP). Through its sixty-four-year history, HP had been organized in a product structure with eighty-three independently run product units. Products were developed with little internal collaboration on how they could be packaged together to create more value and new markets. The new structure combines the product units into two back-end organizations: computers, and printing and imaging equipment. The front-end units sell to two market segments: consumers and corporations. Cross-company initiatives focused on wireless services, digital imaging, and commercial printing are intended to bring parts of the company together to create new marketing opportunities. The idea is to rival both Sun Microsystems's product excellence and IBM's services strength.[1]

Use the following checklist for a front-back structure to determine what criteria your organization meets:

☑ Large organization with multiple product lines and market segments.

☑ Customers are global and cross-border coordination is a must.

☑ The organization needs to maximize both customer and product excellence.

☑ Managers are skilled in managing complexity.

Figure 3-9 summarizes the benefits and drawbacks of each of the structures discussed in this section.

SIZE OF THE ORGANIZATION

The size of the organization is another parameter for decision making. If the organization is small, a functional structure will probably be the most effective. A small organization can't afford to duplicate functions. As it grows, however, there is opportunity to break up the functions into other structures as volumes increase and they reach minimum efficient scale to hit the break-even point. Many organizations are driven to pursue growth, either organically or through acquisition, in order to afford them the size to specialize their products and services by market or industry. For example, U.S. investment banks organized by industry group had an advantage over European banks in bidding for work during the pharmaceutical mergers in the 1990s. Although many of the pharmaceutical companies were European, they chose U.S. banks because they were able to provide the in-depth knowledge that comes from creating a specialized practice area. European banks, which were still largely organized by country, weren't able to pull together a cross-border industry team.

The size of the organization doesn't change the design process. It only changes the number of iterations of the process. A 100-person organization

Figure 3-9. Summary of advantages and disadvantages for each structural option.

Option	Advantages	Disadvantages
1. Function *Organized around major activity groups such as R&D operations, marketing, finance, or HR.*	• Increased knowledge sharing within functions. • Ability to build depth and specialization—attracts and develops experts who "speak the same language." • Leverage with vendors. • Economies of scale. • Standardization of processes and procedures.	• Difficult to manage diverse product and service lines. • Cross-functional processes cause contention. • Different departments have different priorities; the customer's interest can get overlooked.
2. Geography *Organized around physical locations such as states, countries, or regions.*	• Provides a local focus.	• Difficult to mobilize and share resources across regional boundaries.
3. Product *Organized into product divisions, each with its own functional structure to support product lines.*	• More rapid product development cycles. • Focus allows for "state-of-the-art" research. • P&L responsibility for each product is located at the division level with a general manager. • Positive team spirit develops around products.	• Divergence among product lines in focus and standards. • Loyalty to product division may make it hard to recognize when a product should be changed or dropped. • Duplication of resources and functions. • Lost economies of scale when functions are spread out. • Multiple points of contact for the customer.
4. Customer *Organized around major market segments such as client groups, industries, or population groups.*	• Ability to customize for customers. • Ability to build depth in relationships.	• Divergence among customer/market segments in focus and standards. • Duplication of resources and functions. • Lost economies of scale when functions are spread out among customer/market divisions.
5. Front-Back Hybrid *Combines elements of both the product and customer structures in order to provide the benefits of both.*	• Customers can buy multiple products with a single point of contact and one account. • The organization can better cross-sell its products. • Ability to provide value-added systems and solutions when products have become commodities. • Preservation of product focus and product excellence. • Allows for a variety of distribution channels.	• Contention over where resources are allocated. • Disagreements over prices and customer needs. • Difficulty coordinating marketing functions that are split between the front and the back. • Conflicting metrics. • Information sharing and accounting complexity.

may have only one level of design. After the basic framework is determined, the resulting units will probably be only large enough to be structured one level further, if at all. A 10,000-person organization will still have a single organizing structure at the top level. However, there will be multiple levels of design below that. For example, a division may be organized by geography. Each geographic unit may then be structured into functional groups. The functional group may then be divided into local customer teams. The design process needs to be carried down through each level to the front line of the organization. If the organization is expected to grow, the design must be based on the antici-pated future size.

Let's look at how the CBC executive team decided to restructure their organization.

CASE STUDY

George dos Santos met with his executive team from CBC for two days to review the new strategy and look at options for restructuring CBC in a way that was more aligned with the direction the firm needed to go. After mapping, discussing, and testing a few alternatives with the help of a design facilitator, they decided to begin building a front-back structure in order to retain their organization's product focus while creating a capability to build relationships with new customers that would probably want custo-mized packages of products. Figure 3-10 illustrates how the executive team regrouped the product lines into four back-end units: equity, bonds, mort-gage- and asset-backed securities, and finance. They established two new front-end units: CBC and institutional accounts. The front-end units brought together all sales, marketing, investment strategy, and new business expertise into one place, to service CBC's parent company accounts as well as those of new external institutional clients.

Given the small size of CBC, each product line was not large enough to support its own functional units. The lack of functional support and exper-tise had been one of the issues identified in the current state assessment. The executive team didn't want to re-create this problem. Therefore, the sup-port units were put together as centralized functions to be used on a shared service basis. Separate trading and credit functions were established in order to build depth of expertise in these areas and reduce duplication. The exec-utive team also established two new roles—head of marketing and head of information and e-commerce—to focus attention on these needs.

Use Tool 3-1 to confirm your understanding of your current structure, what aspects provide advantage and might be preserved, and what aspects hinder achievement of your strategic direction. Use Tool 3-2 to begin mapping a new structure.

Figure 3-10. New CBC structure.

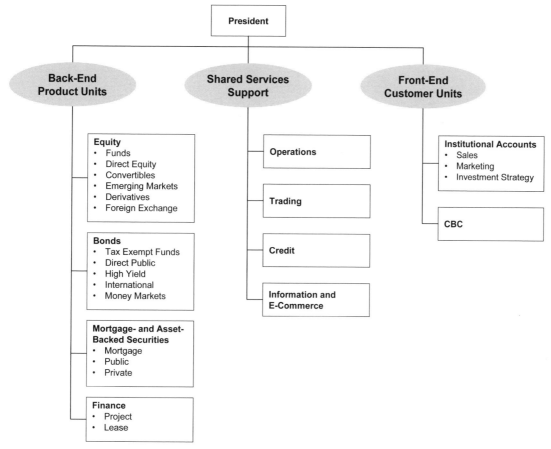

ORGANIZATIONAL ROLES

The change to CBC's structure created new organizational roles. More important than drawing the organization chart is defining the roles that each component in the organization is to play. An *organizational role* is a distinct organizational component defined by a unique outcome and set of responsibilities. An organizational role may be a business unit, a function, or a type of job. Even if your organizational components retain the same names after you have restructured, the roles they will play are likely to change. The relationships and responsibilities for each should be thought through anew.

Probably no other design activity is as important to the employees in the organization. Most current state assessments find some level of confusion over roles, responsibilities, and work handoffs that cause frustration and inefficiency. Time spent on clarifying roles early on will pay off exponentially later.

Figure 3-11 shows the organization chart for the private bank division of a financial services firm. The Private Client Bank has more than 1,000 employees in six states focused on providing investment, trust, and brokerage services for high-net-worth individuals. It is structured into three regions. Each region is then structured into functions—relationship manager, trust, credit, and sales. People in the functions work together on client teams to face off against customers. Services shared across the regions include centralized functions, such as risk management, marketing, MIS, and sales support.

In this example, organizational roles exist at multiple levels. A person in the position of credit specialist in the eastern region is a part of four different organizational roles.

- The credit specialist is a part of the *region*. Each region in this bank is a minibusiness, with a complete P&L responsibility.

- The credit specialist is a member of the *client team*. The team's role is to acquire and service a particular set of customers with the best possible wealth management solutions.

Figure 3-11. Private client bank.

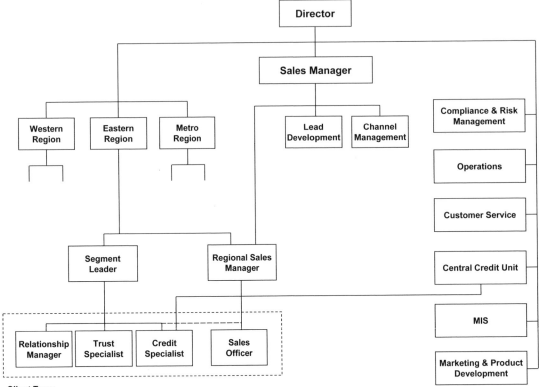

- The credit specialist is a member of the *credit function,* which is one of the specialist units that interface with the client-facing roles on the client teams. The specialist roles provide expert product knowledge to the generalist relationship manager and salespeople. As a member of the credit function, the credit specialist has a dual, or matrix, reporting relationship between the region and the central shared services (making matrix relationships work effectively is discussed in Chapter Four).

- The person in this job is also a *credit specialist* in terms of a positional role, a job with its own set of outcomes and responsibilities.

You can begin to see why even in a fairly simple structure, the interactions among roles quickly become complex and multidimensional. Each role has a counterpart with a different set of needs, goals, and perspectives. This can put them in contention with each other.

Organizations are intended to reflect different functional perspectives. For example, in the Private Client Bank, the market manager for a region will be focused on attracting and retaining clients by creating full-service, customized solutions. The heads of the centralized functional units, however, may be more concerned with creating common standards and solutions that will be cost-effective and efficient to deliver.

Ideally, the differences in viewpoint lead to a fuller view of the issues, identification of potential consequences, better ideas, better decisions, and in-novation. They should result in a balance between the differing perspectives that benefits the company and the customer. To achieve this, the goals for each organizational role need to be aligned to the overall organizational goals so that creative tension doesn't become destructive conflict.

Organizational role alignment requires three steps:

1. *Role Definition*: Defining the expected outcome and responsibilities for each of the various organizational roles

2. *Interface*: Agreeing on the mutual expectations each role has of the other when handing off work, receiving work, providing service, or collaborating

3. *Boundaries*: Clarifying the boundaries between roles, particularly for decision making and responsibility

Too often, role alignment stops at the definition phase. Although this is a start in communicating what each role does, it misses clarifying the "gray areas." No organizational role works in isolation. The gray areas are the points of interface where one role ends and another begins. Frequently there is shared responsibility, causing overlaps. Sometimes, the roles may become redefined too narrowly, resulting in gaps and the work not getting done at all. Role alignment requires defining the nature of these relationships, interdependencies, and handoffs. At the role alignment stage, participation often expands beyond the executive and leadership team, to include people who haven't been involved in the design to this point. Role alignment requires participation by people who will actually be in the roles and have familiarity with the potential conflicts and interface issues.

1. ROLE DEFINITION

Organizational roles are defined by two dimensions: outcomes and responsibilities. The role description is not a job description intended to list every task and activity. Rather it defines what is unique and different in each role and the value it is expected to provide the organization.

An *outcome* is an end state to be achieved. Outcomes are results to be attained. When possible time frames and measures should be included in the outcome statement. Examples of outcomes from the roles in the Private Client Bank illustration are:

- *Region:* Grow market share to 7.5 percent within twelve months.

- *Client Team*: Improve retention of client accounts by 10 percent in twelve months.

- *Credit Function*: Have portfolios and products meet all risk parameters.

- *Credit Specialist*: Have comprehensive credit expertise and technical support for the team and clients.

Focus on those outcomes that distinguish the role from others. Emphasize what is unique.

Responsibilities are the tasks to be performed that will close the gap between the current state of the work and the needed end states (the outcomes). After identifying an outcome, it is tempting to jump to the tasks that need to be performed. However, an important step is to determine the priority problems and obstacles to be overcome and the opportunities that present themselves at this point in time. The tasks then become the means to address the problems and seize the opportunities. Ask yourself the following questions:

- What are the highest-priority gaps?

- What are the plans that must be developed, what actions must be taken, and what resources must be acquired to close the gap?

- What steps should be followed to understand and reach the needed results?

- What would an "expert" do to address these problems and opportunities?

The responsibilities for each of the outcomes defined for the Private Client Bank roles might look like this:

- *Region*

  Outcome: Grow market share to 7.5 percent within twelve months.

  Responsibility: Design and market leading-edge products.

- *Client Team*

  Outcome: Improve retention of client accounts, by 10 percent in twelve months.

  Responsibility: Implement a consistent relationship management process.

- *Credit Function*

  Outcome: Have portfolios and products meet all risk parameters.

  Responsibility: Develop training program for all sales and relationship managers on credit issues.

- *Credit Specialist*

  Outcome: Have comprehensive credit expertise and technical support for the team and clients.

  Responsibility: Provide advice based on most current product and industry information for loans, renewals, and tax issues.

Figure 3-12 illustrates what the role description for a sales officer role might look like for the Private Client Bank example. Use Tool 3-3 to identify

Figure 3-12. Sample role description.

Role: Sales Officer

Outcomes	Responsibilities
Bring in new business from internal and external referral sources—increase new business as a percentage of total revenues to 20 percent.	Develop referral sources to generate new business.
	Increase and manage the lead pipeline.
Grow investment revenue to achieve above-market growth rates.	Assist relationship managers to sell to existing client base.
Cross-sell to enrich existing team book.	Report sales data (input sales data) for sales-tracking purposes.

the outcomes and responsibilities for the roles in your organization. Then use Tool 3-4 to help identify where there may be tension between the roles in your organization.

2. INTERFACE

The next step in role alignment is to define the mutual expectations between roles that are interdependent and have points of interface. Interdependencies may require roles to collaborate to get the work accomplished. It may also mean that one role is dependent on the quality and timeliness of another as handoffs of work are made between roles.

These interfaces are the gray areas that, if not well defined and managed, can easily become visible to the customer as an indication that the organization does not work as an integrated team. One way to identify interdependencies is to start from the perspective of the central business processes. For each business process, chart out the blocks of work and handoffs. Figure 3-13 illustrates a critical process for the Private Client Bank. A key point of interface is between the sales role and the specialist roles when the offer to the client is being developed. A second point is when the sale is closed and handed off to the relationship manager for account setup and ongoing service.

After thinking through the critical processes and points of interface, the sales role can identify the needed information and expected performance stan-

Figure 3-13. Sales acquisition process.

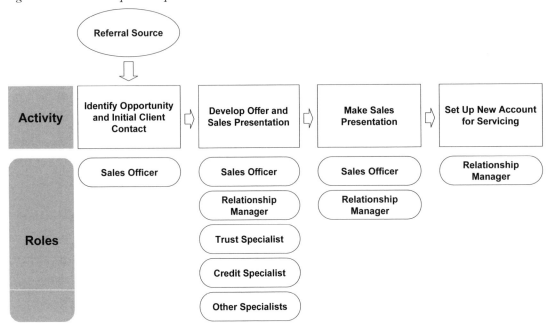

dards from the other roles (Figure 3-14). When the other roles do the same from their perspective, it can yield a rich discussion resulting in a set of agreements that can be monitored and referred to when issues arise. These agreements can also be used as the basis for a cross-evaluation performance feedback system, which is described in Chapter Six.

Another way to generate mutual expectations is to work through common scenarios that cause friction in the current organization or can be expected to do so in the new organization if roles aren't clearly defined. The example provided in Figure 3-15, the role scenario for the Private Client Bank, illustrates a common problem of geographic organizations. Clients don't often stay in one geography. When that occurs, the challenge for the organization is to coordinate its efforts so that opportunities are not lost. Mapping the responsibilities for each role in the scenario up front makes it easier to respond effectively when the situation does arise.

Use Tool 3-5 to begin to identify mutual expectations among roles in your organization.

3. CLARIFYING ORGANIZATIONAL ROLES AND BOUNDARIES

The final step in organizational role alignment is to identify boundary issues. Organizational conflicts occur when people have differing views regarding authority over a decision to be made or who has responsibility for an action.

Figure 3-14. Points of interface.

Role: Sales Officer

Key Relationship	What do they need to give to my role?	What do they need to get from my role?
Credit Specialist	Timely response to requests for loan quotes Accompany sales officer on sales calls when requested _____ _____ _____ _____	Prospective client profile document twenty-four hours before quote is needed _____ _____ _____ _____

Figure 3-15. Role scenario.

Scenario

A relationship manager in the eastern region of the Private Client Bank has just heard that there will be a large profit distribution at the Acme Company. One of the Acme executives has a family trust administered by the Private Client Bank. This executive called last week about another matter and during the conversation informally mentioned that her situation will change due to the windfall she is expecting. She hinted that the other senior executives will receive packages between $5 million and $10 million each. Acme's headquarters and the other executives are located in the western region. How does the relationship manager not only make the individual sale but help secure the broader business opportunity for the Private Client Bank?

Role	Sale to Existing Client	Capitalize on Broader Opportunity
Relationship manager	▪ Informs team leader and regional sales manager of the sales opportunity. ▪ Determines client needs. ▪ Develops strategy and approach for broadening the relationship. ▪ Determines support that will be needed to enrich the relationship; prepares sales presentation and materials. ▪ Calls on client.	▪ Informs the eastern regional sales manager and segment leader of business opportunity so that they can contact counterparts in other regions.
Eastern regional sales manager	▪ Works with segment leader to determine which sales officer on the team will provide support (if required).	▪ Eastern regional sales manager informs western regional sales manager of the opportunity. ▪ New York regional sales manager assesses opportunity and identifies sales officer to pursue the corporate opportunity. ▪ Supports western regional sales officer in developing the strategy for the pitch. ▪ Informs market managers of regional sales opportunities.
Segment leader	▪ Provides support to relationship manager to assemble the team and develop a strategy and approach to enrich the relationship. ▪ Keeps market manager informed of progress.	▪ Before the sale is made, works with the sales officer to determine the relationship manager who will service and enrich the relationship. ▪ May be asked by sales officer to act as part of the sales team.
Sales officer	▪ Works with relationship manager adviser as requested.	▪ Assembles team to address opportunity based on expertise needed. ▪ Coordinates sales team activities to prepare for meeting with client, develops sales strategy, and assembles sales presentation. ▪ Makes presentation to client. ▪ Before the sale is made, works with the segment leader to determine the relationship manager who will service and enrich the relationship. ▪ After sale is made, introduces relationship manager and other team members to client.

When people have differences over the process for making decisions or who should make a particular decision, then the conflict is unproductive and wastes valuable energy and time.

A commonly used technique for identifying where one role ends and another begins is responsibility charting.[2] Key decisions are listed in the left column of a grid. These are major decisions that involve multiple roles and where gaining clarity is important. They can be taken from the business process and scenario work you completed for Tool 3-5. The roles in the organization are listed across the top row of the grid. For each decision, a code is assigned:

R = Responsibility	Has the **R**esponsibility and authority to make the decision.
A = Accountability	May not make the decision but will be held **A**ccountable for it (often a more senior role).
V = Veto	Can **V**eto or block a decision. This is different from the normal veto power that a boss or higher-level role has—it refers here to a role that reserves the right of veto for a specific decision.
C = Consult	Must be **C**onsulted and give input before the decision is made.
I = Informed	Needs to be **I**nformed about the decision after it is made.

Here are some rules for responsibility charting:

- Each decision must have an R. Someone must be responsible for the decision.

- There can only be one R given for each decision.

- Each decision must have an A. It may be the same as the R role.

- The V should be used sparingly. Too many Vs may indicate that responsibility is being placed in the wrong role or that issues of trust and competence have to be examined.

- Ensure that the Cs represent a diversity of viewpoints for important decisions.

Figure 3-16 shows how a responsibility chart might look for the client team members in the Private Client Bank example. The sales officer has responsibility for pursuing new opportunities in the marketplace, but the sales manager has ultimate accountability. The segment leader should be consulted, but the other roles only need to be informed.

Figure 3-16. Responsibility chart.

Key Decisions	Roles					
	Sales Officer	Segment Leader	Relationship Manager	Trust Specialist	Credit Specialist	Sales Manager
Market Pursuit	R	C	I	I	I	A
Product Pricing	R	A	C	C	C	I
Development of Offer	A	C	C	C	C	I

The power of this tool is apparent when people complete the charts individually or in small groups and then compare them and use the differences as a basis for discussion. The overlaps and differing assumptions about role responsibility become clear and can be negotiated and resolved before conflicts happen in the workplace. Also, when conflicts do arise, responsibility charts are a useful tool to use to provide a neutral language for discussing responsibilities and the decision-making process. Use Tool 3-6 to clarify the boundaries in your organization's new roles.

Many of the organizational roles will overlap with individual roles and jobs. Undertaking the work of clarifying organizational roles will make the task of creating individual job descriptions and specifications much easier. These become the basis for restaffing the organization, which is discussed in Chapter Six.

LEADERSHIP ROLES

Special consideration should be given to the leadership and management roles in the new organization. Answer the following four questions:

1. HOW MANY LAYERS OF MANAGEMENT ARE NEEDED?

In order to create more nimble organizations, the current trend is to "delayer" and "flatten" organizations by removing management levels and giving front-line teams more responsibility for managing and coordinating their own work. Removing layers of management can bring decisions and communication closer to customers, develop autonomy and accountability lower in the organization, and decrease costs. Conversely, having more management positions gives people opportunity to develop supervisory skills, provides for closer coordination of work output, and frees managers in levels above to concentrate on more strategic priorities.

The number of management levels you need depends upon the span of control each manager has—that is, how many people a manager can adequately supervise and develop. The span of control depends upon the nature of the work. As summarized in Figure 3-17, if the work is complex and requires a high degree of management attention and control, then the span of control will be narrow. If the work is straightforward or teams have developed a high degree of skill to work autonomously, then managers can support a larger group of employees or a broader range of activities.

The span of control may change over time. If the design requires people to work on cross-functional teams, more management time may be needed in the beginning while the teams are learning to manage their own process and conflicts. As they mature and become more autonomous, less management is needed.

2. HAVE YOU CREATED TOO MANY MANAGEMENT ROLES?

How many of the new roles in your organization are pure "management" positions? The trend in flattening organizations is not just to increase each manager's span of control, but to make management responsibilities just one part of

Figure 3-17. Span of control considerations.

Narrow (managers can supervise fewer people)	Broad (managers can supervise more people)
The work is complex.	The work is straightforward.
Work cycles are unpredictable.	Work cycles are routine.
Work processes require close coordination.	Work processes rely on rules and procedures for coordination.
Workers are unskilled or inexperienced in their work.	Workers are highly skilled.
Workers don't have skills or experience "self-managing" (scheduling, resolving conflicts, making project plans, etc.).	Workers have some skills and experience working in self-managing, autonomous work groups.

a larger role. For example, a professional services firm had regional directors, area directors, and office directors. These directors, although they were partners in the firm, did not interact with clients, but spent full-time managing their designated purview. After a redesign, these jobs were eliminated. All senior partners had client responsibility. Some also had management responsibility. In the Private Client Bank example, the segment leaders and regional sales managers have some client-serving responsibility in addition to their management roles. Revisit the role descriptions that you have created for managers and ask how much value is each one adding.

3. HAVE YOU INCLUDED LEADERSHIP TEAM RESPONSIBILITIES AS AN EXPLICIT PART OF THE ROLE?

In addition to identifying each role's contribution in terms of managing their unit, also define the contribution in terms of the organization's leadership team. Managers have to wear two hats—leader of their unit and member of the organization's leadership structure. Leadership positions increase the demands on individuals. They have to be an individual contributor, lead their own part of the organization, and be a leadership team member. Many people have difficulty getting past seeing the world from a functional perspective. To move from being a leader of a function to a fully contributing member of an organization's leadership team requires a shift in perspective. Some managers will need coaching to help them understand that they are being expected to represent an enterprise view as well as a functional view. This includes:

- Making trade-offs to optimize the portfolio rather than focusing exclusively on individual business strategies

- Making decisions for the "corporate good" rather than narrow functional interests

- Focusing on business results (can we make money?) versus functional concerns (how we do this?)

Make these expectations part of the role so that they don't become performance surprises later on.

4. HAVE YOU CREATED A WORKABLE EXECUTIVE TEAM?

How many people will report directly to the leader in the new structure? Workable executive teams are typically five to ten people. Imagine yourself holding an executive team meeting. Is it clear who would come? Are they the people you really count on for advise and counsel? Would they represent a range of perspectives in the organization? It is always easier to invite more people in than to have to exclude people who believe they are part of the executive team because it is too large and unwieldy. Clarify which roles would be part of the executive team and which would be part of a broader leadership team.

TESTING THE DESIGN

The third major step in developing a new structure is to reality test the design from the perspectives of organizational capabilities, power, workflow, e-commerce impact, complexity, and consistency.

1. Does the structure meet the design criteria?

2. Does the structure create power imbalances?

3. Does the structure support the flow of work?

4. Have you accounted for multiple distribution channels, particularly the impact of e-commerce?

5. Do you have the right amount of complexity?

6. Is the organizational culture congruent with the design?

1. DOES THE STRUCTURE MEET THE DESIGN CRITERIA?

The first test is whether or not the proposed design meets the design criteria and moves you closer to being able to build the organizational capabilities that are essential to your strategy. Refer back to the design criteria you developed in Tool 2-3, in Chapter Two.

2. DOES THE STRUCTURE CREATE POWER IMBALANCES?

STRONG HEADQUARTERS VS. DISTRIBUTED FUNCTIONS

- Have you created a headquarters/field office model in your design?

- Are there opportunities to distribute some functions from the headquarters into the business units?

■ What advantages could you achieve by considering the distribution of functions (cost, competence, etc.)?

If your organization is geographically dispersed, you may have created something that looks like a headquarters with "field" locations. Activities needed by everyone are located in headquarters. In this way scale is achieved, duplication is avoided, and a broad enterprisewide view is maintained. However, you can anticipate conflicts that are likely to arise when these centralized activities are perceived as too far removed from the realities and concerns of the operating units.

HR is frequently configured in this way. HR generalists are aligned with the specific sites or businesses. Specialized functions such as compensation, benefits, and training are located in the headquarters. Predictable tension occurs regarding who works for whom. Are the generalists there to roll out programs from headquarters, or are the specialized staffs in place to support the generalists? In addition, field units generally feel that the services and products provided by headquarters aren't customized enough for them. As a result, they begin to re-create the activities in their local organization. The next step is often a move to decentralize—to divide up an activity and give autonomy back to the local organization.

This swing of the pendulum toward decentralization, while moving decision making closer to the customer, results in duplication that centralization and shared services are intended to avoid. An alternative to consider is a *distributed structure* (Figure 3-18). Distribution gives a whole activity to a local unit to serve its own needs as well as other units. Responsibility is placed where the competence is located. The function or service is centralized but not necessarily in a headquarters or corporate location.

Large consulting firms are typically organized in this way. The center of power and knowledge for a practice is located close to customers, rather than centralized in a headquarters. The financial practice may be in New York, automotive in Detroit, entertainment in Los Angeles, and energy in Dallas.

The distributed structure is less hierarchical than the traditional headquarters model. Local units gain enterprisewide responsibility that ties them more closely to the overall direction of the organization. When different units each have responsibilities, mutual interest is created to ensure that local interests don't supersede broader needs. One unit may provide training, another may provide project management services, and a third may provide application development. Each then has an interest in providing excellent service to the other units.

The distributed organization relies on a set of senior players who can work well together peer to peer.

Figure 3-18. Distributed structure.

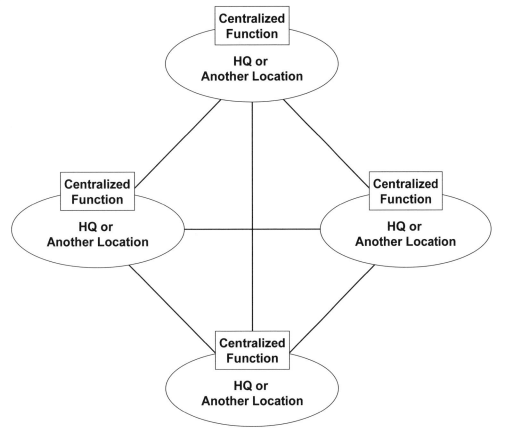

CHECKS AND BALANCES

- Where does the power lie in the new organization?

- What roles, processes, or other mechanisms provide balance to this new power center?

The organization's structure depicts the power and authority relationships among departments. The reality is that once the structure is determined, not all departments are equal. The choice of structure results in some areas becoming subordinate to others in terms of power, influence, and their role in the overall business decision-making process.

In the desire to orient toward the customer or fulfill other design criteria, the design may give too much power to one organizational role and weaken others. Although these checks and balances can be achieved through processes, measures, and management, the design may exacerbate potential problems. For example, if account management, which is more focused on sales than delivery, is overrepresented at the top of the organization, this may skew decision making. The voices of operational and infrastructure units may be drowned out—creating control problems when growth overwhelms the organization's ability to deliver.

3. DOES THE STRUCTURE SUPPORT THE FLOW OF WORK?

- Have units and departments been configured to facilitate a logical flow of work?

- Is work contained, end to end, in one unit where possible?

Look at how work will flow through the organization. If people are grouped together in ways that give them control over an end-to-end process, bottlenecks and weak points in the process can be easily discerned and changed. With one manager responsible for an entire process, it is easier to overcome the resistance to change that occurs when a process is spread among many functions and run by managers with different perspectives and interests.

Typically, however, the work flows across many different units. Most processes in an organization feed into other processes or are part of larger processes. Where one work process ends and another starts is not always clear. Nor does work always flow in one direction. What can look like an end-to-end process may really be a larger process that has been chopped into more manageable pieces. When this occurs, it is even more important to clarify the organization roles and boundaries as discussed in the section on organizational roles in this chapter.

4. HAVE YOU ACCOUNTED FOR MULTIPLE DISTRIBUTION CHANNELS, PARTICULARLY THE IMPACT OF E-COMMERCE?

- What are your distribution channels?

- Do they all hold equal power in the organization?

- How will you ensure that internal competition doesn't distract attention from real competitors?

Distribution channels might be branches or stores, the Internet, direct mail, sales agents, or catalogs. Many organizations use multiple channels to sell the same products at the same prices. Today, an organization's e-commerce initiative is often not just another channel, but a competing business.

For example, Barnes and Noble, in an effort to compete with Amazon, created a full-fledged on-line service. Books were priced differently from those in the physical stores. Although competing effectively on-line with Amazon, Barnes and Noble is in effect cannibalizing some of its own business. People that would have traveled to the store and bought a book now shop on-line and buy it cheaper. The question becomes, "Is it better for us to do it to ourselves if someone else is going to do it to us anyway?" The Barnes and Noble stores survive because through attractive and comfortable design and the inclusion of coffee shops they provide a destination and environment that transcends book shopping. And although some sales are cannibalized from stores, the e-commerce channel also reaches a potentially new market of buyers.

The same challenge is facing a well-known U.S. insurance company. It recently launched an e-commerce strategy that will directly compete with its large, traditional sales force. The Internet channel will reach people who never had access to or wanted to meet with a sales agent. It will also attract people who would have otherwise done business with an agent. More and more businesses are using both "clicks and mortar" to gain an edge, housing competing business models beneath the same corporate roof. Although it is too early to know what the full impact of Internet commerce will be on organizations, the potential impact on your business should be accounted for in your design.

5. DO YOU HAVE THE RIGHT AMOUNT OF COMPLEXITY?

- Is the new organizational structure overly complex? Can the same outcomes be achieved with a simpler structure?

- Have you simplified at the expense of your design criteria?

The organization needs to be as complex as the business it supports. Although managers may prefer to keep things simple, the organization design needs to be simple for only two constituents: the customer and the front-line employees that have to serve the customer. It is the manager's job to handle internal complexity if the business requires it.

If you have a simple and stable business, you probably have a straightforward organization that doesn't require a high degree of complexity. It is more likely, however, if you are trying to create a reconfigurable organization in anticipation of ongoing change, that you have a need for complex internal relationships. If you are doing business globally, with global customers and multiple products, you will certainly need a structure that allows you to operate both globally and locally and that can respond to multiple opportunities and demands simultaneously.[3]

At the same time, you can overdesign and introduce complexity where none is needed, creating a drain on management time and attention. Sometimes, complex design is required by the business strategy, but the current people in the organization don't have the skills or experience to successfully manage the complexity. You may want to adjust the design to account for this.

You will also want to focus on plans for staffing, training and development, and timing of the transition to the new structure. Design the ideal first, and then determine how you will prepare the organization to move toward it and whether you need an interim design.

6. IS THE ORGANIZATIONAL CULTURE CONGRUENT WITH THE DESIGN?

- What cultural values or norms might be challenged by the envisioned organization?

One of the advantages of designing a start-up organization is that there is no existing culture that has to be changed. The organization's designers and leadership can determine what type of culture they want to create. However, one is rarely starting with a blank slate. With an existing organization, the whole point of redesign is change—to acknowledge that what might have worked in the past is no longer sufficient for the future. However, the redesign effort will have to recognize the larger organization around it, its history, and the deeply held values and culture that have shaped it. Some companies are able to have highly entrepreneurial divisions in an otherwise staid and traditional culture. Usually, they are highly isolated divisions, such as R&D, or e-commerce initiative "skunk works." More typically, the people in your organization have to remain an integrated part of the larger whole. Particularly if you are new to the organization, be aware of the potential challenge posed by values and norms. Often they are unstated but can become barriers when you get to implementation. Two examples illustrate the issue:

Protection for Long-Tenure Employees. The insurance company was proud of its 150-year history. Many of its employees spent their whole careers with the company. Some were second- or third-generation employees. The company way was to provide job security for those employees with long service. Managers who let go long-tenure employees were not well regarded. The director of financial control, who had been with the company just nine months, reconsidered the extent of the planned restructuring of his organization when he realized the changes envisioned could not be supported by the culture. If the current employees in your organization are not able to make the shift in skills and knowledge, but still must be retained or redeployed, you may be similarly limited in the amount of change you can make or the speed with which you can make it.

Hierarchical History. At your last company, everyone worked in teams in a flattened, nonhierarchical structure with genuine teams. At your new company, although teamwork is a buzzword just like everywhere else, there are no true teams to be seen beyond the occasional task force. People rarely deal with counterparts before checking with their own manager. If your new structure and roles are built around your past assumptions of teams, recognize that the change is going to be larger and more difficult to make. You'll want to consider interim steps to build this capability and you will need more investment in training and development.

Use Tool 3-7 to assess the options you've generated against your design criteria, current state assessment findings, and the considerations discussed above.

USING A PARTICIPATIVE PROCESS: MAPPING THE STRUCTURE

The sections above presented the initial steps in developing a new organizational structure: considering the options, designing and clarifying roles, and reality testing the potential design. What we haven't discussed is how to actually develop structural options and a new design. How do you figure out what might work?

The design of the new structure and roles is a powerful place to use participation, as we defined it in Chapter One. If there are acknowledged issues with the current structure, people will be eager to create something better. The people working in the organization know what the issues are and can be surprisingly creative when generating alternatives to address them. Even more important, involvement becomes a form of education. Those who participate understand why changes are being made and can speak positively about the changes to their colleagues who are not directly involved in the design. The challenge for the business leader and the HR leader (who is often managing the involvement process) is to structure participation in such a way that you get strong, well-considered alternatives to choose from and people who feel empowered by the process.

This section describes a participative process for using the leadership team to generate and evaluate new organizational structures using the tools described in this chapter.

THE LEADERSHIP DESIGN OFF-SITE

We often suggest to our clients that they accelerate the design process by scheduling a three- or four-day off-site meeting with the leadership team. An off-site meeting yields a number of benefits:

- People are freer to be innovative when removed from their work site and its distractions. They are less likely to move a few boxes around on the organization chart and come up with an "old wine in a new bottle" solution.

- The intensity of an off-site meeting, assuming it is well structured and facilitated, seems to push people to generate more ideas than when they try to do design work incrementally while also responding to the demands of their day-to-day work.

- The design off-site focuses people on collaboration and the common ground they share as members of one organization.

- The investment in an off-site meeting signals the importance of the need for change.

A design off-site is a great way to "kick off" the change process. When in the design process to schedule the meeting depends on when you believe broader participation will yield the most value. There are two points in the process when a design off-site can be held:

- The strategic framework has been set and the leader wants to generate structural alternatives.

- The leader has already defined a new structure and wants to involve the organization in defining and refining organizational roles.

The experience of the United Nations Office for Project Services (UNOPS) illustrates how one organization used a leadership design off-site to generate a new organizational structure and initiate the change process.

CASE STUDY

UNOPS is a 500-person entity of the United Nations that provides project management and procurement services in every field where the UN has a mandate. Projects range from environmental protection, to land mine removal, to poverty eradication. For example, when the World Bank lends money to a country to build schools, it may ask UNOPS to manage the whole project, from hiring architects to buying the cement, from finding electricians to awarding construction contracts and paying suppliers. UNOPS is unique in the UN in that its budget is entirely funded by fees earned for services rendered. As a nonprofit, it prices its projects to cover costs, rather than according to what the market will bear. The requirement for self-funding means that UNOPS operates much more like a business than many other nonprofit and governmental agencies.

UNOPS's major client is the United Nations Development Programme (UNDP), which is focused on funding development projects. In 1999, 74 percent of the UNOPS budget came from projects done on behalf of UNDP. A number of trends that became apparent in the late 1990s forced UNOPS leadership to reconsider its strategy of dependence on one client:

- UNDP funding was declining with predictable impacts on the UNOPS budget. UNOPS needed to diversify its client base if it was to remain viable.

- UNOPS was largely passive toward the acquisition of new work. As a result, it was taking on a large number of small projects that had high acquisition costs and failed to lead to long-term client relationships. There were no strategic parameters for what type of work to pursue and what projects to decline. Few resources had been put toward marketing or building business acquisition skills.

- Competition from the private sector was increasing. Although UNOPS's nonprofit status allowed it to provide services at lower fees than competitors, its lack of experience in marketing and bidding on work and its inability to ensure quick, customized responses placed it at a disadvantage.

- Clients were becoming more sophisticated, demanding speed, value for money, lower costs, and increased flexibility from UNOPS and other project management and procurement providers.

The opportunities, however, were significant. UNOPS had no more than a 25 percent market share in any of the countries that were the top five recipients of UN aid. Reinhart Helmke, UNOPS Executive Director, began developing a new strategy in the fall of 2000 to respond to these trends. The strategy focused on developing new markets, deepening customer relationships, and building a global organization with a strong internal service culture (Figure 3-19).

While the strategy work was under way, a current state assessment was conducted that highlighted issues in each area of the organization. The major issues are summarized in Figure 3-20.

The organizational structure issues were particularly critical for UNOPS. The organization was structured into two areas—support and operations.

Figure 3-19. UNOPS strategy.

The support functions included centralized services, such as legal, finance, IT, and HR. Operations divisions were either geographic or thematic. Geographic areas delivered service regionally. Some were located in the UNOPS headquarters in New York. Some had been decentralized as local offices in the region. The thematic divisions, also split between New York and international locations, focused on particular types of market segments, such as environmental programs, rehabilitation and development projects, or program evaluation (Figure 3-21). When compared to the design criteria implied by the new strategy, the structure created a number of barriers, which are summarized in Figure 3-22.

Reinhart Helmke engaged a design facilitator and scheduled a four-and-a-half-day off-site meeting to share the new strategic direction and begin involving his leadership team in redesigning the organization to meet the strategic design criteria. Planning for the meeting centered on three areas:

■ *Involvement*: Who should be at the meeting?

■ *Agenda*: What needs to happen at the meeting?

■ *Process*: How should the design process be managed?

(text continues on page 106)

Figure 3-20. UNOPS summary of current state issues.

VISION AND STRATEGY

- Lack of connection between the current strategy and day-to-day decision-making.
- Little congruence between business plans and the stated strategy.
- Lack of clarity regarding the UNOPS value proposition.

LEADERSHIP

- Unclear leadership roles, responsibility, and accountability.
- A leadership group that doesn't operate as a team.

MANAGEMENT PROCESSES

- Decision-making roles and responsibilities not clearly defined.
- Lack of input from lower levels in the organization on decisions.
- Project management planning processes are lacking.

ORGANIZATIONAL STRUCTURE

- The current structure perpetuates blurred lines of reporting and accountability.
- There is a lack of role clarity between the thematic and geographic divisions.
- New units have been created without defining their value to the organization.

CONTROL SYSTEMS

- Performance metrics do not reinforce quality or leverage of resources.
- Performance management systems are weak.
- Shared standards for operations and service areas are needed.

SKILLS AND KNOWLEDGE

- Managing in a team environment is not an embedded skill.
- Managers lack marketing skills.

Figure 3-21. UNOPS organizational structure before redesign.

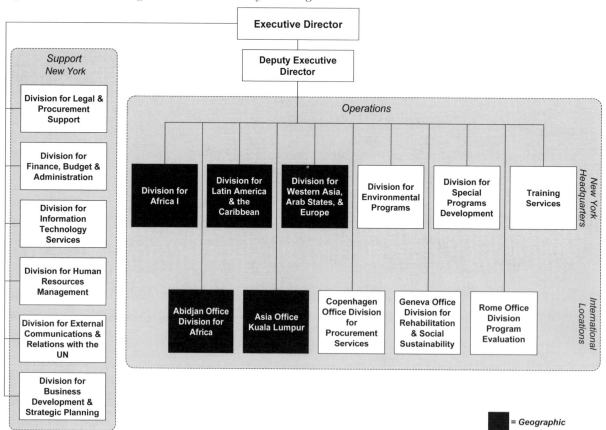

Figure 3-22. UNOPS new strategy requirements.

Current Structural Barriers	New Strategy Requirements (design criteria)
Geographies and themes don't reflect how customers do business. • Clients operate globally but projects are delivered locally.	Organized around customer.

Internal competition for clients.
 	
  • Geographic and thematic divisions compete for the same clients and all have delivery capabilities.
  • Each division has its own budget without a mechanism for sharing revenue.
	Clear ownership for clients.

Multiple points of contact for clients.	Coordinated client contact.
New York centered with offices abroad creates a headquarters/field relationship rather than global perspective.	Global organization located close to customers and work.
An internal focus—multiple managers and management levels.	Fewer management positions focused internally—more people engaged in serving clients.
Duplicate functions.	One pool of shared resources.
Largely immobile staff "owned" by geography, theme, or function.	Flexible deployment of resources around the world.
Status based on attaining higher and higher management positions—limited career paths.	Status based on client results—opportunities to manage larger and more complex projects.

Imbalance of power on the executive team.
 	
  • Support functions report directly to the executive director but the operations (i.e., revenue-producing) divisions report through a deputy director.
  • The seventeen division chiefs perceive themselves as equal contributors to decisions, creating an unmanageable and contentious decision process.
	An executive team representing key perspectives in the organization and of a manageable size.

INVOLVEMENT

Although you may be convinced of the need for change and already have some ideas of how you would like to see the organization look, restructuring is bound to make your leadership team nervous. Although they will publicly support the need for change, they may feel they have the most to lose. They'll be concerned that their area may be subsumed into another department and their position of leadership will disappear, or at least be diminished. Participation from a level or two below is necessary to create the upward pressure for change. People at this level are less concerned with power and position issues, and more concerned with making things work better.

The broader leadership team, comprising of the executive team and one or two key people selected from each of their organizations, makes for more dynamic and robust participation and ideas. Usually this ends up in a meeting of anywhere from twenty to seventy-five people.

For example, Reinhart Helmke decided to invite forty-five people to the UNOPS design off-site. In addition to the seventeen division chiefs, he also chose one or two of their direct reports to bring additional perspective to the discussions.

Use Tool 3-8 to determine participants for your design off-site.

AGENDA

The off-site meeting is a forum for education, decision making, and networking, and it has to be designed to achieve all these objectives. An overview agenda for the UNOPS design off-site is shown in Figure 3-23. The agenda for the meeting should be checked against three criteria:

1. *Is the flow logical? Does each activity link to the one before and after?* The agenda starts with the big picture and then gradually addresses smaller concerns. Participants first need to understand and agree on the changes in the external environment that are driving a change in strategy before they can design new structures and roles or agree on desired behaviors. In the UNOPS agenda, each day has a theme that builds on the day before. The first half-day is focused on understanding the competitive environment and the second day is spent on gaining clarity and agreement on the new strategy. Only then are the participants prepared to generate organizational structure options on the third day. The fourth day begins to focus on roles and behaviors. On the last morning participants wrap up their work, agree to both a transition structure and the assignments for continuing the design work, and decide how to communicate the results of their work to an organization that is eagerly awaiting their return.

Figure 3-23. Sample off-site agenda.

	Day One	Day Two	Day Three	Day Four	Day Five
	Understanding the Competitive Business Environment: What Are the Market Forces and Trends That Impact Our Business?	*Understanding the New Direction: What Are the Implications of the Strategy?*	*Envisioning a New Organization: How Best Can We Deliver on the Strategy?*	*Clarifying Roles and Creating Accountability: What Roles Need to Be in Place and How Will We Hold Ourselves Accountable?*	*Creating a Transition Plan: What Transition Strategy and Plans Do We Need to Move to the Future?*
Morning		Review Presentation: Defining the New Business Strategy (Leader) Table Team Work: Identify Key Messages, Questions, Concerns, and Disagreements Discussion	Review Presentation: Building a Service Organization (Outside Speaker) Question-and-Answer Session Summary: What Can We Learn from this Example? Presentation: Organization Design Parameters (Leader)	Review Presentation of Integrated Design to the Leader Discussion	Review Change Process Check Transition Planning Defining Next Steps

Afternoon	Welcome and Introduction
	
	Agenda, Objectives, and Guidelines
	
	Summary and Discussion of Current State Assessment Findings
		Small Group Work: Understanding the Strategy
		  1. Core Strategy
		  2. Strategic Resources
		  3. Customer Interface
		  4. Value Network
		Report Out and Discussion
			Small Group Work: Developing Organizational Alternatives
			
			Report Out and Discussion
				Clarifying Leadership Roles and Responsibility/ Discussion
				
				Small Group Work: Building a Global Service Culture
				
				Report Out and Discussion
				
				Leadership Behaviors and Accountability
				
				Discussion and Debrief
					Developing Communication and Involvement Plans
					
					Close/End of Meeting

Evening	Presentation: The Changing Market (Industry Speaker) Table Team Activity: Questions and Facts Question-and-Answer Session	Free Evening	Integrating Designs and Presentation Preparation (Two Delegates From Each Small Group)	Free Evening	

2. *Is the expected outcome of each activity clear?* There is a saying in the litigation profession that a lawyer in the courtroom should never ask a question to which she doesn't already know the answer. The same desire to avoid unwanted surprises should guide the agenda design. Open-ended discussions without a clear purpose should be avoided. Otherwise you can end up having the meeting hijacked by side issues that are of interest or importance to only a few people in the room. The objective of each activity should be clearly stated. Is it to:

- Convey information?
- Clarify understanding?
- Generate options?
- Evaluate alternatives?
- Summarize options, issues, or decisions?

3. *Do you have a mix of modalities?* Everyone has sat through meetings that were no more than a series of presentations followed by open question-and-answer sessions. Account for the fact that people have different learning and discussion styles. Use small groups of varying sizes and configurations to allow people to digest and discuss what they have heard before they respond to a presentation. Have people work on flipcharts to draw and diagram their ideas. Provide materials so that they can create three-dimensional representations.

Sometimes having people act out skits that illustrate the new roles in the organization or the new behaviors required can be an effective way to engage all of the creativity and energy of the group.

Consider including the following components in your agenda to prepare the group for design work.

■ *Industry Trends/Competitor Information.* Don't assume that everyone agrees on where your industry is headed or what external forces are driving the need for a strategic shift or redesigned organization. Ensure there is a common agreement early in the meeting. Engage the group in a discussion of the implications of these trends and in identifying the most relevant facts for your business. These can be referred to later to refocus people if they lose sight of the bigger picture.

UNOPS invited the head of a private sector company that operated in the market UNOPS was preparing to enter. As a private sector business, this company had limited access to the UN market and was interested in forming an alliance with UNOPS. Most competitors will not be as eager to share their view of the industry. A speaker from an industry group, an academic, or a consultant can provide this outside perspective. If your organization is one piece of a larger company, this perspective can also be provided by a senior executive from another area of the company, who can speak to how the enterprise is responding to changes in the environment. If a suitable speaker can't be located, send the participants copies of articles for prereading as a substitute. As you prepare for your design off-site, ask yourself:

—What are the key industry trends and facts that you believe everyone at the meeting needs to understand and agree on?

—Who might be able to provide the "big picture" perspective on your industry?

—What recent reports or articles could supplement or substitute for a speaker?

■ *Best Practices.* It is helpful to have a model in mind, an organization that you admire, which is either in your industry or facing some of the same challenges. One option is to invite someone from another company who has gone through a similar transition. Hearing about a similar company's journey early in the off-site meeting reassures participants that while this is hard work, many companies go through it successfully. If the strategic or structural issues are similar, that is even better. The comparisons may spark new thinking. Again, having participants read articles before the meeting and then discuss them at the meeting can also be effective.

Reinhart Helmke invited a former partner from Ernst & Young Consulting Services to speak at the UNOPS off-site. Although their businesses and markets are very different, both organizations share similar operating models. E&Y transformed during the 1990s from a fairly small, geographically based organization, which relied on the larger E&Y audit and tax business for clients, to one of the top five global consulting firms in the world by the end of the decade. The need to streamline and delayer the organization, create profit accountability around customers rather than by geography, and create measures and rewards that support a service culture all resonated with the UNOPS listeners. The group quickly went from believing their situation was unique to exploring how they might be able to apply the lessons of E&Y to their own organization.

—What issues face your organization that people may believe are "unique"?

—What other organizations might have faced challenges similar to yours that could provide lessons learned?

■ *Current State Findings.* Share the results of the current state assessment. It will get the issues out on the table. Rather than spend time rehashing why things don't work well, you can devote more of the meeting agenda to problem solving. By acknowledging all of the issues that currently exist and demonstrating that people's concerns have been heard, you will find it much easier to refocus the participants on the future.

■ *Strategy.* The participants need a good understanding of the strategy and how the organization needs to support that strategy. You will have done this work on your own or with the executive team. It should be presented at the off-site. The strategy is the foundation of the meeting. Be sure that it is presented in a way that is easy for participants to understand, remember, and communicate to their own staff when they get back to the job.

—What has changed in the environment?

—What are the challenges and opportunities?

—What are the three to five most important points of the new strategic direction that you want people to remember?

■ *Design Parameters.* The design parameters set out the boundaries for the process, the nonnegotiables, as well as the criteria by which you will judge the design. The design parameters should include:

1. The success indicators, limits, and assumptions you generated in Chapter Two as part of *Determining the Design Framework.*

2. The decision-making process and the meeting participants' role in it.

3. Whether you are willing to commit to accepting a structural design the group agrees on or whether their work will be input to be taken under advisement. (See Tool 1-5, "Determining Participation.")

4. The time frame. Ask the group to design an ideal structure for twelve to eighteen months from now. It will free them from the "we can't do that today" arguments that will narrow their thinking.

Reinhart Helmke communicated a clear set of design parameters at the UNOPS off-site. These provided guidance on the direction of the design without prescribing what the organization was to look like. He committed to accepting a new structure and design as long as it represented the consensus of the group and met all of the design criteria and parameters. He also recognized that whatever was developed at the off-site would need substantial additional work before it would take the shape of a fully formed recommendation. UNOPS design parameters are summarized in Figure 3-24.

What are your design parameters?

What are the criteria by which you will judge a design to be successful?

■ *Structural Options*. Most people are not used to thinking about structure in a formal sense. You may want to provide prereading or use an activity where participants match scenarios and organizational structure in order to introduce the language of structural design and organizational roles.

Use Tool 3-9 to determine the components of your design off-site.

PROCESS

How do you involve people in the task of redesigning their organization so that they have a high probability of generating good options? As discussed, structuring the agenda to first provide adequate information is essential. The

Figure 3-24. UNOPS design parameters.

■ Account for all current activities but do not limit yourself by their current form.

■ Eliminate overlapping territories and internal competition.

■ Allow for a balanced use of resources.

■ Create a truly global organization—consider moving functions outside of New York to other locations.

■ Integrate client relation management with business development.

■ Allow us to deliver solutions, not just products and services, to our customers.

■ Make it easy for our customers to do business with us and help us build long-term relationships with our customers.

■ Allow us to respond to new opportunities quickly.

■ Increase knowledge sharing and success transfer.

second step is to provide a process and tools to guide the group's work. Some things to think about:

■ *Structuring the Teams.* Divide the group into teams of eight to ten that are mixed by function and location, but not by level. Because restructuring can become such a personal issue for people in leadership positions, they may be tempted to exert their positional power to influence people at lower levels. Keep the leaders together in one or two teams and let other participants work with colleagues at their own level. These different teams probably will come up with strikingly different alternatives.

■ *Leader Participation.* Generally, as the leader, you should not participate in the design process. As the ultimate decision maker, your comments carry too much weight. You may even want to leave the meeting site while the groups are working in order not to influence them or limit their creativity.

■ *Space.* The teams can work in separate break-out rooms or in corners of the main meeting room if it is large enough. Seeing the work of other groups can generate positive competition, but if the groups work in the same room it must be large enough so that they don't distract each other.

■ *Facilitation.* Facilitation is strongly recommended for a design off-site. Use a design facilitator with some experience in the field of organization design, if possible. Organizational structure is a contentious topic and people can easily lose sight of the big picture and the overall goals. Ideally, each team should have its own facilitator to keep it on track.

■ *Tools.* We have found two tools particularly useful for helping people generate ideas.

1. *Post-it Notes®.* Post-it Notes allow people to explore options for visually reconfiguring the organization over and over again without having to redraw it each time. Working on a large piece of butcher paper pinned to the wall, people can use Post-it Notes of different shapes and colors to represent functions, roles, and relationships. If the organizational components are not going to change (e.g., if finance must stay together as one function), then the Post-it Notes can be prelabeled. If more flexibility is desired in reconfiguring the pieces of the organization, allow the teams to label the Post-it Notes themselves.

2. *Cases.* Provide the teams with a short (one or two paragraph) case that illustrates a common, dysfunctional scenario in the current organization. As they design, ask them to consider how their solutions would address the issues raised in the case. The case provides a concrete way of walking through how potential new structures and roles will work.

■ *Reviewing Results.*

1. *Review all alternatives.* One option is to have each team present their suggested design to the leader and the rest of the group. You can ask questions to clarify and identify areas of commonality and divergence among the designs. Reviewing them all allows you to pick the best elements of each. The disadvantage of this approach is that it doesn't gain consensus among the participants and that there may be charges of favoritism if you eventually choose one design over another.

2. *Have the group reach consensus.* The alternative is to have each group present their design and rationale to the other groups before you return. Each group then identifies one or two people to become delegates on a new team that spends time integrating the designs of all the teams, identifying where there is agreement and where there are differences in approach or unresolved issues. When this consolidated design is presented to you for review, you can express your concerns and point out elements that you'd like considered further. The advantage of this approach is that the group leaves with one design that if not complete is at least representative of the new direction and reflects everyone's concerns. A follow-up work group can be configured to continue working on the open issues after the design off-site is over.

■ *Time.* The teams need at least four hours to work and then fifteen minutes each to present to each other and raise questions. If you will be asking them to consolidate their work, structure the meeting so that the design work occurs in the afternoon and the consolidation can occur in the evening. The delegates to the consolidation team should be prepared to work late into the evening because it takes a significant amount of time to negotiate the differences and agree on an integrated presentation.

CASE STUDY

The UNOPS group spent the afternoon of the third day of their off-site working in four teams. Two of the teams comprised lower-level participants. The four teams generated very different design solutions. As expected, the lower-level staff members were bolder and more willing to consider abolishing the division-chief structure. A consolidation team (comprising two delegates from each of the design teams) worked far into the night to merge the areas of agreement and create one integrated presentation.

The final proposal responded to the design criteria shown in Figure 3-25. The proposed customer structure featured account managers able to respond to their UN-funding clients as well as to the local and national governments to which they delivered services. Regions would remain an important dimension in the structure to facilitate the delivery of service and to build both local presence and relationships. However, the geography would be clearly subordinate to the customer dimension. Global account managers would coordinate acquisition, thus eliminating the current internal competition. Four unresolved issues were identified for further examination:

- The need to create decision-making criteria and processes for client allocation, account allocation, and setting up new regional offices

- The need to define who would be on the executive team to ensure adequate representation of all views

- The concern that too much power might be concentrated in the hands of the global account managers

Figure 3-25. Proposed UNOPS structure (generated by participants at a design off-site).

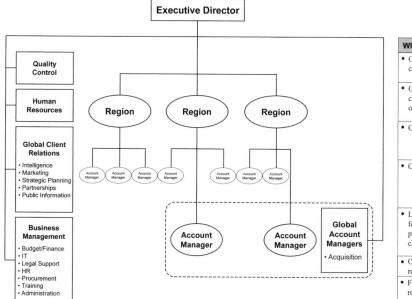

Client: A UN-funding source or a local country or government.

Account: A defined portfolio of work for a client.

Account Manager: Primarily responsible to the client for all activities related to an account; manages the resource flow through a portfolio manager at the regional level; has responsibility for cost management, client retention, and staff development.

Regional Office: Center for delivery that most staff will call home; principle reference point for governments.

Response to Design Criteria

Where we need to go . . .	What we propose . . .
• Organized around customer.	• Organized around accounts (institutional clients (and regions.
• Global organization located close to our customers and our work.	• Based on a network of regional offices where implementation takes place.
• Clear ownership for clients.	• Account managers coordinated with and accountable to clients (accounts)
• Coordinated client contact.	• Regional offices coordinate at country level and account managers at institutional level.
• Less management positions focused internally—more people engaged in serving clients.	• Outward-looking structure.
• One pool of shared resource.	• Global Client Relations and Knowledge Center.
• Flexible deployment of resources around the world.	• Resources can be moved between client accounts based on changing demand.
• Status based on client results—opportunities to manage larger and more complex projects.	• Career path through various levels of implementation and account management.

■ The lack of adequate mechanisms and skills to share knowledge throughout the organization

Four work groups were set up to carry the design forward: structure, knowledge management, HR, and communication.

At the conclusion of the design off-site, you won't have a finished product. Much work will still remain. This is the time to designate work groups to carry the process forward. One group might continue the structural work, while others can begin working on the organizational issues that were identified in the current state assessment or as a result of the off-site. With at least a structural framework agreed upon, the remaining work can proceed with a common context and point of reference.

DESIGN AND IMPLEMENTATION GOVERNANCE: WORKING THROUGH THE DETAILS

One way to move the design work forward and begin planning for implementation is to create a governance structure. A *governance structure* is a set of roles and processes used to ensure that plans progress, activities are coordinated, and the change process is not overwhelmed by current business demands. It acts as a planning group for the organization that provides both consistency during the transition process and models the new behaviors (teamwork, cross-functional cooperation, etc.) that demonstrate visible and tangible evidence of the commitment to change. It is used to gain ownership, participation, and involvement across the organization.

The governance structure combats the inertia that is likely to set in after the initial enthusiasm of the design off-site and of the whole creative process of the design stage wears off. As much as the intensity and excitement of an off-site can focus and accelerate change, there is a danger that as soon as people return to their jobs, the momentum is lost. Follow-up plans get pushed to the side while everyone catches up on the work he or she missed and deals with immediate business needs. The hard labor of working through the details is given low priority. The positive experiences of working together across organizational lines gives way to old patterns of behavior.

The governance structure comprises a parallel set of roles outside of the current hierarchy that is responsible for the day-to-day business. This parallel structure brings together a subset of people in the organization to take ownership of the design process and push the work forward. Involvement in the process is usually in addition to job duties, although you may want to excuse some people from some of their job responsibilities or provide them with extra support so that participation doesn't become perceived as punishment. Figure 3-26 illustrates how the parallel structure is often configured.

Below are definitions of common roles and typical responsibilities in the governance structure. How the responsibilities are allocated among roles is not as important as defining each role explicitly. Demarcating roles early in the process will avoid overlap of effort or conflict over authority among those involved.

SPONSOR

When the organization is part of a larger whole, it is often useful to have a sponsor at a higher level. The sponsor could be the leader's boss or even someone more senior who has an interest in the organization. The sponsor:

Figure 3-26. Governance structure.

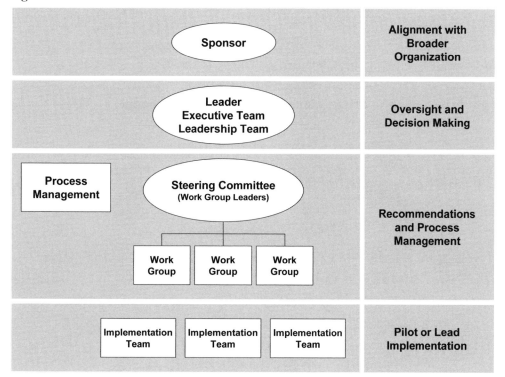

- Provides feedback and advice on design options.

- Ensures that the redesign is aligned to the broader organizational strategy.

- Secures resources for the redesign process outside of the reach of the leader.

- Secures cooperation and participation from other parts of the larger organization that are impacted by the redesign and need to be involved.

LEADER

The leader is the business head of the organization. A leader may be the CEO, the director of a function, or the head of a line of business. Whoever is most senior in the organization undergoing redesign is the leader. The leader:

- Makes the determination that the organization needs to be redesigned.

- Determines the parameters for the process, including how decisions will be made and who will be involved.

EXECUTIVE TEAM

The executive team typically comprises the direct reports of the leader. If the team in place will remain throughout the redesign, most leaders use their executive team as a decision-making body. Sometimes, you may not have a functioning executive team. Key positions may be open or you may not have confidence in the competence of the people you have. If you are contemplating making major changes to the executive team, make them as soon as possible, so that the new roles can be sorted out and the group can begin to operate as a unified body that guides the rest of the organization through the change.

The executive team:

- Sets the boundaries for the redesign—what can be changed and what is off the table.

- Articulates the success indicators—the goal of the redesign.

- Sets the overall timing for the process.

- Makes decisions based upon steering committee and work group recommendations.

- Provides oversight to the process.

LEADERSHIP TEAM

The leadership team may be the same as the executive team for a small organization. In larger organizations, it is about double the size of the executive team and includes people who may not be direct reports of the leader but who do have critical and influential roles in the organization. The leadership team may be involved in the same activities as the executive team. In addition, the leadership team:

- Designs the basic components of the organization design for further development by work teams

WORK GROUPS

Once the boundaries for the change process are determined and the highest-priority actions are identified, work groups can be used to generate options, research best practices, and make recommendations. The work groups focus on the details. They flesh out the design framework and decisions developed by the leadership teams. If the work is complex, it may be organized into work streams with multiple work groups within each stream.

The leader of each work group is usually appointed. The work group leaders should not simply mirror the leadership team. Leading a work group is a great opportunity for high potentials in the organization to get visibility. Depending on the size of your organization, you'll probably want to choose people two or three levels down from you.

One issue you may encounter when setting up work groups is that the work will overlap with the mandate of a functional group. For example, an area of work identified in the design process could be creating a new compensation plan for teams that are being introduced into the design. Clearly, if you have compensation experts in your organization, they should be involved in this work along with representatives from other parts of the organization. The work should also become part of the compensation group's work plan. By creating a work group around the issue, however, you ensure that a topic that is essential for the success of the new teams, roles, and structure doesn't get neglected.

A good size for a work group is eight to ten members. Although a smaller group is easier to manage, the reality is that day-to-day business needs will vary the level of time that participants can devote to the work group. A larger size ensures that there are enough people available for meetings and to keep the work going. The members of the work group should reflect a range of views in the organization. Using representatives, as described earlier, is one way of ensuring that participants on the teams have the support of their colleagues. Work groups:

- Develop project plans, methodologies, timelines, and define the resources required to achieve project goals.

- Research internal and external best practices.

- Generate and evaluate design options.

- Make recommendations to the steering committee.

- Complete all activities to meet project deliverables (i.e., do the work).

- Identify operational implications that arise as a result of the design implementation, and raise these implications with the steering committee.

- Communicate and work with other work groups to integrate and leverage efforts.

STEERING COMMITTEE

The steering committee structure is invaluable for ensuring that plans are moved forward, activities are coordinated, and the design and implementation process is not overwhelmed by current business demands.

The steering committee comprises the work group leaders and the process manager (if one is being used). The steering committee is responsible for bringing forward the options and recommendations developed by the work groups to the leadership team for consideration. It is the planning group that provides both consistency during the transition process and models the new behaviors (teamwork, cross-functional cooperation, etc.) that demonstrate visible and tangible evidence of the commitment to change. The steering committee is charged with the leadership and day-to-day management of the design effort. The steering committee:

- Provides overall guidance and direction to the work groups.

- Reviews and approves the goals, methodologies, plans, and timelines of the work groups and ensures their consistency.

- Provides coaching, feedback, and plays "devil's advocate" to work groups.

- Makes integrated recommendations to the leadership team on behalf of the work groups.

PROCESS MANAGER

The process manager monitors the overall project plan. While the other members of the steering committee are focused on content (the design recommendations), the process manager is focused on how the work is getting done. The role is much more than tracking milestones on a spreadsheet. The process manager needs to be a person with good influence and communication skills who is comfortable dealing with all levels of the organization. The process manager pushes the process forward, generates enthusiasm, and champions the change. In addition, this person helps to identify what resources the groups need to function smoothly and builds the mechanisms to ensure that information is being shared among the work groups and with the larger organization.

The need for dedicated process management will depend on the scope of the change. It may be part of the steering committee role or you may want to make it a part- or full-time position during the design and implementation process. If the organization is already project oriented, then the process manager might reside in an already existing project management office, such as an IT function. The process manager:

- Tracks progress and identifies resource constraints.

- Makes sure work group plans are integrated and coordinated.

- Monitors and reports on project plans to ensure milestones are being met.

- Provides regular updates to the leadership team on the overall progress of the work.

- Gives feedback to the steering committee.

- Provides problem-solving support.

- Maintains an integrated project plan based on input from the steering committee; acts as the "keeper" of the project plans and meeting minutes.

- Shares information across the work groups; captures and summarizes key learnings.

IMPLEMENTATION TEAMS

For large organizations, it often makes sense to use "lead" or "pilot" teams to implement structure and process changes incrementally rather than trying to make radical changes across the whole organization at once. The implementation teams:

- Lead the implementation of the new structure and processes.

- Focus resources, training, and attention effectively.

- Test and refine new operating practices, tools, and systems.

- Build internal knowledge and competence that can be transferred.

- Document learning from experience before an organizationwide rollout.

Implementation teams can also allow for faster implementation with less disruption to the larger business while quickly identifying regional differences that have to be accounted for. Although lead and pilot teams are similar in that they both allow for rollout of changes in selected locations or business units, the terminology can make a difference. Use of lead teams simply means that some sites will go through the change before others. Use of pilot teams means that the change is being tested and may be modified or even scrapped.

Use Tool 3-10 to determine who should fill these roles.

SUMMARY

In this chapter we've looked at various options for structuring the organization and worked through the definition and clarification of organizational roles. We've also illustrated a participative process for generating and evaluating alternatives. Whatever structure is chosen will present disadvantages. Although some of the design criteria will be maximized, others won't be met. These disadvantages can be overcome by designing the lateral organization—the networks, processes, teams, and integrative mechanisms that bind the organization together and help people work across organizational boundaries. Designing these processes and building lateral capability is discussed in Chapter Four.

NOTES

1. P. Burrows, "The Radical: Carly Fiorina's Bold Management Experiment at HP," *Business Week,* February 19, 2001, pp. 70–80.

2. Adapted from R. Beckhard and T. H. Reuben, *Organizational Transitions: Managing Complex Change* (Reading, Mass.: Addison-Wesley, 1977).

3. For more on designing complex global organizations, see J. Galbraith, *Designing the Global Corporation* (San Francisco: Jossey-Bass, 2000).

Tool 3-1. Evaluating the current structure.

Purpose:	You now understand the various types of organizational structures and how they function. Use this tool to evaluate your current organizational structure.
This tool is for:	Leadership Team.

1. Draw your current organization structure for the top three levels.

2a. What is the primary structure of your organization currently at the top level (your direct reports)?

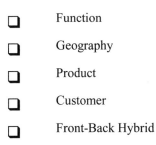

    ❏   Function

    ❏   Geography

    ❏   Product

    ❏   Customer

    ❏   Front-Back Hybrid

b. Describe the structure. Note the rationale for the structure and how it got to be that way.

Description of Structure	Rationale/How It Got to Be That Way

(continues)

Tool 3-1. (Continued).

3.   How have each of your direct reports structured their respective organizations?

_____

_____

_____

4a.   What growth or changes are expected over the next twelve to eighteen months in your organization, if any?
      In what areas are the changes likely to be located?

_____

_____

b.   If you are likely to grow, what should you take into account as you consider a new structure?

_____

_____

Answer the next questions based on the definitions provided in this chapter and the results of the current state assessment regarding the organization structure.

5.   What benefits and advantages does the current structure provide your organization?

_____

_____

_____

_____

6.   What disadvantages and problems result from the current structure?

_____

_____

_____

_____

The information from this tool should guide your decisions as you complete tool 3-2, *Designing the New Structure*. Be sure you have taken all the issues raised above into account as you go forward so that you don't re-create your current problems.

Tool 3-2. Designing the new structure.

Purpose:	Use this tool to consider possible structural options for your organization. Look back at your results from the previous tools, especially those pertaining to your design criteria, assumptions, and assessment of the current structure. Use your current state assessment to help you link the issues raised to your consideration of different structural options.
This tool is for:	Leadership Team.

1. What ideas emerged from your current state assessment regarding changing the structure?

    _____

    _____

    _____

2. Consider the organizational structures that would best suit your organization. For each one, use your criteria and current state assessment themes to identify potential advantages and disadvantages of each for your organization.

Structure Type	Advantages	Potential Pitfalls
1.		
2.		
3.		

3. Sketch one or more new structures for the top three levels of the organization.

Tool 3-3. Defining roles.

Purpose:	Use this tool to help you define the responsibilities and expected outcomes for each role.
This tool is for:	Leadership Team.
Instructions:	For each role you identified in your new structure, focus on the attributes that distinguish it from other roles in the organization. If there are current roles with the same name as roles in your redesign, emphasize how that role will be different. Reproduce this page for use in defining multiple roles. Use the following definitions to guide your thinking:

- *Outcomes:* An outcome is an end-state to be achieved. They are results to be attained. Where possible, set measures and milestones.
- *Responsibilities:* Responsibilities are tasks to be performed that will close the gap between the work that is currently done and the outcomes to be achieved in the new organization.

Role:

Outcomes	Responsibilities

Role:

Outcomes	Responsibilities

Role:

Outcomes	Responsibilities

Role:

Outcomes	Responsibilities

Tool 3-4. Identifying organizational roles.

Purpose:	Use this tool to help you dimension what is unique about each role in your new organization and to consider with what other roles they are likely to experience tension.
This tool is for:	Leadership Team.
Instructions:	List the roles in your new organization. Identify them at all levels—divisions, departments, teams, and functions, as well as individual positions. For each role summarize the unique perspective, goal, or driver that underlies that role's place in the organization. Then identify other roles that may have different perspectives that can create tensions. An example has been filled in.

Role	Its unique perspective is . . .	Likely to have tension with . . .
Marketing	Promoting sales and growth	Finance and operations

Tool 3-5. Defining interfaces, interdependencies, and expectations.

Purpose:	Use this tool to define the mutual expectations that each role has of one another from two perspectives—business processes and scenarios—to identify gray areas and clarify role interface and handoffs.
This tool is for:	Leadership Team.

A. Business Processes

1. Identify the most important processes that will involve multiple roles in the organization:

   _____

   _____

   _____

   For each, draw the process and identify what roles are involved at each point. Use Figure 3-14 as a guide.

2. Start from the perspective of the key role in each process. List the other roles involved in the process in the left column in the table below. For each relationship, identify the expectations in each direction.

   Process: _____   Key Role: _____

Other roles involved in the process . . .	What do they need to provide to the key role?	What do they need to get from the key role to do their work?

3. Compare expectations among roles. Clarify where there are differences in expectation and where there are likely to be conflicts.

B. Scenarios

1. Identify a situation in the organization that causes friction and confusion between roles. Choose one that involves internal or external customers and has business consequences if not handled appropriately.

_____

_____

_____

_____

2. List all the roles involved and identify the responsibility each should play in the scenario. Compare the future scenario to how the responsibilities are handled today and discuss what needs to change.

Role	Responsibility in Scenario—How It Should Be

Use your output from this tool as a basis to begin the responsibility charting process in Tool 3-6.

Tool 3-6. Clarifying roles: responsibility charting.

Purpose:	Use this tool to clarify levels of responsibility in key decisions for each role.
This tool is for:	Leadership Team.
Instructions:	List the key decisions in the left-hand column. List the roles in the organization across the top row. For each decision assign a code as shown below.

R = Responsibility	Has the **R**esponsibility and authority to make the decision.
A = Accountability	May not make the decision but will be held **A**ccountable for it (often a more senior role).
V = Veto	Can **V**eto or block a decision. This is different from the normal veto power that a boss or higher-level role has—it refers here to a role that reserves the right of veto for a specific decision.
C = Consult	Must be **C**onsulted and give input before the decision is made.
I = Informed	Needs to be **I**nformed about the decision after it is made.

Key Decisions	Roles						
1.							
2.							
3.							
4.							
5.							
6.							
7.							

Adapted from R. Beckhard and T. H. Reuben, *Organizational Transitions: Managing Complex Change* (Reading, Mass.: Addison-Wesley, 1977).

Tool 3-7. Testing the design.

Purpose:	Use this tool to test your organizational structure, roles, and executive team.
This tool is for:	Executive Team.

1. Transfer your design criteria from Tool 2-3. Assign a rating from 1 (= unlikely) to 5 (= highly likely) that the proposed structure and roles will achieve the design criteria.

Design Criteria (Tool 2-3)	Rating of Proposed Design				
	1	2	3	4	5
1.					
2.					
3.					
4.					
5.					

2. Assess your proposed design against the characteristics of a reconfigurable organization.

Reconfigurable Elements (Tool 1-1)	Rating of Proposed Design				
	1	2	3	4	5
Active leadership					
Knowledge management					
Learning					
Flexibility					
Integration					
Employee commitment					
Change readiness					

(continues)

Tool 3-7. (Continued).

3. Assess your proposal design's leadership and management roles.

Leadership and Management Roles	Rating of Proposed Design				
	1	2	3	4	5
Do management spans of control reflect the nature of the work?					
Have you minimized pure "management" roles?					
Have you included leadership team responsibilities as an explicit part of new leadership roles?					
Is the size of the executive team small enough to be manageable, yet provide all the needed perspectives?					

4. Assess your proposed design against these additional elements.

Other Elements	Rating of Proposed Design				
	1	2	3	4	5
Does the structure create a balance of power?					
Does the structure support the flow of work?					
Have you accounted for the impact of e-commerce?					
Do you have the right amount of complexity?					
Is the organizational culture congruent with the design?					

5. What issues can be anticipated that will not be resolved by the new structure?

_____

_____

_____

_____

_____

Keep the list of items you rated a 3 or below to focus your decisions as you work through Chapters Four to Six.

Tool 3-8. Deciding who should be involved.

Purpose:	Use this tool to determine who should be involved in the design off-site.
This tool is for:	Leader.

1. What is the primary focus of the design off-site?

   ❑ To generate structural options

   ❑ To introduce a new structure and develop the organizational roles

2. List the members of the executive team. For each identify one or two other people from their organizations that would contribute a balance of perspectives.

Executive Team Member	One or Two Reports for Each

3. Identify other key people in or outside the organization to participate (internal partners, customers, suppliers) who have something unique to contribute based on their position, perspective, knowledge, or some other factor.

Name/Role	Expected Contribution to the Meeting

4. Check the list and identify any imbalances in function, gender, tenure, location, background, race, or other attribute that is important in your organization.

Use this tool to not only define who should attend a design meeting but also to identify the expected contributions they make. This will also be helpful as you configure small groups at the off-site meeting.

Tool 3-9. Developing an off-site agenda.

Purpose:	Use the checklist below to ensure that important elements are being addressed in your off-site agenda.
This tool is for:	Executive Team.

	Included?	Notes
Design Parameter		
Logical flow and structure	❏	
Activity outcomes are clear	❏	
Mix of learning modalities used	❏	
Agenda Items		
Industry trends	❏	
Competitor information	❏	
Best practices in the industry	❏	
Current state assessment	❏	
New strategy presentation and discussion	❏	
Design parameters	❏	
Structural options	❏	
Meeting Process		
Small groups mixed appropriately	❏	
Leader's level of participation and decision making role clear	❏	
Meeting space adequate	❏	
Time for adequate discussion	❏	

Share your output of this tool with the HR professional or outside facilitator/consultant who will be assisting you in developing the off-site.

Tool 3-10. Governance structure.

Purpose:	Use this worksheet to clarify the roles each group in the governance structure will have in maintaining momentum in the design and implementation process.
This tool is for:	Leadership Team.

Group	Participants	Role in the Design and Implementation
Leader		
Executive Team		
Leadership Team		
Sponsor		
Steering Committee		
Work Group #1		
Work Group #2		
Work Group #3		
Work Group #4		
Process Manager		

CHAPTER FOUR

PROCESSES AND LATERAL CAPABILITY

CASE STUDY

We left CBC in Chapter Three after they completed their initial structural design work after designing the new structure, the CBC executive team was eager to start moving people into their new roles and begin implementation. Although George was comfortable with the new framework, he slowed them down. Their design work was not done. There were still a number of important issues from the current state assessment that he believed needed to be addressed up front. These included decisions about:

- Aligning the executive team around priorities

- Sharing learning and knowledge across the organization

- Allocating resources in the trading and credit functions—whether to assign them to divisions or to leave them as a flexible pool—and how to resolve conflicts over the use and allocation of these resources

■ Effectively utilizing the marketing and information roles, which would probably necessitate expensive new hires

Like the CBC executive team, it's tempting to jump from designing a new structure right into implementation. A new organization, however, means new ways of working together. Making these new relationships explicit and building the capability that allows people to work together effectively is an essential step. Every day, companies ask people to operate in concert and to channel their energy for the good of the organization. To do that, they must be provided the best mechanism to give shape to that energy.

The *lateral organization* comprises all the coordinating mechanisms that augment the vertical structure to create a complete structural design (Figure 4-1). It comprises the networks, lateral processes, roles, teams, and reporting relationships that move information and work through the "white spaces" between the boxes on the organization chart and across organizational boundaries. The lateral organization:

Figure 4-1. Star model.

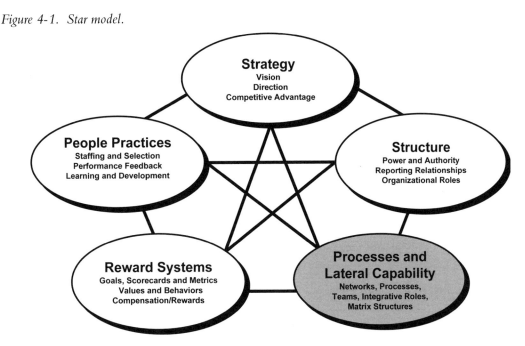

Source: Jay R. Galbraith, *Designing Organizations: An Executive Briefing on Strategy, Structure, and Process* (San Francisco: Jossey-Bass, 1995).

- Allows work to get done at the level it occurs; people interact and communicate directly without having to go up through the hierarchy and through their managers.

- Brings together the relevant players with the right perspectives to solve problems, make decisions, and coordinate work.

An organization's *lateral capability* is its ability to build, manage, and reconfigure these various coordinating mechanisms to achieve its strategic goals.

Designing the lateral organization ensures that the efforts of each role add up to more than the sum of the parts. It is also critical for creating a dynamic and reconfigurable organization. Since the lateral organization is more flexible and easily changed than the vertical structure, a focus on its design will allow the company to respond quickly to shifts in strategy without having to restructure the entire organization.

The vertical structure provides the clarity and sense of stability that people need in order to function in large organizations. It provides the "home base" for goal setting, reporting, and performance management. However, the vertical structure doesn't necessarily provide flexibility. Each structural option brings a defined group of people together into departments focused by function, customer, product, or some other dimension. Yet, most organizations must be customer-centric *and* a product leader *and* operationally excellent. Companies struggle to build global product design capability while delivering those products in different local markets. There is pressure to grow in order to gain the advantages of scale yet remain nimble and entrepreneurial to compete with start-ups. The reality is that most organizations operate in a complex, multidimensional world.

The dilemma is that by improving the organization's ability to respond to one constituency or market force, it is easy to fragment its ability to deal with others. It is the lateral organization that allows you to get the "and" by optimizing multiple capabilities.

Following a section that further defines *Lateral Capability*, this chapter is a guide to building five types of lateral capability:

1. *Networks* are the interpersonal relationships and communities of practice that underlie all other types of lateral capability and serve to coordinate work informally.

2. *Lateral Processes* move decisions and information through the organization in a formalized flow.

3. *Teams* are cross-business structures that bring people together to work interdependently and share collective responsibility for outcomes.

4. *Integrative Roles* are managerial, coordinator, or boundary-spanning positions charged with orchestrating work across units.

5. *Matrix Structures* create dual reporting relationships in order to manage the conflicting needs of functional, customer, product, or geographic forces.

The final section, *Building Lateral Capability,* presents some points to be considered when choosing among the options.

These five types of lateral capability can be placed on a continuum both of complexity and of whether they will occur on their own or need to be purposefully put into place (Figure 4-2). Networks and lateral processes tend to occur naturally and are the easiest to build and manage. People form and use personal relationships to get work done. Deliberately or not, work, information and decisions flow through processes between organizational units. How effective these networks and processes are, however, depends upon how well they were designed and implemented.

Teams, many integrative roles, and matrix structures are elective mechanisms. They exist to respond to complexity in the business environment, but when used, each also introduces a degree of internal complexity that must be managed. They require more management time and employee skills to make full use of their potential and to avoid introducing dysfunctional behaviors and relationships. Lateral capability is cumulative. You can't have effective teams or matrix structures if your organization doesn't have strong networks and well-designed processes. The key is to use only the lateral mechanisms that are re-

Figure 4-2. Continuum of lateral capability.

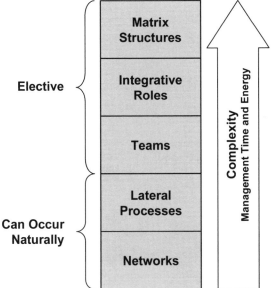

quired by the strategy and structure in order to minimize complexity and to build them on a strong foundation.

LATERAL CAPABILITY

Organization design is still evolving as a field of study. As a result, the terminology used by different observers is varied and inexact. What we define here as lateral organization and lateral capabilities are sometimes referred to by other authors as horizontal, flattened, networked, or process-based organizations. We refer to them as integrating or coordinating mechanisms as well. All these terms convey the important idea that an organization operates in multiple directions and dimensions and must be linked together.

The structural design is not complete without the design of the lateral organization. You may also find that it is the only part of the structure that you can impact. For example, imagine you have just been made head of the product development area in your division. The company is organized functionally. Your peers are the heads of operations, sales, marketing, finance, etc. (Figure 4-3).

The general manager has made it clear that increasing the speed of getting new products to market is a key goal. You may not be able to change the overall structure but you may be able to influence the creation of cross-functional product development teams that can help overcome the barriers created by the functional structure.

Another way to look at the need for lateral capability is to consider what we ask people to do each day when they come to work. We've hired them on

Figure 4-3. Cross-functional lateral team.

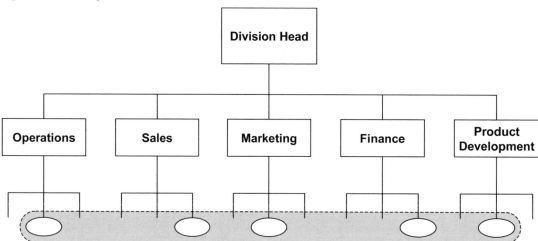

Team decked against customer segment

an individual basis, one by one, and usually pay them for their individual accomplishments. But we ask them to work together in teams and to collaborate with people in other parts of the organization and even on the other side of the world.

More often than not the organization itself creates barriers to their success. Examples are likely to abound in your current state assessment, such as:

- People don't know who has knowledge or experience outside of their own department that they might be able to draw upon.

- People have never met their counterparts in other areas of the organization in order to establish relationships with them.

- Policies inhibit the internal mobility that would give employees opportunities to work in other areas of the company and broaden their perspective.

- Processes cause conflict because no one is sure who has the authority to make a decision.

- Team members lack group process skills, causing more time to be spent on navigating the group dynamics than creating results.

- Matrix relationships are created, but the "two bosses" have neither the common ground nor the skills to negotiate collaborative solutions.

Building lateral capability provides a number of advantages.

+ *Better Return on Management Time.* Perhaps the greatest driver for designing a robust lateral organization is the limited resource of management time. If all decisions must flow up the hierarchy, management becomes a bottleneck and a barrier. Given that most organizations face continual change and given that the number of decisions to be made increases geometrically with the rate of change, decision making needs to be pushed to lower levels in the organization. Coordinating mechanisms designed into the lateral organization increase the organization's capacity to make decisions. People closest to the front line and customers make day-to-day decisions, freeing senior managers to focus on long-term strategic issues. In addition, the data that rise up through the hierarchy tend to get sanitized as people avoid having to deliver bad news. Building the capability to deal with issues at the level they occur can make for more accurate decisions and actions.

+ *Speed.* People closer to the customer, the product, and the business processes are often better able to make informed decisions than managers reviewing MIS reports. Lateral capability generates speed. It is certainly quicker to make some decisions by decree at a senior level.

However, significant time and energy will be spent by managers communicating the decision and the rationale down the organization to those who need to carry it out. Peer-to-peer collaboration can increase buy-in and decrease the time between decision and implementation.

+   *Flexibility.* The lateral organization is multidimensional. It allows a focus on whatever issue requires attention. Therefore, the company can be responsive to multiple constituencies and deal with unforeseen issues without having to reorganize. Lateral capability allows adaptability. Although the organizational structure is focused on maximizing the ability to execute today's strategy, the elements of the lateral organization can be configured to anticipate tomorrow's strategy. For example, customer teams operating across a functional structure can be an interim step toward reorienting the entire organization toward the customer.

+   *General Management Perspective.* Many business leaders are trying to get their employees to think like owners, to make decisions as though it was their own money on the line. Integrating mechanisms help employees to think more broadly and to understand and incorporate other perspectives into their own decisions and actions.

In order to make the lateral organization effective, you will also need to be aware of potential challenges:

—   *Parochial Interests.* Lateral mechanisms often allow for the delegation of decisions not only downward but across organizational boundaries. It may be difficult for some people to make decisions that go against their own interests unless they are rewarded for decisions that reflect an enterprise view.

—   *Increased Need for Information.* As with any delegated decision, the quality of the outcome is only as good as:

•   The information provided

•   The skills and judgment of the decision makers

•   The support and monitoring by the person or group delegating the decision

In order to make good decisions, people need to understand the strategy and be able to translate it into criteria against which they can test their decisions. They also need to understand the broader business and how their decisions will impact other people and other systems.

—   *Increased Time and Meetings.* Many lateral capabilities can't be dictated from the top. For example, people in the organization have to be involved in designing and developing the processes or working out team operating agreements. All of this takes time and is an internally focused activity. Although the hope is that the effort will pay off in better products or services for the customer, if not managed the discussions centered on how to work together can cut into time spent actually producing results.

— *Increased Conflict.* The coordinating mechanisms in the lateral organization bring people together from different parts of the organization to address an issue or make decisions. The participants still represent their part of the organization and will have differing points of view. The contention resulting from different viewpoints should make for better decisions, but this doesn't always occur. One area might "bully" other areas into accepting its point of view. This would be a bad outcome. A worse outcome would be when people make compromises to preserve their relationships but don't really resolve the issue. Lateral teams need skills to manage their meetings and discussions and resolve conflicts successfully.

— *Requirement for New Leadership Behaviors.* Lateral capability is closely linked to empowerment of employees. The organization's leadership needs to be willing to trust decisions that no longer rise up the chain of command but get made at the front lines by people working together across unit lines. The success of these mechanisms depends not only on new designs but on new skills and mind-sets among managers as well.

Building lateral capability requires an up-front investment of time and energy. If people are to be empowered to make decisions, they need:

- To have tools and information systems to give them access to required data
- To have skills to manage conflict, work on teams, and to reach optimal rather than compromised solutions
- To have time for increased communication and meetings
- To be rewarded for working across organizational boundaries

Lateral capability doesn't happen by chance. It needs to be designed and supported. The next sections provide guidance on how to develop each type of lateral capability: networks, lateral processes, teams, integrative roles, and matrix structures.

NETWORKS

Networks are the interpersonal relationships that people form across an organization. Networks are the foundation of the lateral organization and are created naturally as people interact with other employees in their office; with their boss, peers, and subordinates in their department; and with colleagues in other parts of the company. People use these networks on an informal, spontaneous basis every day. An issue arises and a few people get together to resolve it. An unanticipated event occurs, and someone calls a colleague in another office who has had the same experience.

It is common knowledge that people get things done in big companies by going outside of formal channels. Successful people rely on their "know-who" as much as their "know-how." This natural tendency can be a resource to be developed as a capability for the company. The stronger the interpersonal networks—the more people know who the right person is to reach out to, and the more that others are willing to respond—the stronger the foundation for building lateral capability and breaking down the silos that tend to form in any organization.

Organizational competencies are built upon relationships. The capacity to outperform the competition can't be considered separately from the social fabric of the organization. Conscious attention to networks is particularly important as an organization grows or disperses into multiple locations. When everyone is located together, information gets communicated in the hallway or by someone dropping in to a colleague's office for some advice. Everyone knows the level of other people's knowledge, experience, and interests. As people are moved to different offices and new people join a growing organization, however, this informal network can fall apart.

FOSTERING AND SUPPORTING NETWORKS

Most people are aware that cultivating a strong network is a personal asset. Networks are also an organizational asset. They smooth the way for information to be exchanged and developed into ideas and solutions that benefit the company. Networks provide the foundation of the dynamic organization. When it is time to reconfigure, a robust web of networks allow new relationships will fall into place faster and therefore speed everyone's adjustment to the new environment.

Fostering networks encourages spontaneous knowledge sharing across functions, businesses, and geographies, as well as serves as a fertile ground for innovation. Whenever you provide opportunities for different groups to learn or work together, the process of interaction itself becomes a learning experience: an experience of broadening one's perspective, learning from one's peers, valuing knowledge sharing and collaboration, and an experience that further embeds and reinforces the organizational culture.

Although the interpersonal interactions that create these experiences will remain somewhat spontaneous and informal, the underlying networks can be strengthened through deliberate design decisions. At some level there is no substitute for face-to-face interaction, but many of these efforts can be aided by technology. Since bringing people physically together is expensive, particularly for national and global companies, the challenge is to get the most from network-building practices. This section discusses six ways to foster networks:

1. Co-location

2. Communities of practice

3. Annual meetings and retreats

4. Training programs

5. Rotational assignments

6. Technology and e-coordination

CO-LOCATION

Physical proximity increases the probability that people will initiate, build, and productively leverage relationships. While e-mail, voice mail, and video conferencing can bridge some of the communication barriers caused by people working remotely, the predications made just a few years ago—that time and space won't matter with more use of the Internet—haven't come to pass. Pixar, the computer animation studio associated with Apple Computers, consolidated all of its employees into one building in San Francisco in the fall of 2000. They had previously been scattered among four different sites, but CEO Steve Jobs found that creativity and collaboration suffered when people weren't able to work in the same physical space.[1] Co-location is particularly important in organizations that depend on teams and high levels of collaboration.

A by-product of co-location is the increased chance that people will form personal relationships that will allow them to handle work conflicts better. For example, engineering and manufacturing departments might be co-located to facilitate formal workflow communication. People meet each other in the cafeteria, at the coffee machine, at the copier, and in the parking lot. Relationships start with conversations about the Super Bowl, elections, or a new mall in town. Then, when controversial design changes need to be hammered out between engineering and manufacturing, the participants already have a relationship within which a problem-solving dialogue is more likely to happen.

BMW used co-location as a temporary design intervention for facilitating cross-functional collaboration when introducing the 300 Series model. During this period, all groups responsible for the redesign efforts were moved into the prototype factory: product designers, manufacturing process designers, purchasing negotiators, designers of training programs, marketing product managers, and financial analysts. The groups communicated as the design process proceeded from concept to drawings to models to full-scale clay models to driveable prototype.

Co-location can also improve internal customer service relationships. For example, an operations group in a large insurance company was dependent upon three different technology platforms for processing claims. The information technology (IT) function that supported these systems was located in another city and provided service remotely. System updates, enhancements, or fixes would be sent by work order to the IT group. There were continual conflicts between the two areas around issues of responsiveness, accuracy, speed, and flexibility. A new head of IT decided to co-locate a small IT group on-site at the operations facility. Immediately, the relationship improved. The technologists could talk to users; observe how they used the system; and suggest when training, rather than enhancements, was needed. This IT outpost still worked closely with the centralized IT department for making systems changes, but co-location allowed for better service overall.

When you are able to locate people together, design the space to encourage interaction and reflect the new organization's spirit.

■ *Provide communal space.* To save on real estate costs, companies are squeezing the amount of office space dedicated to individuals. Particularly in consulting, IT, and other knowledge work where employees are frequently out of the office or are able to telecommute, "hotelling" has gained popularity. Rather than having a fixed "address" when they are in the office, employees are assigned a fully equipped office for the day, which reduces the amount of space that sits empty at any given time. Despite the obvious cost advantages, hotelling has some negative impacts on morale. People lose the sense of identity that comes with having "my space" decorated with the photos, mementos, and other decorations we use to mark our personal space. Therefore, the design of communal space becomes even more vital for creating a shared identity with the organization and colleagues when people can't retreat into personalized space.

Communal space in the reconfigurable organization is central to supporting a flexible organization. Communal space should be more than the traditional conference room that must be reserved days in advance. Create collaborative workspaces in a variety of sizes. Some spaces can even be open, allowing others to notice and easily join the discussion. Make finding an inviting, functional meeting space on the spur of the moment almost effortless if you want people to work together.

■ *Create natural interaction hubs.* Michael Bloomberg purposefully designed the headquarters of his Bloomberg media group to allow the elevator from the lobby to stop only on the middle floor of the six floors he leases on Park Avenue. This forces everyone to come in and leave by the same door, passing and interacting with other people on the way to their desk. A central spiral staircase becomes a vertical meeting room as people share information before heading in opposite directions.[2]

■ *Base the design on function, not privilege.* Office size and location still communicate status in most companies. Some companies have switched from walls and cubicles to open plans to reduce the sense of hierarchy but found they are less than optimally functional. Organizations that implemented open space plans—with low walls and joined desks instead of traditional cubicles and offices—found that it made it difficult for employees who wanted to conduct private conversations, who had to discuss sensitive matters with clients, or who just needed a quiet place to work. On the other hand, supervisors, who should be out on the floor coaching their teams, would have little need for enclosed offices. The idea, however, of allowing people to see their colleagues working and being able to initiate discussions without having to knock on doors has merit. The trend when designing private offices is to use a lot of glass when a quiet environment is required but a sense of openness is desired. Allocate and design space based on function, not status.

■ *Provide tools.* Flipcharts, markers, and walls uncluttered by pictures and suitable for posting visual displays are the basics for meeting rooms. Many companies go further by installing computers with projection displays, so that ideas and notes can be captured immediately and shared with others, and encouraging video conferences when in-person meetings are impractical. Consider IT and connectivity needs as part of the design so that people can plug in their laptops and access information remotely without having to return to their own space.

COMMUNITIES OF PRACTICE

Communities of practice are networks of employees with shared organizational interests. They allow people to learn and share knowledge for their personal benefit. They also help to avoid the divergence of procedure and standards when people with similar positions work in isolation from each other. They can be informal networks that depend on the group's members to initiate and sustain, or they can be formalized with dedicated budgets and administrative support.

The education practice in Andersen Consulting, now renamed Accenture, created formalized communities of practice in the mid-1990s to promote networking and sharing of learning-related ideas. The groups are open to all employees and structured around projects and topics that are of importance to the firm, such as computer-based education, classroom learning issues, or virtual learning. Although the intention is to encourage the generation and testing of ideas in a safe, internal environment before they might be developed into products for clients, the other goal is to create time for reflection and learning within the groups. To support them, each employee is allowed to spend about two hours of billable time per week involved in community of practice activities.[3]

Communities of practice can have even more direct business results. When Xerox connected its 17,000 technical representatives around the world on an intranet site for sharing ideas, knowledge, and experience, it found it had created a rich source of direct feedback from Xerox customers around the world. The role of the technical rep, previously one of the lowest in the company, changed to one of the most important. The company saved $100 million a year from the suggestions posted by technical reps. Rather than being viewed as merely repairpersons, they became a source of intellectual capital for the company.[4]

The Ford Foundation created an informal community of practice to knit its IT people closer together. The Ford Foundation has thirteen offices around the world to support regional grant making. Most of the IT infrastructure as well as the technology specialists are located at the New York headquarters. Each field office has one or two technical advisers who support local technology needs. It was becoming apparent that although there was frequent communication between New York and each individual office, there was limited communication among the offices. The result was little sharing of learning or experience. In fact, the technical advisers were developing duplicate solutions to common problems occurring in multiple offices.

The chief information officer brought together all the technical advisers for a five-day meeting. At the meeting they spent extensive time reviewing the technology capability and projects in each office. Time was also allocated to structured socializing in order to allow this group to create personal relationships. During the meeting, the group developed the specifications for an intranet-based "virtual forum" to share information, post help requests, and discuss IT issues.

Communities of practice are most successful when:

■ *They are formed around common interests.* Functional or staff groups make natural communities of practice. The lawyers dispersed across a product or customer structure may be working in different business lines but will have a lot to share in terms of methodology and the types of issues they encounter. Communities of practice rely on the voluntary participation of their members to make them useful. They have to be formed around topics people care about and to which they see some self-interest in contributing.

■ *They use both technology and face-to-face meetings.* Most communities of practice are sustained on-line through bulletin boards, chat sessions, discussion forums, databases, frequently-asked-question lists, and directories. They are aided, however, by occasional live meetings, where people can establish personal connections and put names to faces.

■ *They have a dedicated coordinator.* Successful communities of practice designate a coordinator or facilitator to identify topics of interest, set agendas for discussions and meetings, and promote participation in the group. This can be a rotating role within the group or a permanent part-time role. At the World Bank, communities of practice are so highly valued as a tool for learning and coordination that the budget for each community includes funds to pay for a staff person to organize meetings, edit each group's newsletter, and perform other administrative chores so that the group members can focus solely on their subject.[5]

ANNUAL MEETINGS AND RETREATS

Your organization's annual meeting or retreat is probably a significant expense in terms of travel and hotel costs in addition to the cost of taking people away from their day-to-day jobs. Use the meeting not only to accomplish the stated agenda, but as an investment in building the organization's networks, building commitment, and improving interpersonal relationships. For your next meeting think about maximizing these elements:

■ *Participation.* If you tend to have the same people attend each time, consider whether there is an opportunity to broaden the participation for your next meeting. Invite some high-potential people from a few levels down. You will help them build their network by introducing them to the organizational leadership. Another option is to invite partners from other parts of the company outside of your organization. Too often these people are only engaged when there is a service problem, a conflict, or an issue to negotiate. Use the meeting to build relationships with them in a more neutral setting.

■ *Small Groups.* The agendas for many meetings consist of one presentation after another followed by questions and answers. Interaction among participants is limited to breaks and meals. Structure the meeting so that people have multiple opportunities to discuss issues in small groups. Configure the group assignments to mix people as much as possible. The small group discussions not only allow for better responses to the presentations, but permit people to hear other people's perspectives, observe their working styles, and plan for how they can engage them as resources in the future.

■ *Structured Social Time.* Designers of multiday off-site meetings face the "social time" dilemma. Do you build social time into the agenda hoping that it will pay off in networking, or do you work people from morning until night in order to get them back to their offices and their families as quickly as possible? Either way, some people will be unhappy. If there is an afternoon off, or even if social time is limited to meals or a free evening, deliberately shape some of it to encourage participants to meet new people. Sign up cross-functional foursomes for golf. Assign seating at meals. Plan an evening murder-mystery entertainment so that people don't just wander off to their rooms after dinner. Although it is important to allow some completely unstructured time for participants, get the most out of each element of the meeting.

TRAINING PROGRAMS

Enterprisewide training programs are another forum for connecting the organization. If you structure participation and use the programs as a forum for creating shared values and understanding, you can achieve two goals in addition to the stated training objectives:

■ *Networks*. Training programs that bring people together from different departments are most effective when they create relationships across the shared work flow interfaces. Rather than just allowing open enrollment, participants can be assigned to programs that will bring them in contact with others whom they could benefit from knowing.

■ *Shared Values and Understanding*. Each training event, even if as mundane as business writing or time management, is an opportunity to communicate the direction of the organization, the leadership's key messages, and the values of the organization. Customization of programs can be justified when it is employed not just to make the material more relevant to the participants, but to create a shared culture, language, and set of organizational values. For example, case studies, vignettes, and role plays that are used to illustrate the course material can be written to reinforce behavioral norms. A management skills course can incorporate practice scenarios that illustrate the new performance expectations or new roles of the organization. When seen this way, course design becomes not only a matter of teaching the topic at hand, but an opportunity to build common organizational understanding among a group of diverse participants.

ROTATIONAL ASSIGNMENTS

Rotational assignments move people laterally through the organization at defined intervals. Rotational assignments can be used to broaden skills, promote and reinforce best practices and knowledge transfer, and embed an enterprisewide perspective. Many companies have used cross-functional rotational assignments as a two-pronged organizational strategy: to train functional managers to become generalists and prepare them for their next career move, and to help them to build networks of contacts and communication channels that they can use to leverage knowledge across the organization.

Dow-Corning, for example, places new chemical engineers in the product development function. From there, they follow their new product into manufacturing. Once in the factory, they may move to the quality function and then become a controller for the plant. The next move may be as a controller in a factory in Europe to gain international experience. Careers are designed to move people among line positions, as well as between line and staff positions. Each rotation reinforces some roles that are familiar while introducing new ones. With each new move, the engineers learn to adapt more quickly and effectively. Over time, they spend time in different functions, in different businesses, in different geographies, and in both line and staff roles. They learn to be accountable for results and to influence staff without necessarily having formal authority.

Another organization that uses rotational assignments is McDonald's. As an organization with a strategy focused on operational excellence, it is essential that all functional fast-trackers rotate through operations and actually have the experience of running a restaurant. No one is considered for senior leadership positions who hasn't had this experience.

In large, multibusiness companies, the audit function can be used to build cross-functional and cross-business knowledge and networks. Citigroup rotates high-potential managers through audit positions not only to build their appreciation for the discipline of good control practices but to expose them to the workings and issues of different business lines. Audits are opportunities to learn and develop, both for the unit being audited and for the auditors themselves. When correctly positioned, the function can spread best practices, develop talent, and build networks across borders. A corporate banker participating in a cross-geography audit team looking at the Malaysian consumer business for three months will get to know the other team members, while also meeting people in the Malaysian subsidiary. Each experience provides another opportunity to extend one's network of contacts.

Shell Oil uses job rotation to tie together an otherwise highly decentralized organization. Although local operating companies are empowered to make almost all sourcing, recruiting, and selection decisions concerning management staff, all units give a new manager at least two assignments during his or her first five years. Directors of the local operating companies conduct a series of swaps and negotiations in order to provide the best possible development opportunities for their people. The local company absorbs any costs associated with a swap (e.g., moving other people into new positions to make room for a high-potential manager who is ready for a new developmental assignment). The ethic of growing management talent internally permeates the entire company. Many, if not most, of the senior executives started as junior management partners.

Rotational assignments are typically lateral moves that add new skills and experience but not necessarily a greater scope of responsibility. To avoid having people perceive that they are missing opportunities up the career ladder, rotational assignments have to be part of a defined career path with a set time limit and clear next steps. People who participate in these assignments also have to be rewarded commensurately so they don't feel they might have done better financially if they had stayed in a narrow functional career path.

TECHNOLOGY AND E-COORDINATION

One of the most powerful current and future shapers of informal networks is IT. Although it can't replace face-to-face interaction completely, technology has the potential to remove significant time and space barriers to communication as well as organizational barriers of hierarchy and department. The organization becomes opened up to virtually limitless communication. Informal networks or communities of interest spring up naturally through chat groups and electronic mail distribution lists on a company's intranet. LotusNotes, Microsoft Exchange, and other group interaction tools allow instant messaging, group discussion, scheduling and group calendar management, and document and work flow management.

It is the role of the organizational designers to shape relationships and networks that can be facilitated by the new technology available. Most companies have a personnel database, which is accessible via the company intranet. Often it is little more than an electronic Rolodex with name and contact information. CARE International, one of the world's largest private international relief and development organizations, took its existing contact database and enhanced it with the kind of information that would make it easy for people with congruent interests and needs to find each other. Each person has listed past responsibilities and experience, current responsibilities, language abilities, country knowledge, emergency experiences, skills and core competencies, and interests. This searchable database has increased the ability of people working across borders and across projects to seek each other out and share ideas, information, and solutions. The cost of creating and maintaining it is very low.

Even more promising are the enterprise technology packages, such as customer relationship management (CRM) systems that are beginning to harness all the customer information that is dispersed throughout organizations. CRM systems have the potential to integrate all relevant data so that a company can truly present "one face" to the customer.

You most likely will agree that fostering strong interpersonal networks, collaboration, and knowledge sharing is a good thing to do. However, if you look at your organization's reward and recognition systems, they may tell a different story. They may not reward people at all for reaching out to others or providing help when requested. Use Tool 4-1 to assess your current networks and identify ways that they can be enhanced and supported in your organization.

LATERAL PROCESSES

Lateral processes provide information and shape decisions in order to co-ordinate activities spread out across different units of the organization. They are the business and management processes that provide value to customers and get work done. They are the major activity and decision flows that cut across functions and deliver the end products and services that create customer value. Some needed lateral processes may not exist in the current organization and will have to be created for the redesigned organization. Others will need to be reconfigured.

Although numerous processes exist within any organization, typically there are three to five that are critical to the business and involve multiple parts of the organization to carry them out. For a strictly product-focused company, new product development, innovation management, and market research and intelligence might be essential processes. For a customer organization, building relationship management, knowledge management, and solution development processes might be more important. Figure 4-4 lists some typical lateral processes.

Such critical business processes should not be informally coordinated but should be formalized and documented. These processes should be revisited as part of any design effort. Over time, the processes in all organizations tend to get bureaucratized and reflect old routines and remnants of "how things used to be" rather than the business's current needs.

HOW TO DESIGN LATERAL PROCESSES

The leadership team should define the lateral processes that are critical for the organization. The people who will have to make each process work, however, should be involved in mapping it out and negotiating handoffs, time frames, and expectations. The major steps in mapping a process are:

- Setting the objectives
- Determining the start of the process
- Determining the end of the process
- Establishing key interfaces

Figure 4-4. Typical lateral processes.

MANAGEMENT & FINANCIAL
- Project planning and management
- Priority setting
- Resource (people) allocation and assignment
- Budgeting and forecasting
- Asset management and tracking
- Problem escalation and conflict resolution

PEOPLE MANAGEMENT
- Performance management
- Succession planning & development
- Recruiting and selection
- Communication and feedback
- Talent management

CUSTOMER SERVICE
- Service requests and satisfaction
- Service pricing
- Service-level agreement setting & monitoring
- Account executive/CRM
- Solution development

OPERATIONS
- Change management (infrastructure)
- Supply chain management
- Storage management
- Capacity planning
- Order fulfillment

RISK MANAGEMENT
- Contingency planning
- Disaster recovery
- Information security
- Quality assurance

TECHNOLOGY
- Standards development
- Technology transfer (from development through testing to production)
- Application development
- Software licensing and distribution
- Desktop service & support

BUSINESS DEVELOPMENT
- Service and product design
- Prospect and lead development
- New business/customer acquisition
- New product development
- Market research

LEARNING
- Knowledge management

- Setting measures
- Detailing activities or subprocesses
- Creating new tools

An example of the project management process for a software development division illustrates the process for thinking about and mapping a lateral process. Employer Services is a division of a large asset-management company. It was formed early in 1995, after senior management in the company realized that the proprietary software created in-house and used to manage its own employee accounts could be a valuable product to sell to other large companies considering outsourcing payroll and benefits record keeping.

By the fall of 1996, Employer Services had grown to 400 people, doubling in size every six months since its creation. As the organization grew, it became clear that while Employer Services had done a great job servicing its one, internal client, it had failed to build any discipline or capability around simultaneously managing complex projects for multiple clients. The linkages among the product developers, the business analysts, and the implementation teams were weak. Decision making was slow, deadlines were being missed, and accountability was diffuse. Lots of time was being spent trying to establish blame for mistakes rather than find answers. People felt they were working hard, but there were not enough results to show for it. One of the quotes from the current state assessment captures the feelings at the time:

> *We're making noise, not music. We need to balance and coordinate project, resources, deliverables, and timing. We all work hard. Give us a task and we'll do it as best we can. The problem is that we may not pick up our heads to see if it's even the right task to be doing. We're missing a mechanism, a traffic cop.*

The head of Employer Services met with his executive team and identified ten key lateral processes for the organization (Figure 4-5). They then scheduled a three-day meeting with *thirty-five* people from the leadership team to collaboratively develop the three most important processes: Project Management, Service Definition, and Technology and Development Standard Setting.

The Project Management team mapped a new project planning and management process (Figure 4-6). The discussion yielded a number of agreements regarding the new process.

Objective of Process	Provide a framework to enable project managers and their teams to deliver on their commitments within agreed-upon budgets, schedules, and resources in an organized and well-communicated fashion
Start of Process	Clearly defined project that has a sponsor and assigned project manager

Figure 4-5. Employer services lateral processes.

PROJECT PLANNING AND MANAGEMENT

- To plan and manage projects to accomplish agreed deliverables on time within budget, optimizing the use of scarce resources across all projects

SERVICE DEFINITION

- To provide a standard methodology for collecting and analyzing customer needs, and producing and documenting system requirements and designs that provide the required functionality

TECHNOLOGY AND DEVELOPMENT STANDARD SETTING

- To identify the need for corporate standards, and analyze, recommend, and select among alternatives in a way that ensures "buy-in" and implementation across Employer Services, taking into account existing company standards

STAFFING RECRUITMENT & CAREER DEVELOPMENT

- To ensure that the best people available are recruited into Employer Services in a proactive and timely way, to ensure that the staff is in place to accomplish the agreed-upon strategy and goals; to provide a career path and necessary training to support individuals in Employer Services transition to new positions that are opportunities to grow and develop professionally

COMMUNICATION

- To ensure a regular flow of information between all levels of Employer Services about company direction, strategy, priorities, and successes

QUALITY ASSURANCE

- To provide a process to ensure that new applications transition smoothly through the various phases, from requirements gathering to production, and meet customer needs and operations standards

COMPLIANCE

- To ensure compliance with all internal and external audit and regulatory requirements

PERFORMANCE MEASURES

- To establish and monitor a set of performance measures that proactively enable Employer Services to improve customer satisfaction and financial performance

INFORMATION SECURITY

- To provide appropriate and agreed-upon levels of access to data and applications in a timely manner

---

Figure 4-6. Employwer services project planning and management process.

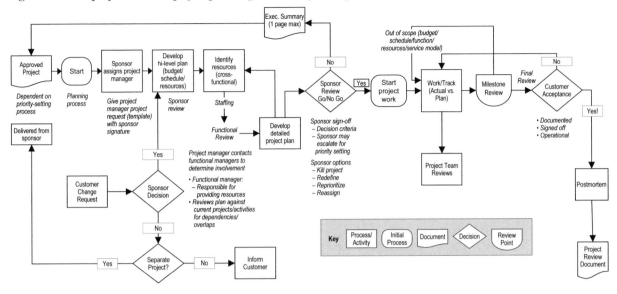

End of Process	Product delivered to internal or external client; post-mortem review is finished
Key Interfaces	Leadership team (priority setting) Service definition Staffing and recruiting
Performance Measures	Quantitative—schedule and budget Qualitative—quality, standards, functionality (meets business requirements, customer satisfaction

New Tool	Detailed project plan that is not just a Gantt chart or list of activities but includes:
	    Risk assessment on key deliverables
	    Trade-offs and cost/benefit analysis
	    Clear statement of links to employer services imperatives and goals:
	        Issues and constraints
	        Complexity assessment
	        Dependencies

If mapping lateral processes sounds a lot like reengineering, it is related. Both are about creating a work system based on efficient, clearly defined business processes that add value to customers. The difference is that reengineering projects begin and end with process redesign. Lateral processes, on the other hand, are just one tool among many in the organization design tool kit. The goal of mapping lateral processes is not only to create efficiency, but to identify the nodes in the fundamental business processes that link parts of the organization together.

Use Tool 4-2 as a guide for teams to define and revise the critical lateral processes in your organization.

TEAMS

Teams bring people together to work interdependently and share collective responsibility for outcomes. They are a formal mechanism for integrating work. Most organizations use teams in some way. They can be thought of in three categories:

■ *Issue Teams.* These are the teams that are put together to solve a short-term, particular problem, such as organization design, cost cutting, or strategy development. Although the work of these task force–type teams is important to the business, it is not the work of the business. While participation on these teams can provide important networking opportunities, they are not integrative mechanisms in and of themselves.

■ *Work Groups.* Work groups are clusters of employees in the same unit who do the same or similar work and must coordinate their efforts. Everyone on the team reports to the same manager. Although they may have different jobs, the people in a work group don't represent different functions or organizational perspectives, nor do they usually have collective responsibility for outcomes of their work; that is, they are not compensated in any significant way based on the overall group's efforts or results. Work groups are the most common types of teams in an organization. When job descriptions and performance appraisals refer to "teamwork," they are typically describing the behaviors of listening, responding, providing support, and respecting others' views. Work groups can exist in very hierarchical cultures because they don't change the role of management or the upward, hierarchical decision-making process.

■ *Cross-Business Teams.* Cross-business teams are true integrative mechanisms. They pull together people with different organizational skills and perspectives to create or deliver products and services to customers. We use the term *cross-business* to encompass all teams comprising of people from different areas. People can be from different functions, business units, or geographies.

Cross-business teams reduce the need for hierarchy in decision making by pushing decisions closer to the customer. They are an essential component of an integrated, flattened organization. When cross-business teams become the basic organizational unit of the business, the organization is described as "team-based." Building cross-business teams is the focus of this section.

Cross-business teams are used both to complement the vertical structure and to overcome any disadvantages introduced by it. The cross-functional team is a common type of cross-business team. People are pulled from their functional "home" to participate on a product or customer team. The example of customer teams in the Private Client Bank illustrates this concept (Figure 4-7).

Each person who potentially needs to interact with a particular client is a member of a functional group: relationship management, trust, credit, or sales. By organizing into functions, the Private Client Group can build depth of expertise in each of these areas. However, no one person has all the information that the client needs. This could be addressed by putting one function in charge of interface with the client, say the relationship manager. The relationship manager would then have to coordinate all the resources she needs to serve clients across the functional boundaries and, because she lacks any formal authority, hope that her colleagues would cooperate. If there were disputes, they would have to be escalated to senior management levels to be resolved.

A better alternative is to configure representatives from each function into a team to deliver to the client as one unit, as shown in Figure 4-7. This provides the organization with a number of advantages:

- *All relevant skills and information are available to the client.* The client needs the capabilities of all of the functions presented in an integrated package. No

Figure 4-7. Private Client Bank, "client team."

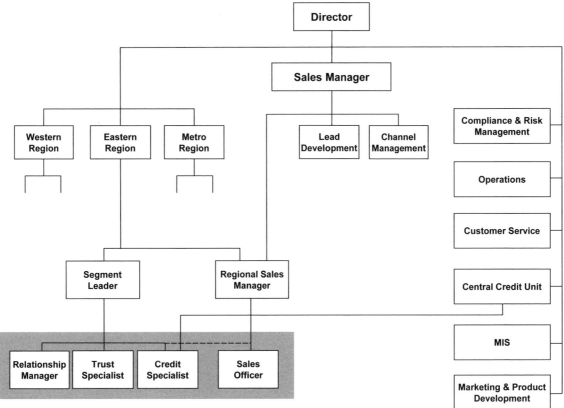

one function or person can have all the knowledge or skills necessary to provide what the client desires. Therefore, they must work as a team. As a team they are more likely to generate innovative solutions than work as individuals in isolation.

■ *Interface is coordinated*. The client can be assured that whoever is the "face" of the company is representing all the views and knowledge in the company. The client doesn't have to go to multiple places to gather information. Quality is improved when work is better coordinated.

■ *Decision making occurs at the client level*. The knowledge of the organization is re-created at the team level. Except in rare cases, decisions don't need to rise to management levels and issues can be negotiated within the team. This speeds response time.

Cross-business teams can be permanent or flexible. In this example, the customer teams may be fixed in order to target particular client segments in their regional market, such as inherited wealth, entrepreneurs, or corporate executives. Fixed teams are generally stable, although members may change over time. The teams can also be designed to be flexible with a different team configuration for each account, based on the particular skills needed by each client. Flexible teams give the organization the ability to deck exactly the right mix of people against each client or project. However, people can end up working on multiple teams simultaneously. This increases the complexity of managing the internal team workings. Permanent teams allow for team members to build effective working relationships over time and avoid the distractions of a continuous "start-up" phase that all new teams must go through when establishing themselves.

TYPES OF TEAMS

The autonomy of a team depends upon the nature of the work, the maturity of the team as a unit, and the need for management oversight and coordination. People assigned to a team need to be clear where authority resides. An analogy to the world of sports sometimes helps people understand the difference between being *in* a team, being *on* a team, and working *as* a team (Figure 4-8).

Football players work *in* a team. They are either defense, offense, or part of a special team, similar to the work groups described earlier. Each team works as a single unit, pushing forward with plays planned in advance. The coach and the quarterback make most of the decisions. The new business, remittance, and quality teams in an insurance-annuity processing department are like a football team. Within each unit, people have similar roles. Although all three units must coordinate their work, they operate generally independently of each other.

Figure 4-8. Types of teams.

		Football 	Baseball 	Basketball 
Team Elements	**Setting**	*In a Team*	*On a Team*	*As a Team*
	Tasks	• Programmed • Working in parallel	• Serial • Independent	• Integrated • Interdependent
	Decisions	• Centralized	• Combination of centralized and decentralized	• Spontaneous
	Personal Focus	• Hierarchical	• Individual expertise	• On-the-spot flexibility
	Management Focus	• Having the answers	• Distributed leadership	• Coordinated • Participative
	Weakness	• Lacks flexibility • Time-consuming to move up hierarchy for decisions	• Individuals can't help others when role-focused	• Requires time to build familiarity and trust

Baseball players work *on* a team. They are part of a team working toward the same goal, but make their contributions largely as individuals, which is reflected in the extensive individual statistics kept for each player. It's difficult for players to help each other, particularly when batting, pitching, or catching. As with football, decision making rests largely with the manager. The baseball team model might look like a project team where each person makes a contribution, but where that contribution is largely independent of the other members.

Basketball players work *as* a team. Their abilities and actions need to be integrated and interdependent. Many times decisions are made spontaneously; where the ball goes depends on who is open and who has the best chance of scoring. While there are prearranged plays, whoever has the ball has the flexibility to change those plays to adjust to circumstances as they unfold. These are the teams that many organizations would like to build.

Basketball teams, while having a bench, don't have duplication of resources. Players play offense and defense. Everyone is involved and contributes all the time. No one is standing in the field waiting for his or her skills to be called upon. The players communicate continually with each other and make most of the decisions. The coach builds their skills and encourages them, but the team shares fully in making decisions once the game is under way. Success depends as much on one's own skill as knowing the skills of others. A player who assists others to score is as highly valued as the one who scores the points. The trust that is needed to create a high-performing team of this sort takes time to develop. An example could be a team of consultants working on an assignment together, where each person's contribution is dependent on the timeliness and quality of the work of the others on the team.

MANAGING TEAMS

When true cross-business teams are embedded in an organization, the manager's role evolves and a different type of leadership is required (Figure 4-9). Traditional supervisory responsibilities are gradually taken on by the team as trust develops among team members as well as the skills to manage its own group process. These include such activities as work coordination, administrative functions, group process facilitation, mentoring and training, introducing improvements, and managing performance. A manager's leadership style also needs to shift when teams are introduced and embedded into the organization. Managers move from a supervisory style based on directing others, to a team style oriented toward coaching, and finally to a facilitative leadership approach focused on building team capabilities (Figure 4-10).

Managers are able to increase their span of control as their teams become less dependent on management involvement in decision making. The facilitator and adviser roles are essentially integrative roles rather than management roles. They replace traditional supervisors and managers, allowing the organization to flatten without adding layers or head count. The remaining managers are able to concentrate on more strategic concerns.

Teams also provide new career paths and development opportunities for their members. Leadership roles within the team are not necessarily hierarchical. Assignments can be based on technical ability or rotate among members. By taking on these duties, team members develop competencies that make them more valuable to the organization and raise the overall level of management skill in the organization.

CONDITIONS FOR SUCCESSFUL TEAMS

Teams are popular, but not every need is best served by creating teams. To gain the power inherent in teams, the organizational leadership has to be ready to support them and accept how other systems, roles, and procedures will need to change to accommodate them. Although people are social animals, the skills for working cooperatively don't come naturally. Many people prefer to work

Figure 4-9. The manager's evolving role.

Manager

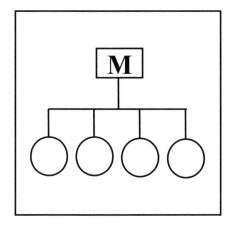

The traditional hierarchical structure where manager is at the hub of decision making. The team has responsibility but not authority.

Team Leader

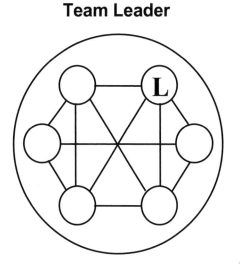

The team leader shares decision making with the team and straddles roles of team leader and member. The team leader helps facilitate the growth of the team.

Facilitator

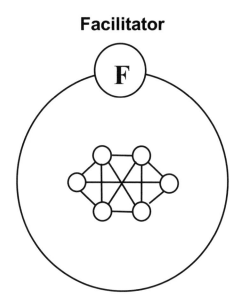

Primary decision making is equally distributed among team members who all have equal authority and power. The facilitator supports the process of reaching consensus but rarely imposes opinion or decision.

Adviser

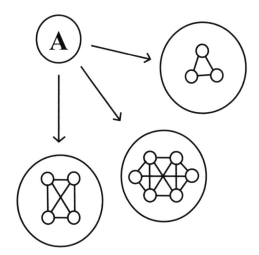

Team members are able to take on facilitator role as well as leadership role. The adviser functions as boundary manager between teams, and the larger organization. The adviser provides consultation and support and ensures the teams have the resources they need.

Figure 4-10. Evolving leadership styles.

SUPERVISORY LEADERSHIP	TEAM LEADERSHIP	FACILITATIVE LEADERSHIP
Direct people.	Coach people.	Build trust and inspire teamwork.
Explain decisions.	Use team input for decision making.	Facilitate and support team decisions.
Train individuals.	Develop individual and team performance.	Expand team capabilities.
Manage one-on-one.	Coordinate group effort.	Create team identity.
Contain conflict.	Resolve conflict.	Encourage and utilize team differences.
React to change.	Implement change.	Foresee and influence change.

independently even when they see the compelling business need to collaborate. Teams work best under the following conditions that meet both business needs and individual needs:

■ *Common Purpose.* The need for people to work together must be compelling if a cross-business team is to add value. Members need to believe that the effort involved in working directly with their peers across organizational lines will yield better results than if they worked only within their business unit. People share a common purpose when they need timely information from others to do their own work, and when this information can't be automated. Their tasks are interdependent and what one does will impact the actions and decisions of others.

■ *Team Members Influencing Goals.* When people have the opportunity to shape a goal, they have a higher commitment toward meeting the goal. This is especially true in teams where achieving a team goal may require some members of the team to forgo meeting individual goals.

■ *Clear Priorities.* Most teams are overlay structures. Team members are still part of their "home" unit (functional group, business unit, geography, etc.) but may spend most of their time contributing to the team. Conflicts occur when the team's goals or activities contradict the priorities or resource needs of a person's home unit or when the work of the team diverges from common standards. For example, an IT specialist working on a team that provides outsourcing is prompted to employ a new processing platform to meet a particular customer need. This decision may diverge from the IT function's goals of using a common platform for all clients so that system enhancements and features can be shared among clients. How time is allocated, what activities take priority, and how conflicting priorities are resolved are questions that need to be decided among the members of the management team directing the teams and functions. If one depends on lower levels to resolve such issues, much confusion and anger can result.

■ *Right Skill Level and Mix.* Teams depend on members trusting each other. Trust develops when a person believes that others can and will deliver what they promise. If the team is not designed to contain the right skill level and mix of skills to achieve the team goals, not only will the team fail to meet expectations but team members will be discouraged. Not all skills need to be in place in order for the team to get under way, but the team members need to have assurance that there is a plan to develop or hire in the right skills.

■ *Team Accountability.* Work teams in hierarchical organizations have responsibility for the work, but not accountability. In a cross-business team embedded in a team-based organization, accountability shifts to the team. This not only requires that the team be prepared to take on accountability for its performance and accept it, but that the manager let go and resist jumping in and taking over when things go wrong. Managers need to be skilled in coaching, teaching, and facilitating so that the team can begin to resolve its own performance issues.

■ *Clear Criteria for Leadership Positions.* As some management activities are transferred to the team, the way in which these team leadership activities are assigned can create friction. Some roles may be more coveted than others. By making the criteria clear, time spent on debating how to assign leadership roles is minimized and resistance to accepting peers in leadership roles is decreased.

■ *Decision Norms.* If teams are to be used as the organizing unit of the business, then they have to be able to make decisions effectively. Members of cross-business teams bring not only their different knowledge bases, they bring different values, styles, and norms of decision making. Someone from operations, where systems changes have far-reaching impacts, may be much more deliberative than a freewheeling marketing specialist used to a quickly and frequently changing course. Whenever team members have differences, each person will need to individually decide whether pushing for their desired outcome is worth the possible harm that may be done to his or her relationship with other team members. Figure 4-11 illustrates the possible stances a person can

Figure 4-11. Task/relationship balance in conflict management.

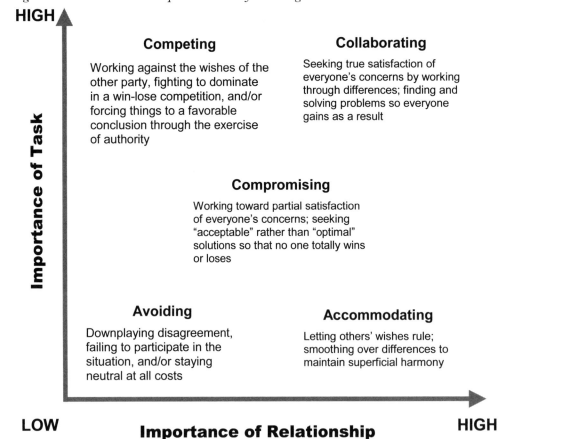

HIGH

Importance of Task

Competing

Working against the wishes of the other party, fighting to dominate in a win-lose competition, and/or forcing things to a favorable conclusion through the exercise of authority

Collaborating

Seeking true satisfaction of everyone's concerns by working through differences; finding and solving problems so everyone gains as a result

Compromising

Working toward partial satisfaction of everyone's concerns; seeking "acceptable" rather than "optimal" solutions so that no one totally wins or loses

Avoiding

Downplaying disagreement, failing to participate in the situation, and/or staying neutral at all costs

Accommodating

Letting others' wishes rule; smoothing over differences to maintain superficial harmony

LOW   **Importance of Relationship**   **HIGH**

Adapted from *Kilmann Conflict Mode Questionnaire* (Xicom, 1974).

take when a conflict arises. A fair amount of work must be done in the early stages of the team's development to build awareness of different decision outcomes to ensure that "collaboration" is the most common result when the team engages in group decision making.

■ *Information.* Communication and information must be widely distributed and equally available to all team members. Introducing teams into the organization may change the way that information is managed and controlled. Since work is being performed and coordinated laterally as well as vertically, information needs to flow in all directions. Information that was formerly held by managers and shared only on a "need to know" or by-request basis will need to be shared more openly. In addition, the responsibility for moving information through the organization broadens. People will need to get used to proactively sharing information with others on their team or on other teams. Mapping these needs and the new information routes and determining what changes to the IT systems are needed to support information flow is essential to supporting teams.

■ *Performance Measures and Rewards.* A major source of initial resistance to introducing teams into the organization may come from a fear that individuals will lose control over how their performance is measured and rewarded. Establishing measurement and compensation systems that drive and reward business and team goals as well as individual results is fundamental for ensuring that actions and efforts are aligned. Measures and rewards communicate the values of the organization and help to build the collective responsibility that will actually change behaviors.

Use Tool 4-3 to assess your organization's readiness to support team structures.

INTEGRATIVE ROLES

Integrative roles are managerial, coordinator, or boundary-spanning positions charged with orchestrating work across organizational units without formal authority. Leaders and managers should play an integrative role in the organization, ensuring that the work of each component fits with the overall business objectives and that resources within the organization—people, knowledge, time, etc.—are optimally leveraged and coordinated among units. In a small organization, the leader may be all that is needed. For large businesses, it is impractical for the leader to be coordinating work except at the most senior level of the organization. Other roles are necessary to link work, share information, and keep the components of the organization aligned with one another. Whenever possible, it is desirable to leverage existing resources rather than add head count for the purpose of coordination.

EXPANDED MANAGERIAL ROLES

From an organizational perspective, increasing the capability of managers to think from an enterprisewide perspective in addition to their functional perspective increases an organization's lateral thinking and adaptive capability overall. We've all observed individuals who naturally take on an integrative role. They are curious and interested in how other parts of the organization work, and they reach out to peers to learn from them. They easily see the complexities of situations and help others meet on common ground to solve problems. They are the first ones thought of when a leader is needed to take charge of a change project that involves varied or contentious stakeholders. Social scientists call this "extrarole behavior," meaning behavior that goes beyond role expectations in a way that is organizationally beneficial.[6] There are some specific ways to encourage managers to make extrarole behavior an integral part of their work.

■ *Communicate and reinforce expectations of extrarole behavior.* Rarely is integration an explicit part of a manager's role. Increasing awareness among managers of the expectation that they will serve as a catalyst for organizational improvement and effectiveness is a first step.

■ *Provide opportunities that build lateral experience and confidence.* The most powerful tool for building confidence is hands-on experience. Providing managers with opportunities to build confidence through rotational assignments and the opportunity to manage cross-business teams will increase their receptivity, initiative, and performance in managing laterally.

■ *Identify individuals who naturally think and act as integrators and use them as role models.* Even within the same organization, some individuals will be more naturally inclined to take initiative, making linkages between what they are doing and what others are doing to identify new opportunities. These behaviors should not only be recognized, but held up as an example for others to follow. Encourage them to teach others to do what they do intuitively.

COORDINATORS

Coordinator roles are dedicated positions that integrate the work of other people. In some situations, the objective of the liaison role may be to ensure that critical information gets transferred on a regular basis between functions or teams that have interdependent goals or work streams. In other situations, the primary role of the liaison may be to proactively monitor activities in other functions or teams to ensure that opportunities are not missed or issues affecting multiple units are raised.

Product, service, project, or quality managers are typical integrative coordinators. They don't control resources but they may chair a council or team that identifies areas where functional strategies and product or customer needs are in conflict and that tries to achieve resolution. For knowledge-intensive firms, the key integrative role may be to deploy people against projects and to manage how talent is allocated. For example, Ernst & Young Consulting Services uses staffing coordinators whose sole task is to coordinate resources against projects in order to maximize industry, functional expertise, and organizational knowledge.

BOUNDARY-SPANNING ROLES

There has been a recent proliferation of new job positions in organizations with names such as "chief knowledge officer," "chief learning officer," or "chief innovation officer." These positions arise in response to a business need that doesn't fit neatly into a traditional box. By definition, these are "boundary-spanning" roles specifically created to integrate work and knowledge. Usually, people in these positions have small staffs and are dependent on the information, knowledge, and resources provided from other units for success. Three examples illustrate the boundary-spanning role:

- *E-Commerce.* The drive to do business on the Internet has created a host of challenges for traditional businesses in the way that they conceptualize the market, and how they define external boundaries with suppliers and customers. Textron, a diversified company whose businesses include helicopters, golf and lawn care equipment, and corporate financing services, created the role of chief innovation officer to lead its foray into e-commerce. The CIO heads up an e-business council that is charged with helping Textron units incubate ideas, launch start-ups, and create external alliances. As the CEO describes the role, "It underscores the importance of changing our perception of e-business— from one that focuses on technology to one that focuses on fundamentally redefining our business model."[7] The Internet is an inherently integrating force. Organizational units that never coordinated their activities must find ways to produce integrated responses to customers and suppliers.

- *Knowledge Management.* Knowledge officers are increasingly being deployed to identify opportunities for knowledge creation that will create value for the company or coordinate knowledge sharing. Typical activities include defining the intellectual capital that differentiates the company and creating systems for capturing, sharing, and using the knowledge resident in the employees. For example, at Ernst & Young the chief knowledge officer is charged with organizing, capturing, and cataloging the firm's collective knowledge as well as encouraging the firm's employees to share and use that information. A study of chief knowledge officers found that they describe themselves as change agents, charged not only with overseeing the development of knowledge management systems but creating the environment and culture that will stimulate knowledge sharing.[8] At all levels, they try to break down barriers between divisions so that anyone can quickly find out who has expertise in which areas.

- *Project Management.* Organizations undergoing large-scale change efforts (e.g., converting legacy technology systems) often employ an Office of Project Management to oversee and integrate the multiple initiatives under way. The persons in this unit can have significant impact if they define their role as being broader than simply monitoring project plans and keeping work on track. The role is boundary spanning when it is used to surface unrealistic deadlines, identify training needs, see opportunities to leverage or redeploy resources.

Boundary-spanning roles are typically senior-level positions, often reporting to the organization's leader, in order to give them the status necessary to "nose around" into other areas of the business. Not all boundary-spanning roles have to be at the CEO direct-report level. Staff functions at all levels of an organization are naturally boundary-spanning roles that are often underutilized.

The human resources (HR) function provides a good example. Over the last decade, HR professionals have struggled to move from being perceived as administrative processors to being "strategic partners" with the line of businesses they support. With the introduction of technology-enabled service centers that reduce the administrative component of their role, many HR staff have gained the ability to dedicate time to diagnosing and addressing systemic organizational issues and counseling business leaders on the human impact of strategic choices. In many companies, HR has become a full member of the executive team, actively contributing to business decisions.

HR people gather a lot of business information, but it often isn't transferred beyond their business unit. When HR people get together, they don't talk business; they talk HR. Opportunities to pollinate other businesses, to create linkages above and beyond HR processes, even the ability to "get ahead of the game" by finding out what is going on in other businesses, are missed. Not only is the organization hurt when staff functions don't serve as integrating roles, individuals diminish their own influence by limiting the definition of their role. IT, finance, audit, and other functions have similar opportunities to span boundaries because their work takes them into all areas of the business, if not as individuals, then as representatives of their functions.

SELECTING AND SUPPORTING PEOPLE IN INTEGRATIVE ROLES

The integrative role is difficult to implement because of the internal conflict it inherently generates. In traditional organizational structure terms, most people come to identify with and represent a specific specialty. The role of integrating these various groups in the organization, which see issues from a perspective of self-interest, is not a simple one. Integrative roles, irrespective of type, rely heavily on the holder's interpersonal skills to build credibility. People in integrative roles usually do not command resources or have the authority that comes from overseeing a revenue-producing department. A person must be able to convince and motivate others to work across business lines, be solution-driven even when it's "not their problem," and be willing to see things from multiple perspectives. To be successful in his or her role, the person must exercise power through networking, persuasion, and influence. When designing and staffing integrative roles, keep the following in mind:

- Select and develop people who can influence without formal authority.

- Select people who thrive in spaces, roles, and processes that are not clearly defined.

- Select people who are comfortable accessing and leveraging the resources of others without having to build or own their own.

- When possible, have the role report to a senior person in the organization, if not the leader, to legitimize the importance of the integrative role.

- Provide the integrator with access to the facts and knowledge he or she can use to influence others.

MATRIX STRUCTURES

Ideally, each person in your organization would approach problems and decisions holistically. He or she would bring his or her personal expertise to bear but have the knowledge and perspective to make trade-offs to ensure that each action taken is for the good of the organization, free of narrow parochial interests, political considerations, or individual concerns. Assets and HR would be shared easily and deployed wherever they were most needed. Unfortunately, this doesn't happen. Where people are placed in the organization shapes their worldview. They advocate for positions that reflect their particular perch in the organization. When views collide it is often left for senior management to sort out.

But what if you really need particular people or units to embody both a functional and a customer perspective? Or, a balanced geographic and product outlook? Essentially, you want to design an organization where power is shared equally among two or more dimensions. These dimensions are most often functions, geographies, customers, or products. Figure 4-12 illustrates how different lateral mechanisms shift power from one dimension to another. The left side of the diagram represents an organization structured by geographic profit centers. Point A represents loose coordination of product interests across regions or countries. This coordination is dependent on networks and informal contacts. All of the power lies with the managers who head up the geographic business units.

As you move to the right on the diagram and introduce cross-business teams (Point B), there is more linkage among the product activities across the geographies, but the power structure is still dominated by the geographies. A product manager may be on a global product team but reports in through the local management structure in the country or region where he or she is located. Only when you reach Point C is there an equal balance of power between the geographic and product organizations. At this point the product manager would have two bosses—a local market manager and a global product manager. To the right of Point C, power shifts to the product organization. At points D

Figure 4-12. Power shifts in the lateral organization.

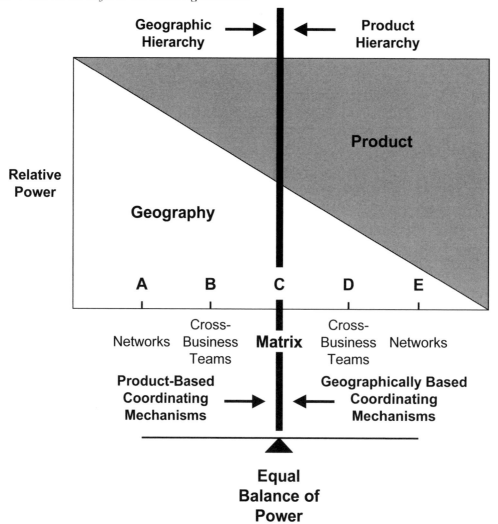

and E you have a product structure with geographically based coordinating mechanisms.

Point C in the diagram represents a matrix relationship. A matrix allows the organization to focus on two or more dimensions simultaneously. In a matrix relationship, a person has two bosses, each of whom represents equally important strategic dimensions. In Figure 4-13, the regional sales manager is in a matrixed position. The regional sales manager reports to both the eastern market manager (geography) and the director of sales (function). Matrix relationships force all of the parties in the matrix—the two "bosses" as well as the people they manage—to give equal weight to multiple perspectives. The regional sales manager is going to try to maximize overall sales (a goal of the functional sales organization) yet pursue those sales that are most profitable in the eastern market (a goal of the geography). The matrix forces a multidimensional worldview.

Figure 4-13. Matrix relationship.

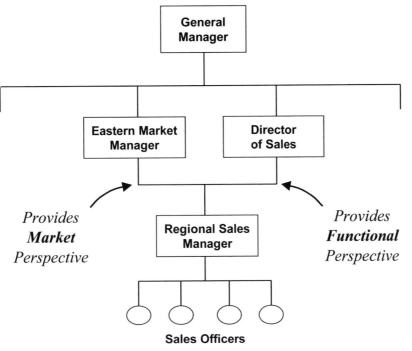

Matrix relationships introduce complexity. Selection decisions are more complex, goals have to be set jointly, and evaluations are conducted by multiple managers. Balance has to be maintained between both dimensions. The organization and its individuals must have the ability to surface and manage conflict productively without having to continually escalate to the management level above for tie breaking. Ideally, the matrix is a transitional structure—a way to build "matrix thinking." Matrix thinkers are comfortable with having a foot in two or more worlds at one time without having to formally report into two places.

Until people can think intuitively with a matrix mind-set, formal matrix relationships can reinforce this plurality of thinking. Two desired behaviors result from matrix structures:

1. *A Simultaneous Focus on Multiple Perspectives.* A matrix makes a person or unit responsive to two or more market forces at once. This introduction of multiple perspectives can be expected to improve decision quality just as using a team would. The matrix allows for a middle manager to make trade-offs from a "general management" perspective more easily than would be expected if he reported only through one channel in the organization.

2. *More Effective Use of Technical and Specialized Resources.* Every organization has specialists that are needed by various business units. These experts are too expensive to duplicate across the organization. The matrix allows for shar-

ing of HR without having one division or unit own them. For example, a major disadvantage of a product structure is that functions are spread among the product divisions. Scale and expertise are diffused and the ability to flexibly move functional talent between divisions is limited. By matrixing the functions with the product lines, the functional units retain their ability to specialize and build depth of expertise. At the same time, product lines have access to the entire pool of functional resources.

The matrix reflects the complexity of the customer's world. Customers don't care about internal organizational design. They care only about the composite output in terms of product, quality, cost, and time. The matrix allows for complexity to be managed internally rather than trivialized or disregarded.

MANAGING IN A MATRIX

Matrix structures were popular in the 1970s and 1980s, when large manufacturing companies, particularly in the aerospace industry, employed them to solve the dilemma of creating depth of technical expertise while focusing on new product development. They were also employed by multinational companies seeking to build global products while continuing to operate close to local markets. Both Asea Brown Boveri (ABB) and Citibank built a three-dimensional matrix around countries, global products, and global customers.

Matrix structures fell out of favor in the 1990s when a number of companies that had very visibly employed them failed to meet their stated goals and then restructured without using matrix relationships in their new designs. In retrospect, most of the failures can be attributed not to the inherent problems with matrix relationships but the lack of other supporting lateral capabilities necessary to make them work.

Matrix structures have evolved from a highly touted "solution" that served as the organizing framework for a whole business to simply another tool that can be used in concert with other structures and mechanisms to integrate a business. The following are some things to keep in mind when considering matrix structures:

■ *Employ matrix relationships sparingly.* Organizational designers get into trouble when they try to adopt structures from admired companies as "best practices." Each organization is unique. Use the matrix where a team or integrative role alone is not strong enough to gain the dual perspective necessary, not just because a competitor uses it.

■ *Align the management team.* Since most people grow up with two bosses (i.e., parents) the idea of reporting in two directions shouldn't seem so foreign. But just as in families, problems arise when the two supervising bosses in the matrix don't share the same goals or agree on outcomes, and the subordinate (child) is left to negotiate between them. The subordinate in a matrix has to reconcile sometimes conflicting directions from each of the dimensions he or she reports to. If they aren't easily reconciled, both bosses have to get together and resolve the matter. These peer debates often result in healthy trade-offs and better decisions than if they had been made from one viewpoint alone. When the peer "bosses" can't agree, then the issue escalates up to the senior manager common to both bosses. A downside to introducing matrix relationships is that it introduces more conflict into the organization and more time is spent resolving these conflicts.

It is incumbent upon the senior manager to push these disputes back to the peer managers to resolve. Percy Barnevik, the former CEO of ABB, is often remembered for telling his managers that they could escalate a problem to him once, that they could escalate it to him twice, but that if they escalated it three times, he would probably know it's time to replace them. If problems are not resolved at the lowest level possible, the matrix will be defeated by the drain it creates on senior management time. Senior managers support the matrix by:

—Ensuring a balance of power between the managers in the matrix

—Arbitrating disputes that cannot be resolved at the next level down

—Creating common ground around the strategy, values, and priorities so that managers don't receive mixed messages and can make joint decisions for the good of the organization

—Introducing performance management and reward systems that reflect the multiple foci of the organization

■ *Keep it simple.* Even when matrix relationships are used extensively, not everyone will be in matrix relationships. Some midlevel managers may have two bosses, but everyone who reports into them has only one. Matrixes become overly complex and unwieldy when there are multiple layers between the two bosses and the senior manager who must function as the tiebreaker for disputes. When everyone is matrixed and dozens of people must become involved to resolve an issue, operations can't function effectively. For example, in the simple matrix that was illustrated in Figure 4-13, the regional sales manager must balance the market and functional perspective, and this duality of perspective will be translated down to the sales officers in the group. However, the sales officers all report into the regional sales officer, keeping the reporting relationships well defined.

■ *Install accounting and reporting systems to support it.* A matrix relationship creates dual accountability. The organization needs to have reporting systems that allow information to be aggregated and desegregated along all the dimensions of the matrix. This may require only a few modifications to current systems or it may necessitate the development of an entirely new system. The most famous of matrix reporting systems is ABB's ABACUS system. ABACUS allowed for performance data to be collected at the level of its 4,500 operating companies and then analyzed within and across sixty-five product lines and 140 countries simultaneously.

BUILDING LATERAL CAPABILITY

If you view the organization as a set of shared resources and competencies that collectively define the organization's capability, the challenge is to create mechanisms to ensure that these resources and competencies create value for customers. The design of structures and mechanisms is only effective to the extent that it changes individual and collective mind-sets. The goal in design is to make it easy for people to think in new ways, and to make it more likely that they will operate with full appreciation of how their decisions and actions impact the entire system. As more organizations move toward conducting work in reconfigurable project-based teams, the strength of lateral connections becomes as important as the vertical structure.

Building each type of lateral capability has benefits and costs, which are summarized in Figure 4-14. The goal should always be to build the capability that gets the job done while introducing the least amount of complexity.

A last visit to the CBC case illustrates what design decisions an organization might make regarding building lateral capability.

CASE STUDY

The CBC executive team determined that they needed to build the firm's lateral capability on a number of fronts to address the current state assessment findings and support the front-back structure they had designed. Given the poor history of collaboration, the team was wary of creating too many team or matrix structures that depended on either management or employee skills to resolve issues. In fact, they decided that addressing issues among the managers was the highest priority. They developed a work plan focused on four topics:

Figure 4-14. Summary of integrating mechanisms.

Type	Benefits	Drawbacks
Networks	▪ Tend to occur naturally. ▪ People are eager to form them—provide personal benefit as well as organizational benefit. ▪ Relatively inexpensive to foster. ▪ Rely on simple communication. ▪ Do not add levels or meetings.	▪ Dependent on spontaneous interactions—just because they are there doesn't mean that people will use them. ▪ Too informal to rely on for critical processes. ▪ No documented processes. ▪ Difficult to capture learning across the organization.
Lateral Processes	▪ Formalize the flow of work and information across organizational boundaries. ▪ Help the organization focus on the critical requirements of business processes. ▪ Reduce reliance on individual managers to make systems work.	▪ Require dedicated time from staff to develop and implement processes. ▪ Processes owned across units may be owned by no one. ▪ May increase bureaucratic tendencies—documentation and compliance with the process create rigidity.
Teams	▪ Utilize multiple organizational perspectives and resources for real-time problem solving. ▪ Push decision making downward. ▪ Can be a permanent or ad hoc part of the organization structure. ▪ Focus units on resolving differences and conflicts. ▪ Use existing staff—do not increase head count.	▪ May increase conflict in the organization and the time required to resolve it. ▪ Require investment of internally focused time to build team skills and develop operating agreements. ▪ May waste resources if there is no clear charge or charter. ▪ Rely on healthy informal systems and networks.
Integrative Roles	▪ Resolve conflict through mediation and negotiation instead of escalation. ▪ If it is an expansion of the definition of an existing role, then it does not add to head count. ▪ Create formal point of responsibility for communication.	▪ Cost associated with hiring individuals for newly created roles.
Matrix Structures	▪ Mirror the reality and complexity of the client world. ▪ Enable more flexible utilization of technical depth. ▪ Force employees to adopt a multifunctional perspective. ▪ Enhance communication and information transfer by multiple channels.	▪ Dual reporting relationships can cause conflict. ▪ Decision strangulation—severe "group-itis." ▪ Increased need for complex communication due to ambiguity. ▪ Employees may feel lost without a permanent "home."

1. *Management Team Alignment and Skills.* The executive scheduled a series of combined meetings/training sessions for all CBC managers to roll out the new strategy, introduce the new structure and organizational roles, and define the responsibilities of managers in their roles as members of the executive and leadership teams. The training component of the meetings would focus on negotiation and conflict management. Scenarios drawn from real conflicts in the organization would be used as a basis to establish new operating ground rules. The managers also agreed to schedule training sessions to develop their own people-management skills in order to address the concerns from employees in the current state assessment.

2. *New Product Development Lateral Process.* A work group was put together to map the product development process, analyze it, and reconfigure it. The charge to the group was not only to reduce internal delays but to create mechanisms to allow for better and faster execution in the operations area. Most important, the work group was to build clarity and transparency into the process.

3. *Information and Marketing Integrative Roles.* A search for a marketing director and chief information officer was started. The marketing and information/e-commerce roles would be positioned as integrative roles. Each would have a small staff, but they would also chair cross-business teams. The marketing team would work closely with the sales officers and product areas to create integrated responses to those customers that bought multiple products from CBC. It would also serve as a vehicle to collect and act on customer feedback. The chief information officer would lead the effort to develop an e-commerce strategy as well as build more cross-product knowledge-sharing capability.

4. *Trading and Credit Matrix Relationships.* A work group was assembled to define the new roles for traders and credit specialists and to make recommendations on how best to utilize these roles. The goal would be to allow traders the continuity with clients necessary to support the deepened customer relationships that CBC was trying to develop, and to build depth of expertise among the credit specialists. The work group was to consider, among other options, the implications of creating teams and matrix relationships for these roles.

When choosing which types of lateral capability to build or design into the organization, there are some considerations to take into account in addition to those discussed in the chapter.

■ *Existing Strengths.* Start by assessing and enhancing the foundation. Teams and matrix relationships will be much more difficult to implement if the organization's networks are weak, if current units have poor working relationships, and if people have few skills or experience working in teams across organizational boundaries.

■ *Management Skill.* The most important enabler of the lateral organization is the mind-set and skill level of the managers. Managers need to feel comfortable letting go of decision-making authority. They need the skills to serve as facilitators and coaches and be able to work across the organization, in addition to the traditional mode of managing up or down. They also need to exhibit the behaviors that model flexibility and appreciation for multiple perspectives. Building these skills and attitudes is a prerequisite to building lateral capability.

■ *Maturity of the Workforce.* Just as with the management team, the skill and experience level of the workforce will impact how quickly the organization can develop lateral capability. Three skills are essential:

1. *Communication,* including informing others, consulting, gathering perspectives, and presenting issues

2. *Conflict management,* including legitimizing but not presuming conflict, working with conflict resolution processes, and determining when to escalate issues

3. *Influence,* including negotiating win-win solutions, building trust through understanding of other viewpoints, and creating buy-in for initiatives

The more the skills are embedded as organizational skills, the more effectively the lateral organization will operate.

Use Tool 4-4 to determine which types of integrating mechanisms are most appropriate for your design.

SUMMARY

This chapter defined the concept of lateral organization and presented five different types of lateral capability that can be designed to complement the vertical structure: networks, processes, teams, integrative roles, and matrix structures. We have looked at how these coordinating mechanisms can overcome barriers to collaboration created by the vertical structure. This brings us to the conclusion of our discussion of structure and roles.

The next two chapters focus on the last two points of the star model—reward systems and people practices—both of which must be aligned with the organization's structure. In these chapters, we look at how you can make choices in the design of these systems to drive and reinforce the behaviors required by your strategy.

NOTES

1. P. Tam, "Pixar Bets It Can Boost Output to One Movie Feature a Year," *The Wall Street Journal*, February 15, 2001.

2. N. Hass, "The House the Bloomberg Built," *Fast Company*, November 1995, p. 97.

3. W. Graham, D. Osgood, and J. Karren, "A Real-Life Community of Practice," *Training and Development* 52 (May 1998): 34.

4. J. S. Brown, "Unfreezing the Corporate Mind," *Fast Company*, June 16, 1998.

5. E. Raimy, "Community Zest," *Human Resource Executive*, August 2000, pp. 34–38.

6. E. W. Morrison and C. Phelps, "Taking Charge at Work: Extrarole Efforts to Initiate Workplace Change," *Academy of Management Journal* 42, 4 (1999): 403–419.

7. "Textron Promotes Bohlen to Executive Vice President and Chief Innovation Officer," *Textron News*, www.textron.com, April 10, 2000.

8. M. J. Earl and I. A. Scott, "What Is a Chief Knowledge Officer?" *Sloan Management Review*, Winter 1999, pp. 29–38.

Tool 4-1. Building networks.

Purpose:	Use this tool to assess your current networks and think about how you can foster and support them in your organization.
This tool is for:	Leadership Team.

Co-Location

1. What areas in your organization would benefit by being co-located?

    _____

    _____

    _____

2. What are the opportunities to move some service and staff functions closer to their internal clients?

    _____

    _____

    _____

3. What are the opportunities to redesign your physical space to encourage interaction and make it easy for people to spontaneously collaborate?

    _____

    _____

    _____

Communities of Practice

1. If you have a functional group dispersed into your business, product, or customer organizations, what mechanisms are in place to maintain their functional identity?

    _____

    _____

    _____

2. Do you have communities of practice in existence? What formal encouragement or support is in place for them?

    _____

    _____

    _____

Annual Meetings and Retreats

1. What are the norms for inviting people to management retreats and off-site meetings? What are the opportunities to use participation as a means to build networks?

    _____

    _____

    _____

2. What mechanisms could be used at these meetings to encourage networking and to help people stay connected afterward?

    _____

    _____

    _____

(continues)

Tool 4-1. (Continued).

Training Programs

1. How could participants in enterprisewide training programs be more deliberately selected to maximize network and relationship building?

_____

_____

_____

2. What key themes should be included to ensure that the scenarios, cases, and role-plays used in customized programs reinforce the desired messages, values, and cultural norms of the organization?

_____

_____

_____

Rotational Assignments

1. Does your organization use rotational assignments? What are the typical paths? How are people rewarded for taking lateral moves?

_____

_____

_____

2. If your organization does not use rotational assignments, what are the key positions that could provide managers or high-potential talent the skills, exposure, and experience that would prepare them for the next level of responsibility?

_____

_____

_____

Technology and E-Coordination

1. Does your organization's use of technology support creation of networks? If so, specify how.

_____

_____

_____

2. What type of systems, access, and technological tools beyond e-mail would allow people to better communicate and collaborate?

_____

_____

_____

Rewards and Recognition

1. List your organization's "heroes" and role models.

   _____

   _____

   _____

2. What are they known for? Are they people known for learning, teaching, and sharing or only for delivering the results?

   _____

   _____

   _____

		Yes	No
3.	Are people rewarded for taking time away from their own job to help someone else even if, as a result, they deliver less on their own objective?	❏	❏
4.	Are people given the same recognition for borrowing and modifying an existing solution as inventing something new?	❏	❏
5.	If people want to create a community of practice are they given time and resources or do they have to do it in their own time?	❏	❏
6.	If people make a lateral career move to broaden their skill set and perspective, does their career advance as rapidly as those who choose to climb a narrow functional ladder?	❏	❏

If you answered "no" to any of the questions above, what reward systems need to be examined? What changes would make your organization more integrated?

Tool 4-2. Mapping lateral processes.

Purpose:	Use this tool to guide the design of lateral processes in your organization.
This tool is for:	Leadership Team.

Identify three to five critical processes for the new organization. Refer to Figure 4-4, *Typical Lateral Processes*, to guide you.

Name of Processes: 1. _____

2. _____

3. _____

4. _____

5. _____

For each process follow the steps below.

Name of Process: _____

Step 1—Scoping the Process

1.1 What is the overall objective of this process? What are the anticipated results? Describe how it will function ideally.

_____

_____

1.2 Start of Process:
a. What is the input to the process?

_____

_____

b. When does the process begin and with whom?

_____

_____

1.3 End of Process:
a. What is the output?

_____

_____

b. When does the process end? To whom does it go?

_____

_____

Step 2—Defining the Process

2.1 Brainstorm a complete list of activities or subprocesses that need to take place from beginning to end.

_____   _____

_____   _____

_____   _____

_____   _____

_____   _____

2.2 Use this list to create a flow chart of the process. Use the following symbols to denote different activities:

Step 3—Interfaces

3.1 a. With what other processes does this process interface?

_____

_____

b. With what business/technical functions does the process interface?

_____

_____

3.2 Measures:

a. List the quantitative measures of performance.

_____

_____

b. List the qualitative measures of performance.

_____

_____

c. How will they be tracked?

_____

_____

Tool 4-3 Team readiness assessment.

Purpose:	Use this tool to assess the extent to which the new organizational design is able to support team structures.
This tool is for:	Leadership Team.
Instructions:	For the series of statements listed below, assign a rating based on how much you either agree (1) or disagree (5) in terms of your organization.

	Agree Strongly	Agree Somewhat	Neither Agree nor Disagree	Disagree Somewhat	Disagree Strongly
1. There is a clear business reason for using teams.	1	2	3	4	5
2. Our customers would be better served if we used teams.	1	2	3	4	5
3. The work can be organized in such a way that responsibility can be shared among team members.	1	2	3	4	5
4. The culture of the organization, its vision, and its values support shared responsibility and team initiatives.	1	2	3	4	5
5. Technology systems and physical settings can be restructured to accommodate a team environment.	1	2	3	4	5
6. When we ask for involvement we get many volunteers.	1	2	3	4	5
7. Employees are not afraid to speak up.	1	2	3	4	5
8. Systems are in place to provide teams with timely and useful performance information.	1	2	3	4	5
9. Our human resources function fully understands the requirements of a team-based structure (compensation, feedback, training).	1	2	3	4	5
10. There is willingness to share authority, decision making, and responsibility.	1	2	3	4	5
11. Employees are both willing and able to try new behaviors.	1	2	3	4	5
12. Employees have the necessary skills to work effectively in teams.	1	2	3	4	5
13. Management is willing to give employees time to participate in team-associated activities (meetings, etc.).	1	2	3	4	5
14. Managers/supervisors are willing to change their roles and responsibilities.	1	2	3	4	5
15. Our organization has strong networks and relationships.	1	2	3	4	5

For the items that are scored a "3" or higher, identify what needs to change in order to prepare your organization for teams.

Item	Changes Needed

Tool 4-4. Building lateral capability.

Purpose:	Use this tool to determine which types of integrating mechanisms are most appropriate for your new design.
This tool is for:	Leadership Team.
Instructions:	Use the grids below to consider each type of integrating mechanism discussed in Chapter Four.

I. Networks

1. Specify where networks might be most useful.

_____

_____

_____

2. Assess the potential benefits and drawbacks of your design.

Benefits:	Drawbacks:

II. Lateral Processes

1. Identify key lateral processes that your new organization design will require.

_____

_____

_____

2. Assess the potential benefits and drawbacks of your design.

Benefits:	Drawbacks:

III. Teams

1. Where might you use teams? Which type of teams?

_____

_____

_____

2. Assess the potential benefits and drawbacks for your design.

Benefits:	Drawbacks:

IV. Integrative Roles

1. Identify key integrative roles. What need would each role address?

_____

_____

_____

2. Assess the potential benefits and drawbacks for your design.

Benefits:	Drawbacks:

(continues)

Tool 4-4. (Continued).

V. Matrix Structures

1. Where would a dual or multiple focus be most useful?

_____

_____

_____

2. Assess the potential benefits and drawbacks for your design.

Benefits:	Drawbacks:

VI. Does your workforce have the communication, conflict management, and influence skills necessary to implement these capabilities in the design? On a scale of 1 to 5, rate your leadership team, middle managers, supervisors, and others.

	Low 1	2	3	4	High 5	Where do they need more skill development?
Leadership Team						
Middle Managers						
Supervisors						
Others						

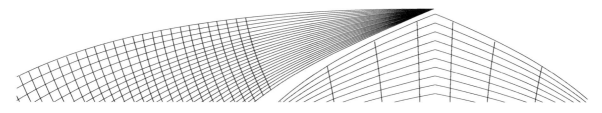

CHAPTER FIVE

DEFINING AND REWARDING SUCCESS

We have discussed how organization design is a means to implement strategy and how design decisions regarding the structure and lateral organization shape work flow, communication, power, and decision making in an organization. Regardless of the structure, employees make choices each day regarding how they work and interact. These choices are influenced by the unique combination of experience, personality, skill, and internal motivation that each individual brings to work. They are also shaped by the measures and rewards that the organization uses to communicate to employees what behaviors and results are most important. Creating these systems is an integral part of your design process. The final two steps on the star model are the design of reward systems and of people practices (Figure 5-1). While there is an inherent sequence in the first three points on the star—strategy, structure, then processes and lateral capability—the design of reward systems and people practices systems is closely linked and frequently done simultaneously. The order of these chapters doesn't imply a strict sequence in how these topics are considered.

Every organization has a different definition of success. Changing other parts of the organization design may mean that your organization's definition of success has changed. In order to perform at their best, people need a clear view of what success means in their organization—in terms of business results

Figure 5-1. Star model.

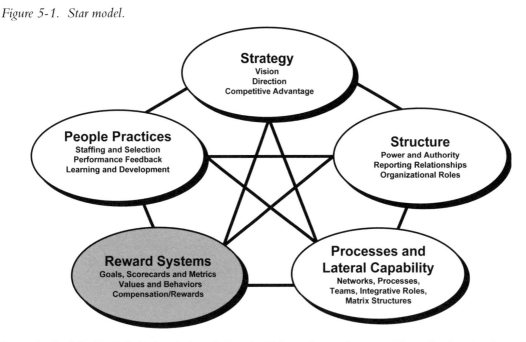

Source: Jay R. Galbraith, *Designing Organizations: An Executive Briefing on Strategy, Structure, and Process* (San Francisco: Jossey-Bass, 1995).

as well as individual performance expectations. While it is important that people understand the business strategy and how their work contributes to it, understanding the goal is usually not enough to shape behavior. There is no guarantee that people will use their skills, knowledge, and capabilities for the good of the organization. How people are measured and rewarded will influence how they carry out their work each day. The challenge of designing measurement and reward systems is to motivate and reinforce the behaviors that add value to the organization.

Reward systems define expected behaviors and influence the likelihood that people will demonstrate those behaviors. They ensure that everyone is pulling in the same direction. An aligned reward system reduces internal competition and the frustration and diffusion of energy that comes when people are given competing goals.

Reward systems have four components:

1. *Metrics*: The systems that identify measures and targets for enterprise, business unit, team, and individual performance

2. *Desired Values and Behaviors*: The actions that are most likely both to produce desired business results and to reflect the organizational values

3. *Compensation*: The monetary means intended to recognize a person's past contribution as well as motivate continued or improved performance

4. *Reward and Recognition*: The nonmonetary components that complement compensation systems to let people know that they are valued

The first two components, metrics and values and behaviors, have to be addressed before the compensation and reward and recognition systems are designed. Metrics translate the strategy into the day-to-day actions and expectations of employee behavior. Metrics serve to clarify the vague terms used in vision statements that appeal to our emotions, pride, and sense of belonging—such as "superior service"—and turn them into concrete directives that appeal to our needs for measurable accomplishment and progress. Metrics take what are often abstract and intangible strategic concepts and make them meaningful to everyone in the organization. "You get what you measure" has become an axiom of organizational life. Given that measures can drive unintended behaviors as well as desired results, it is important to measure the right things.

The trend in reward and compensation systems is to value people for the skills and knowledge they bring to the organization and how they use them, rather than for the particular position they are currently filling.[1] This shift from job focus to person focus helps build a reconfigurable organization. It changes the definition of success from moving up a job ladder to increasing skills and developing additional capabilities that are of value to the organization.

This chapter summarizes recent thinking in the field of performance measurement and metrics and compensation and reward practices and provides tools to guide your design of measurement and reward systems. It is divided into four sections:

- *Metrics* describes six principles to consider when designing a performance measurement system.

- *Values and Behaviors* provides a process for defining the behaviors that will underlie the kind of culture that supports performance and success.

- *Compensation* reviews the advantages and disadvantages of different pay approaches.

- *Rewards and Recognition* presents a thought guide for creating noncompensation-based reward and recognition programs.

METRICS

Before you can reward people, you have to be able to measure their contribution. The design of any performance measurement system should reflect the operating assumptions of the organization. If growth is important, the metrics should stress growth objectives. If the organization competes on the basis of quality, then those should be featured prominently. Measurement systems can become quite complex as you attempt to measure and track all the dimensions of the organization. The design of sound metrics rests on six principles, which are summarized in Figure 5-2 and discussed in detail next.

1. BREADTH

Financial results are the foundation of business metrics. They are generally regarded as reliable and consistent. They provide hard data on which to base reward and accountability systems and they provide a performance measure consistent with the objective of generating profits for shareholders, which is a dominant pressure for senior management in public companies.

While financial measures are good for reporting past results to shareholders, they don't give managers the decision-relevant information that tells them what they must do differently to change those results.

During the 1990s, the concept of the "balanced scorecard" took hold as a way to broaden business metrics beyond financial measures and build a comprehensive view of the operational measures that impact business performance. The balanced scorecard was originally described by Kaplan and Norton in 1992.[2] It includes four categories of performance:

Figure 5-2. Six principles of metrics.

	How to Measure Success
1. Breadth	Go beyond financial measures. Balance financial measures with operational indicators.
2. Criticality	Measure what's most important. Measure the drivers of performance that will make a significant difference if they change.
3. Time Orientation	Look backward and forward. Use lagging indicators for accuracy; use leading indicators to predict future trends.
4. Consequences	Beware of unintended consequences. Check that measures don't drive undesirable behaviors.
5. Alignment	Avoid conflicting measures. Cascade metrics down from the top and align them among interdependent roles at each level.
6. Targets	Set targets to be challenging but not impossible. Use standards to communicate expectations and ensure equity.

Financial	How do we look to shareholders?
Customer	How do customers see us?
Internal Business Processes	What do we have to excel at?
Innovation and Learning	How can we continue to improve?

When using a balanced scorecard, you develop a set of performance indicators unique to your business for each performance category. Then measures are identified for each indicator focused both on short- and long-term results. The advantage of the balanced scorecard is that it allows the user to see if improvement in one area is being achieved at the expense of improvement in another. The balanced scorecard approach is now widely used. It has become a generic term to capture the idea of running a business based on a set of measures that reflect all of the important activities that impact the strategy.

Figure 5-3 summarizes the steps for creating a balanced scorecard. First, the strategy and vision for the organization are translated into broad *performance categories*. Some companies have expanded Kaplan and Norton's original four categories to include such topics as People, Community/Environment, Strategic Cost Management, Risk, and even Partners to focus on contributions to sales by alliances, partnerships, and suppliers. The performance categories used should be selected to reflect the unique purpose and direction of your business.

Figure 5-3. Translating the strategy into measures and behaviors.

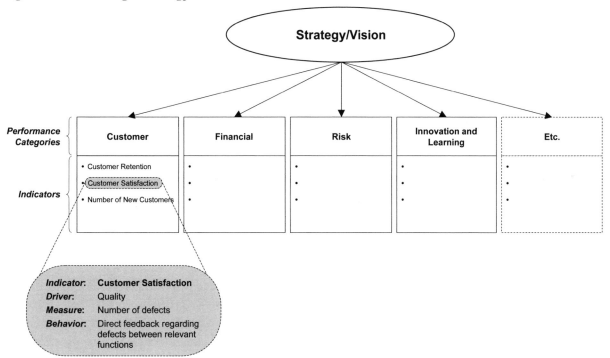

The second step is to determine a set of three to five *performance indicators* for each performance category. Performance indicators reflect the most important organizational capabilities that have to be developed or measured. They should be quite similar to the organizational capabilities you defined as design criteria in Chapter Two. Performance indicators should not be a comprehensive list of everything the organization must achieve, but rather what it must focus on. Some examples are given in Figure 5-4. The performance categories and indicators are likely to be consistent for the entire organization. How each indicator is then translated into specific measures will differ by unit, department, or function. For example, customer satisfaction might be an important performance indicator for your production, customer service, and finance functions. How it is measured in each department, however, will differ.

For each unit, the performance indicator is translated into drivers, measures, and behaviors, as Figure 5-3 illustrates for the performance indicator, "customer satisfaction." *Drivers* are those components of performance that if changed positively or negatively, impact the performance indicator. A cause and effect relationship is believed to exist between the driver and performance. For example, customer satisfaction generally comprises a combination of qual-

Figure 5-4. Sample performance indicators.

FINANCIAL	**INTERNAL BUSINESS PROCESSES**
▪ Return on capital employed ▪ Cash flow ▪ Profitability ▪ Average age of receivables	▪ Gross margins ▪ Quality ▪ Project management ▪ Cycle time, unit cost
CUSTOMER	**INNOVATION AND LEARNING**
▪ Customer satisfaction ▪ Customer retention ▪ Growth of new customers ▪ Share of wallet (depth and breadth of relationships)	▪ Percentage of revenue from new products ▪ Employee suggestions implemented
PEOPLE	**COMMUNITY/ENVIRONMENT**
▪ Turnover ▪ Climate survey results ▪ Internal mobility of talent	▪ Litigation ▪ Employee involvement in community

ity, cost, timeliness, and convenience. But not all of these will be equally important for all businesses. If for a particular product or service, a change in delivery time has little or no impact on customer satisfaction, then it is not a driver and shouldn't be measured. In this example, which might be a production-oriented department, quality is a driver, and it is the driver of customer satisfaction that the production department has control over.

Once the drivers are identified, then a few measures can be determined that will tell you how you are doing. In this example, a key measure might be number of defects. Behaviors that impact the measure can also be identified. This department determined that timely and direct feedback among functions within the department is the behavior that is most likely to reduce defects overall.

The process of creating a balanced scorecard is iterative and ongoing. The framework stays the same, but measures may be added or dropped as conditions change or capability is built. If the organization has identified poor quality as a problem, measuring quality will help to provide the focus needed to improve it. Once a quality discipline is embedded, it may not be necessary to measure quality to the same degree. Other capabilities may become more important and need to be emphasized through inclusion in the scorecard.

2. CRITICALITY

The idea of broadening and balancing measures is powerful. A danger when developing any measurement system, however, is that everything gets measured. The act of gathering, analyzing, and interpreting the data lessens your ability to attend to other business. What is actually critical can get obscured. Some things to consider:

■ *Too many measures overwhelm the system.* A rule of thumb is to limit any component in a measurement system to three to five items. Therefore, translate the strategy into three to five performance categories, identify three to five performance indicators for each category, determine three to five drivers for each indicator, and so on. It will keep people focused on determining what is most critical. One way to do it is to close your eyes, project yourself a few years out, and imagine that your strategy has failed. What went wrong? What failed? This intuitive, emotional component will complement the analytical approach and help determine which are the performance variables that really matter.[3]

■ *Not all measures are equally important.* Among categories and within each category, measures should be weighted by importance. For example, community issues may be important enough to include as a category, but they may not be as critical to overall business success as customer or financial outcomes.

Don't make the measurement system so all-encompassing that it doesn't provide guidance about priorities.

■ *Choose items that can be measured with confidence.* There might be performance dimensions that would be nice to measure but data can only be collected manually or anecdotally. While no reporting system is 100 percent accurate, ad hoc spreadsheets are particularly prone to error, no matter how good they look. Whenever there is manual intervention, inaccuracies are introduced. If current systems don't allow information to be gathered with confidence, it will make for poor measures. People will tend to dismiss any feedback on their performance based upon such data. If the measure is important enough, then develop systems to gather the data with accuracy.

3. TIME ORIENTATION

A robust measurement system needs to look backward and toward the future simultaneously. This can be accomplished through the use of lagging and leading indicators.

■ *Lagging indicators present past results.* They tell you how you did and typically have a high degree of confidence and accuracy. But as the mutual fund companies caution, past performance is not always an indication of future performance. Relying solely on lagging indicators has been likened to steering a boat by examining its wake. They tell you where you've been, but not where you need to go.

■ *Leading indicators help to predict future performance.* They are typically the drivers of performance that we discussed earlier. The indicator is assumed to correlate with some desired outcome. Leading indicators not only give early warning of problems and negative trends, but can also highlight future opportunities. They are more prone to inaccuracy than lagging indicators, however, because assumptions regarding causality may prove to be false.

The challenge of measuring the success and value of a Web site on the Internet illustrates the challenge of developing good leading indicators. The first generation of metrics for valuing a Web site in order to set prices for advertisers was number of Web site hits—how many people visited the site in any given period. The assumption was that more visits meant more people were likely to "click" on a banner advertisement, and that click would result in sales for advertisers. The number of hits was the leading indicator. Owners of sites with large volumes of visitors were able to price advertising space and time higher than other sites. Unfortunately, after some time it became apparent that there was little correlation between the activity (number of visits) and the outcome (eventual sales). The popularity of the site didn't actually predict buying behavior. Analysis showed that the number of new visitors ("eyeballs" in cyberspeak) and length of stay ("stickiness") were better predictors of sales for advertisers. Metrics and valuation formulas were changed accordingly.

In the diagram shown in Figure 5-3, the performance indicators are lagging indicators. Customer satisfaction is measured after the fact. The drivers, on the other hand, should be leading indicators. As product quality, on-time delivery, and accuracy increase and returns decrease, customer satisfaction can be expected to increase commensurately.

4. CONSEQUENCES

The purpose of having metrics is to influence your employee behavior. Although changing employee behavior is clearly the intent, there is a danger of creating unintended consequences that result from an imbalance among measures or from not thinking through the difference between the desired degree of behavior and too much of a good thing. Revenue growth is a common business goal. Setting it as a goal and measuring it focuses everyone on marketing, selling, and getting the product or service out to the customer. However, if revenue growth is not balanced by the goals of profitability and risk, revenue is growing but so are costs. Unless the explicit objective is to gain enough market share to lock out potential competitors, the business is no better off from the growth. Profitability remains the same. More dangerous is that the pace of marketing may outstrip the ability of the operational areas to deliver the product or service. Corners are cut, risks are taken, and the business craters when an ignored control problem explodes.

Call centers experience the dilemma of "you get what you measure even if that wasn't what you wanted" all the time. A classic example is the call center that rewards people for the number of calls answered per hour. Managers soon find that the quality of customer interaction drops as employees focus on getting to the next call. Customer problems don't get solved, but lots of calls get answered. In one center, there was no measure of repeat calls. Employees got high marks even if some percentage of the calls they answered were unsatisfied customers calling back. Most measures have a corollary that you need to be considered as a balance to avoid unintended consequences. For example:

- Increasing speed can lead to reductions in quality.
- Pressure to increase sales may result in sales to less desirable customers.
- Increased manufacturing volumes may lead to more shipped defects.
- Requiring on-time delivery can result in unsafe behavior.

Dominos Pizza experienced this last unintended consequence when it found that pizza delivery people were causing serious accidents, harming themselves and others, in their efforts to meet the company's promise of a hot pizza in thirty minutes or less. Most measures can result in unintended consequences when the relationship between the measure and behavior it is likely to provoke is not thought through.

5. ALIGNMENT

The final step in creating a system that defines and measures success is to ensure that all your metrics are aligned vertically—from the top of the organization down—and horizontally across units that must work together. Consistent goals:

- Define what an organization wants to/needs to accomplish in a given time frame.

- Provide a single purpose and direction around which the organization can focus energy and attention.

- Set the standards against which the organization's performance can be measured.

Goals and metrics should cascade down the organization and be communicated in relevant terms at each level. For example, profitability margins are a fine measure for a senior manager to focus on, but a team on the factory floor needs to know how increasing productivity in terms of units per hour translates into profitability.

The key is to cascade measures down. There is a danger of beginning the definition of measures at the front line and then rolling them up under the assumption that they will result in organizational improvement. A paradox of measurement systems is that organizational performance is not a simple additive function of the performance of individuals and units, but rather a result of the complex interrelationships of all the organization's component parts. So, what may seem like good measures because they encourage desired behaviors or results at the individual or team level, may in fact discourage some more subtle behaviors that will benefit the whole organization. Goals and measures also need to be aligned across the organization. If developed in isolation they can result in conflicts, particularly when units are interdependent.

6. TARGETS

As important as determining the measures is setting the targets. For example, a measure for a manufacturing unit may be number of defects. The target might be to hold defects to no more than one per 10,000. This number is meaningless, however, unless it is compared to a current baseline and external industry benchmarks. The right amount of stretch needs to be built in so that the goals are challenging but not impossible to reach.

Who sets the targets is another decision. Even in highly autonomous teams, managers usually need to be involved with setting targets. It is too tempting for people to set targets low in order to ensure that they can be met or exceeded, particularly when achieving the target is tied to compensation or other rewards.

Use Tool 5-1 to highlight any weaknesses in your current system.

Values and Behaviors

Behaviors are often an overlooked component of defining and rewarding success. Behaviors are not a design component. Rather they are the desired outcome of other design decisions. The logic is that the structure, processes, measurement and reward systems, and people practices encourage employees, and make it easy for them, to act in ways that support the goals of the business.

So, although behaviors don't get designed per se, they need to be made explicit. When they have been articulated and agreed upon by the organization, it will be clearer when other design choices fail to support the desired behaviors. In addition, they can be reinforced through choices made in the design of the reward and measurement systems.

Behavior is the manifestation of an organization's culture. No matter how clearly the organization's values are stated, it is the way that people act that defines the culture. Most organizations identify aspects of their culture that will need to change as a result of their strategy. The current state assessment will usually identify some dysfunctional behaviors, particularly among managers, that reduce the effectiveness of the organization. Changing the culture is difficult. The people who are in the current organization are there because they were attracted to the current culture and feel comfortable in it. Even if they say they would like it to be different, most of them contribute to reinforcing it every day.

Your organization's vision and values are the basis for defining the new behaviors that will be critical to shaping and creating the desired culture. Unfortunately, vision and value statements have become something of a cliche, an exercise for management to produce and proclaim before relegating to the shelf. It is true that most visions statements are indistinguishable and by themselves have little power. Further, few, if any, organizations have objectionable values in their value statement. The real work is to take these documents from the shelf and translate them into a corporate compass that guides employee behavior.

Values are the principles that a company stands for. Johnson & Johnson's response to the Tylenol scare of 1982 remains the hallmark of how a company's values shape decisions and behavior. After seven people died from cyanide-laced Tylenol capsules, management immediately made the decision to inform consumers, halt production, and pull 22 million products from store shelves. The decision was made and enacted without the need for a meeting among senior management. They all acted in concert, knowing that it was the right response. Almost twenty years later, a study conducted by Harris Interactive found that Johnson & Johnson was still rated as having the best corporate reputation in America.[4] By contrast, the Bridgestone/Firestone company was roundly criticized during the summer of 2000 for initially denying any connection between documented car accidents and the quality of its tires, and for only reluctantly agreeing to provide replacement tires. Not surprisingly, in the same poll it was rated as having the worst reputation overall.

Federal Express is another company known for its strong values and the impact it has on performance. During the UPS strike in the summer of 1997, many new customers turned to Fed Ex. After the company was swamped with 800,000 extra packages a day, thousands of employees voluntarily poured into the hubs to sort them, visibly demonstrating the company's values regarding how it serves customers. It was only after the strike was over that employees were rewarded with extra pay tied to the profit gained during the strike.

As an organization is undergoing change, there may be behaviors that were highly functional in the old organization but which are detrimental in the new organization because they directly contradict new values. For example, the Lone Ranger–type decision maker may have been reinforced and rewarded in an organization where individual contributors had a high degree of autonomy. After the organization incorporates teams into its structure, this very same behavior would no longer be as desirable if the new values emphasized consensus decisions. Some of the behaviors and actions that are commonplace in your organization now will need to be stopped as new behaviors become the norm. Many of these can be deduced from the current state assessment. Two processes for turning vision and value statements into behaviors are outlined next. One uses storytelling to translate the vision. The second links behaviors to organizational values.

VISION STORYTELLING

People don't seem to have much capacity for remembering vision and value statements. Dry recitations of bullet points on slides at company meetings are quickly forgotten. Even the pretty brochures, posters, and wallet cards are stowed away and become background visuals. By contrast, people do remember stories. A number of companies are using stories to communicate their vision and make it a substantive part of the culture.

People remember stories better than facts, as our memory is episodic in nature. While people can generally remember just five to seven facts for an extended period, they can easily remember five stories, each one full of facts.[5] When people recall experiences, they recall them in images. Linking facts or information to a ministory provides an image that can be recalled easier than the words.

Vision stories ask people to tell about a time they or someone else in the organization did something that illustrates the vision in action. The stories might be about going above and beyond the call of duty to help a customer or another department. They might illustrate trust, risk taking, or learning. By linking the element of the vision to a story, people can recall and relate the story to their own experience. They can share it with others. The stories, when used by managers, become the oral history that make employees into role models. When done as a group exercise, vision storytelling builds shared understanding of the behaviors that the organization values most.

Even if the vision is new and the organization is undergoing change, it is likely that people are already doing things that support the new direction. Gathering and sharing stories that illustrate the vision in action can reinforce these behaviors. The exercise reinforces what people are already doing right to support the organization's direction, even if it has changed. The act of sharing stories gives life and texture to behavioral norms.

Use Tool 5-2 to gather and share stories that illustrate the vision.

DERIVING BEHAVIORS FROM VALUES

This activity is usually done initially with the leadership team, although other employees should be involved over time. For each of the organization's values, the group determines what an employee might do to demonstrate the value:

- In front of clients

- With colleagues

- With his or her own team (if a manager)

An example is shown in Figure 5-5. For each value, the leadership group of this organization identified how a generic value, such as "place clients first," would "play out" in their particular organization in front of clients and in front of colleagues. For each value, two levels of behavior are defined: expected and exceptional. After additional refinement, these behaviors can be incorporated

Figure 5-5. Sample values and actions.

	Behavior in Front of Clients	Behavior in Front of Colleagues
Value:	**Place clients first.**	
Expected	Follows up on customer requests or problems; keeps customer informed of progress.	Evaluates all work from a client perspective; says "no" to projects or activities that interfere with attending to client-related work.
Exceptional	Takes the initiative to track down and solve systemic service delivery problems.	Can manage multiple internal and client projects; manages requirements and time needs to ensure deadlines are met.
Value:	**Conduct business with integrity and honesty.**	
Expected	Is direct, even when delivering bad news.	Focuses on the issue, not the person.
Exceptional	Takes ownership of bad news and proactively delivers it in a way that maintains customer goodwill.	Takes ownership of decisions made and can explain, sell, and defend them to others.

into the performance management and reward systems for reinforcement. Use Tool 5-3 to translate your organization's values into specific behaviors.

COMPENSATION

Compensation is a fundamental tool for aligning behaviors to your organization's goals. When other elements of the design change, the compensation system may need to be updated as well. Compensation is commonly used to:

- Pay people for the time they give to the business.

- Acknowledge and reward past results.

- Motivate improved future performance.

- Retain employees.

You can think of compensation as giving employees both an income statement and a balance sheet. The income statement tells them how the company views their current contribution, their output for the year. The balance sheet reflects the person's overall value as an organizational asset. The challenge of creating effective compensation systems rests in sending the right messages through changes in pay. A pay raise is wasted if the receiver doesn't know what it is for. Is it because I did a good job last year? Is it because the market price for my job went up? Is it to let me know that I have potential and the company wants me to stay?

Although many would agree that poorly designed compensation plans can encourage the wrong behaviors, it is not so clear whether compensation on its own can have a significant positive impact on performance.[6] The complex interaction between the work environment and the intrinsic motivation that employees bring to their work makes it difficult to sort out the impact of compensation on motivating sustained improvement. Inadequate compensation is clearly a source of dissatisfaction and can cause employees to leave the organization, but how potent money is as a motivator varies from individual to individual.

Over the past ten years, there have been some significant changes in compensation practices among U.S.-based businesses (Figure 5-6). These trends reflect an attempt better to link individual performance with overall business results, increase the flexibility of pay practices, and create compensation packages that will attract and retain scarce talent. Each is reviewed next.

Figure 5-6. Trends in compensation practices.

From . . .		To . . .
A focus on salary	➡	Total compensation philosophy
Predictable merit increases	➡	Variable compensation
Paying for time	➡	Paying for performance
Valuing the position	➡	Valuing skills and knowledge
Rewarding individuals	➡	Rewarding teams and business units

TOTAL COMPENSATION

Total compensation is the combination of salary, cash payments, and benefits received by an employee. For most employees below the very top executive levels, salary remains the largest component of their pay package. However, more and more companies are putting an emphasis on the total value of compensation packages, as opposed to just salary, to attract and retain employees.

One element is a greater use of bonuses and incentive pay above and beyond salary for all levels. In 1998, 72 percent of American companies offered at least one variable pay plan to employees, up from 47 percent in 1990.[7] In addition, many companies are offering menus of benefit packages for employees to choose from, both to meet individual needs and to accommodate the different populations within an organization. For example, a recent study found that working mothers highly value control over their time and are less likely to leave a current job if it provides flexibility, not even for a higher salary at another position.[8] Companies have introduced a whole range of new benefits, including on-site day care, concierge services, gyms, and free lunches, not only to make the work environment more inviting (and make it easier for employees to work longer hours), but also to increase the perceived total value of the compensation package.

VARIABLE COMPENSATION

Over the past few years, despite low unemployment and high competition for skilled workers, annual salary increases have hovered near 4 percent, just around the rate of inflation. Most growth in compensation has been in the form of variable compensation. *Variable compensation* comprises performance-based awards that have to be reearned each year and don't permanently increase base salaries. These can be in the form of cash bonuses or stock options. Over 60 percent of companies now use variable pay below the officer level.[9]

Some variable pay plans are in the form of "add-ons." An employee's base salary is set at the market average, and any bonus or payout is in addition to that salary. Other firms, particularly cash-strapped start-ups, offer salaries well below the prevailing market but provide employees with an opportunity to come out far ahead of the market by earning variable pay. These are "at-risk" plans. If the target for the variable pay bonus isn't met (due to individual, team, or business reasons) the employees risk ending up worse off financially than peers in other companies.

Variable compensation provides a number of benefits for designing compensation systems, particularly when you want to encourage a more performance-oriented culture.

■ *Allows for differentiation in performance.* Variable pay is a tool for rewarding excellence and differentiating top performers. Traditional merit-based compensation systems that give a yearly salary increase allow for little differentiation among employees. Typically, the difference in yearly salary increases is a few percentage points between below-average and outstanding performers. An old-line, tradition-bound insurance company that was trying to create a more nimble, performance-oriented culture, introduced a variable pay plan. Employees who were rated a 4 or a 5 on a five-point performance-rating scale each year would earn significantly more than those who earned a 3, which represented the average rating. In preparation, a study was conducted of past ratings in order to determine how many employees were likely to receive a 4 or 5 rating. Much to management's surprise, they found that over 65 percent of the company had been rated "above average" in the past year! Variable pay plans tend to reduce the sense of entitlement that pervades traditional plans. They give the whole performance management process more meaning by linking the outcome to significant impact on pay. Managers are forced to differentiate performance in order to justify bonuses. This is particularly important when a new organization design requires that people break out of comfortable modes of behavior and act in new ways.

- *Holds down costs.* Probably the biggest driver of variable pay plans is that it reduces overall costs for employers. Even when payouts are large, they are not permanently added to the base wages. Therefore they don't impact other costs that are calculated against salary, such as benefits and retirement contributions. When times are bad and goals aren't met, the company isn't stuck with an inflated salary base. Theoretically, this should provide more flexibility and avoid the need for as many layoffs during downturns, thereby benefiting employees with more job security.

- *Retains high performers.* When variable pay is given in the form of stock options it can build long-term commitment to the organization and a sense of ownership. During the late 1990s, many companies increased the amount of stock they gave and, to compete with dot-coms, distributed it lower in the organization than they had in the past. The promise of wealth creation through ownership in a growing business lured MBAs and lawyers away from established corporations to Internet start-ups. Of course, this only works when the value of stock rises.

PAY FOR PERFORMANCE

The most prevalent compensation metric remains time. People are paid for how much time they work. Even those not paid by the hour are paid an annual salary on the premise that they will work a certain amount of time a year. Closely associated with variable pay is the trend toward pay for performance. *Pay for performance* rewards people for their results and contributions rather than their time and effort.

At the individual level, performance rewards are often given as bonuses for meeting certain goals. Pay for performance is also commonly tied to unit or division results. For example, when the unit achieves its objectives, a bonus pool is divided among all the employees in that unit.

Commissions for salespeople are the most common type of pay for performance. There is a clear link between results and compensation. Paying people in the organization for results rather than time and effort has proven to be a compelling idea and has taken a number of forms.

■ *Gain-sharing plans* began in the 1940s as a collaboration between union workers and management in manufacturing plants and represent one of the earliest forms of paying for performance. The plans are based on the philosophy that workers should share in any of the gains that result from their contributions. A baseline of performance is established. If the business unit does better than the baseline measure, the workers share in the gains. The attractiveness of the plan is that it funds itself. Gain-sharing plans work best when the variables of productivity are under the control of employees and can be accurately measured. Gains are typically highest in the first years of the program when the easiest and most obvious improvements can be identified and addressed. Problems arise when all possible productivity improvements have been exhausted and the company is no more efficient or effective then competitors. Most plans are used as a way to stimulate productivity improvements and are then phased out after a few years.

■ *Business incentive plans* are next-generation gain-sharing plans. They are widely used in a broad range of businesses to meet any number of goals and go by a variety of names. The goal in a business incentive plan is usually a strategic, financial, or operating outcome that management wants to focus everyone's attention on, such as profitability, cost, or customer satisfaction. A target and time frame are set. If they are met, everyone in that unit shares in the rewards. The advantage of these plans is that they can change with business needs. After the expiration of the time period, the targets shift in response not only to internal gains but to the competitive landscape as well. As the business reconfigures, so can the incentive plan. The challenge in designing these plans is to ensure that by focusing energy around a few important goals others are not neglected or compromised. Business incentive plans have to be adjusted periodically to ensure that the targets are fair and achievable and that they are motivating the right response.

■ *Long-term incentive plans* link rewards to company or business unit performance over a period of three to five years. They are usually reserved for senior executives. The intent is to foster long-term thinking in decision making as well as for retention. One large bank instituted them after finding that its aggressive program of rotating senior managers every two years was causing problems. The managers would make very short-term-oriented decisions to boost revenues during their tenure in the position, often leaving "the house a mess" for the next person taking over. In a common scenario, revenues would jump as a result of aggressive marketing and sales incentives. Few investments would be made, however, in infrastructure or customer support in order to keep expenses low. Just as the next manager was to take over, profitability would plummet as customer attrition increased due to service issues.

The challenge with all pay-for-performance plans is identifying and measuring the behaviors and results that individuals or teams have control over and that will add up to the division or company performance that is desired. As was raised in the discussion of metrics, if on-time delivery is the goal, employees will find a way to achieve on-time delivery. The question then becomes, Does on-time delivery impact the overall financial performance of the company, and will singling it out and rewarding it compromise other important goals?

VALUING SKILLS AND KNOWLEDGE

Another compensation trend is a shift from paying for a job to paying for a person. *Skill-based pay* (also called knowledge-based pay) values the skills and knowledge a person is able to contribute to the organization. Skill-based pay rewards learning and versatility. It has particular applicability:

- When the redesign requires the existing workforce to invest time and energy to develop new skills. Skill-based pay is a way to provide incentives that can make the transition easier.

- When the product of the company is knowledge (law, accounting, or consulting) and building knowledge is a source of competitive advantage.

- When there is a shortage of a particular skill in the marketplace. Technology companies frequently use skill "premiums" to help attract people to the company or encourage existing employees to learn sought-after skills.

Traditional compensation methods value a job, regardless of who is in it. When jobs are well defined, stable, and provide little opportunity for development within the job boundaries, this system works well. What many companies have found is that it doesn't work well in environments characterized by:

- Integration of activities across many individuals

- Fluid tasks and responsibility definitions

- High dependence on exchange of knowledge

- Interactions among multidisciplinary people

As more and more organizations fit this description, they are looking for ways to motivate and reward learning, collaboration, and the application and sharing of knowledge. The intent is to move away from a focus on jobs and job descriptions that can create "not my job" responses. To reinforce this, the word *role* is replacing the word *job* in many knowledge-work firms.[10] Role conveys a set of responsibilities. The person's work and activities may change depending on what needs to be accomplished. The focus changes from what a person did or is doing at the moment to the larger contribution he or she is able to make.

Skill-based pay is often accompanied by broad banding of jobs—consolidating the number of job titles—so that people can earn more without having to be promoted into new jobs. Skill-based pay helps to encourage horizontal growth and lateral career moves. It works particularly well in new or high growth organizations where employees don't have well-developed skills and there is a business need to develop additional skills.

The application of skill- and knowledge-based pay plans may present you with some challenges.

■ *How do you know when a person has really acquired the new skill?* Skills that are visible and straightforward, such as the operation of a particular type of machinery, are easy to measure. White-collar work skills can require more subjectivity. It is less clear-cut to determine when someone has mastered report writing or selling. A lot of management time and effort has to go into discerning levels of skill and how they will be measured and certified.

■ *Do you pay for only those skills that are used?* People may develop skills that become obsolete or they may move on to positions where those skills are no longer needed. Policies have to be developed to address how these skills will be paid for or the business will be paying for something it doesn't value. One approach some businesses are trying is to give one-time bonuses for learning new skills rather than to increase base salaries.

■ *What if the learning can't be directly applied?* Some organizations reward all learning—whether it is directly applicable to the work or not—in order to encourage a culture of learning. The organization has to decide whether it will reward a college degree or training certification even if it is in a field other than where the person is currently working. Employees may want to be rewarded for learning new skills that will position them for promotions even if those skills don't immediately benefit the organization.

■ *When do people get training?* Finding time for training is a challenge for any organization. Some organizations do on-the-job training by peers, others develop training modules and classes. The opportunity to attend training has to be equal if people are to be able to gain skills equally.

REWARDING TEAMS AND BUSINESS UNITS

Organizations are relying more on team- and unit-based compensation than they have in the past. If your organization design assumes cooperation will be necessary because of the interdependence and complexity of the work, then the work should be motivated and rewarded through rewards that don't just focus on more than individual contributions. Team and unit incentives usually combine aspects of performance and skill-based pay.

■ *Performance Incentives.* A performance goal is set for the team or business unit. It may be based on hard criteria, such as cost savings, output achieved, or deadlines met, or it may include some softer criteria, such as effective problem solving. When the goal is met, a bonus is given, either in the form of cash, stock, or noncash rewards. When it is linked to a gain-sharing or profit-sharing plan, the amount is tied to the overall financial performance of the unit.

■ *Skill-Based Pay.* Teams can be rewarded for the collective skills they accumulate. The team is not rewarded until all team members reach a certain level, in order to encourage the more skilled employees to help others achieve competence. It is most commonly applied in team settings where the tasks of the team are specific and measurable and where there is a desire to make the team more flexible and autonomous by increasing the skills of all team members. As each team member learns and applies the skills that are needed by the team overall, that person's pay is increased. Team members cross-train in the work of others in order to lessen the impact of absenteeism on productivity. People are also rewarded for developing management skills. As these responsibilities are moved to the team, the organization can reduce the number of managers needed.

Rewards based on collective effort and outcomes have some potential hazards.

■ *Distinguishing Which Organizational Level to Reward.* Team incentives work well to motivate members within the team but may create conflict or even competition between teams. This can be avoided by creating business-unit-level plans that reward the contribution of all teams and employees when there is interdependence among the teams. On the other hand, the danger of setting performance goals to be rewarded at too high a level in the organization is that the line of sight between the team's action and their results is blurred. The responsibility for achieving the goal becomes diffuse and the motivational aspects of the incentive are lost.

■ *Free Riding.* Controls need to be in place to ensure that group members who don't contribute their share don't benefit, or at least don't benefit for long. Only a few organizations reward people based completely on team performance. Most mix individual measures and rewards with a team component to control for differences in individual contribution.

■ *Allocating Rewards.* Even if all members of the team or unit contribute equally, there is the problem of how to allocate the rewards: by percentage of salary or in equal amounts. If the payout is a percentage of salary, then some people will get more than others, unless all earn exactly the same amount. On the other hand, an equal amount will mean that some will find the reward less meaningful because it represents a smaller portion of their total compensation.

DESIGNING COMPENSATION SYSTEMS

Changes in compensation practices typically lag behind other change initiatives due to the time it takes to study a pay system, reevaluate jobs, pilot the new plan, and roll it out. Management tends to be conservative when contemplating compensation changes. As a result, most systems:

■ Are based on custom, tradition, habit, and administrative convenience.

■ Tend to maintain the status quo since compensation is a highly sensitive employee issue.

■ Are expensive to change in terms of studies required, implementation of new systems to capture data, and the management time required to reach agreement on standards.

New pay systems also exact a psychological cost on employees, which has to be anticipated and managed. Putting a higher percentage of compensation at risk is good for companies. It allows them to move dollars out of the fixed-cost category and into the variable-cost category, and it provides tangible evidence that things must change. For employees, however, it means trading something that is sure—base pay tied to time and seniority—for an incentive that may or may not be paid out. There are a few things to consider when contemplating introducing new pay structures:

■ *Is there agreement on what is important and is there a way to measure it?* Any rewards given for meeting specific production, quality, or service goals need to have clear criteria. Without clear measures, decisions made by supervisors and managers can seem arbitrary and create resentment between business units if some managers are perceived as easier than others.

■ *Are rewards for changes in behavior built into the system?* Some work needs to be done as part of the planning process to identify the behaviors that people need to do more of—and less of—to impact the culture and business results. Although the management team can determine these behaviors, involving a representative sample of the people impacted will improve the result. They will identify the *management* behaviors that need to change in addition to what they and their peers need to do differently. They will also ensure the language is direct and descriptive. Finally, the involvement process will increase buy-in to the overall plan.

■ *Are people enabled and empowered to control the variables?* It is impossible to ask people to excel if they are not enabled to achieve excellence. Whether it is pay for performance, skill-based pay, or some team incentive plan, it will only work when the people participating have some control over the outcome. Nothing is less motivating than for a person to work as hard or harder than before, meet their personal goals, and find out there is no upside because of factors out of their control. These could include:

Another business division not making their goals

Lack of reasonable authority to make decisions and solve problems

Lack of tools and resources to do the job well

■ *Is the performance management system adequate?* Performance management processes are closely linked to compensation and reward systems. No matter how solid the metrics or innovative the compensation system, if managers don't set goals, coach their people, and give candid feedback, the outcome will be compromised. There's no one best system among the all the performance management systems available. The scales, forms, and process are less important than the consistency and honesty with which they are applied.

■ *Is there a plan for when times are bad?* Alfred Lord Tennyson said, " 'Tis better to have loved and lost than to never have loved at all." The same may not be true of variable compensation. It is hard to have it one year and lose it the next. Some people are comfortable with wide fluctuations in their pay, but a lot of people join corporations for the predictability. They will be unhappy if a down business cycle means they make less for the same amount of work. Many start-up dot-coms that gave stock instead of salary or bonuses found that people were all too ready to jump ship when their stock options became worthless, no matter how exciting the work environment.

■ *Can the system be manipulated?* Time is easy to measure. Jobs can be compared externally and their value set. Once you get into valuing skills, rewarding learning, and creating complex incentive plans based on softer performance measures, you introduce opportunity to manipulate outcomes. Create pay plans that are simple, valid, and transparent so that the outcomes can be neither debated nor perceived as unfair.

■ *What is the time orientation?* The closer rewards and compensation are given to the time when the goal is met, the more motivating and reinforcing it will be. A mix of short-term and longer-term rewards will ensure that while current actions are rewarded, it is not done at the expense of long-term goals.

Use Tool 5-4 to assess how well your current compensation systems build cross-unit skills and capabilities and contribute to a reconfigurable organization. Be sure to allocate time and resources to the evaluation of your compensation system as part of your design activities.

REWARDS AND RECOGNITION

Reward and recognition programs complement compensation as a way to let employees know they are valued and to communicate what the company believes is important. They are another tool in the organization design process for aligning behaviors to business outcomes. They are valued in the reconfigurable organization because they are easily implemented and customized to meet the needs of specific teams or work groups. Unlike compensation systems, reward and recognition programs don't require significant investment in design time, although they must be well-thought-out, of course, to be effective.

A major difference between reward and recognition programs and compensation is that recognition has a public aspect—the company communicates its values and priorities through the choice of what achievements and behaviors it recognizes and rewards. If the redesign requires that the organization build new capabilities and that people work together in new relationships, rewards and recognition can quickly and publicly reinforce when things go right. A well-designed reward and recognition program can:

- *Support business goals* by reinforcing desired values, behaviors, and results.

- *Build a high-performance organization* by creating an environment in which people want to perform to the best of their abilities.

- *Increase retention* by communicating each employee's importance to the success of the organization, and by building a sense of belonging and pride.

"REWARD" OR "RECOGNITION"?

Most people use the words *reward* and *recognition* interchangeably. Although the meanings of the two words overlap, there are important differences.

Rewarding	Communicates: "Do this" and you will "get that." Focuses on extrinsic motivations (tangible paybacks). Is usually delivered through a centralized program.
Recognizing	Communicates: "The work you do is meaningful, and you've done it well."

Reinforces intrinsic motivations (positive feelings about work).

Requires new management behaviors.

Too often, reward and recognition programs focus primarily on rewards and fail to address the underlying behaviors and work environment issues that they are intended to improve. When designing a program, conscious consideration should be given to maintaining a balance between recognition and rewards.

THE FOUR DIMENSIONS OF RECOGNITION

Within any organization there are dozens of things that employees do that can be recognized. What you choose to focus on sends a clear message about what is most important to the company at this point in time. Recognition opportunities can be grouped into four dimensions: goals and results, values and behaviors, special achievement and effort, and overall contribution (see Figure 5-7). When any one dimension is rewarded to the exclusion of others, just as with any performance measurement system, unintended and undesired outcomes can occur.

GOALS AND RESULTS

Most commonly, reward and recognition programs are established to boost productivity. However, when rewards and recognition are given only for meeting production targets, people tend to focus on the ends over the means. If salespeople are rewarded for quantity of sales, they have little incentive to worry about the quality of the customer or the long-term value of the customer to the business. The same issues identified in the Metrics section regarding unintended consequences apply to reward and recognition programs.

VALUES AND BEHAVIORS

Values and behaviors are the basis of the organizational culture, influencing not only employee morale, commitment, and satisfaction, but ultimately the customer experience as well. The behaviors that are rewarded need to balance improving internal interactions (e.g., between managers and employees or between business units) as well as those that more directly influence customers.

Rewarding only values and behaviors can result in people losing sight of business results. For example, in one company a program intended to promote teamwork encouraged people to increase the number of meetings held, memos circulated, and people involved in projects. Without any measure of outcomes, however, there was no way to ensure that all of this activity produced a better business result.

Figure 5-7. The four dimensions of recognition.

Dimension	Characteristics
1. Goals and Results *Focuses people on which outcomes are most important.*	▪ Recognizes individuals or teams that hit a production, time, budget, quality, or service target. ▪ Easiest to implement with a group of people who have similar types of job. ▪ As productivity improves, the targets can be raised. ▪ Recognizes high performers.
2. Values and Behaviors *Highlights the desired behaviors that support organizational values.*	▪ Recognizes people at all levels who demonstrate desired values and behaviors. ▪ Is especially important in an environment of change when reinforcing the *behavior* (e.g., risk taking) is as important as getting the *right outcome*. ▪ Helps sustain interest when time frames for outcomes are long term or if outcomes may not materialize (e.g., an information technology project gets canceled because business priorities change). ▪ Reinforces borderline performers who are improving.

3. Special Achievement and Effort
 	
Celebrates success, innovation, learning, and extraordinary effort.
	▪ Allows recognition of unique events/contributions and those that occur irregularly, such as:
	  – Completion of special projects
	  – Successful passing of work-related classes and exams, or completion of degrees
	  – Extraordinary overtime
	  – Perfect attendance
	  – Innovative ideas
	▪ Creates role models for others.

4. Overall Contribution *Shows appreciation for day-to-day contributions and service to the organization.*	▪ Recognizes service to the company and communicates that everyone is valued. ▪ Often includes families to recognize their contribution and sacrifices. ▪ Doesn't differentiate based on performance (e.g., events to which everyone is invited or service awards based on anniversary date).

SPECIAL ACHIEVEMENT AND EFFORT

The plan should include opportunities to highlight the contributions of the few—whether for a money-saving idea or perfect attendance—while still honoring the majority who constitute the "backbone" of the organization.

Steady performers who are responsible for managing the continuity of the business need to feel that they have an opportunity to achieve at least some of the rewards and that they aren't left out of the game. For example, many employees are content to do their jobs and don't have aspirations to become managers or project leaders. They aren't interested in taking on the special projects that might earn them glory. But they still want to be appreciated and recognized for their contribution day in and day out.

OVERALL CONTRIBUTION

If everyone is rewarded the same way regardless of contribution, or if recognition is given only to teams and never to individuals, high performers may feel their contributions are taken for granted. They may continue to be high performers, but they may resent that others share the glory resulting from their achievements.

DETERMINING WHAT REWARDS ARE MEANINGFUL

A recognition plan can't fix fundamental problems that create barriers to excellence. Putting a plan in place as a "Band-Aid" without simultaneously addressing some of these problems can cause the plan to backfire and actually reduce morale.

A key question to ask is, "Are people paid fairly?" Although most people would like to be paid more, most will admit when they are paid *fairly* compared to their peers and the marketplace. On the other hand, when people believe that they are not fairly compensated for their work, the introduction of a reward and recognition program, especially if it involves cash payments, can have negative impacts. Small payments will be seen as insulting, and managers will try to use larger rewards to make up the compensation gap for their high performers. Adjustments to salary levels to reflect the local marketplace should be made before rolling out a recognition plan.

As discussed above, the first component of the program design is determining what outcomes and changes are important to the organization. The second component is determining what is meaningful for the employee to receive in exchange for making an extra effort.

THE PROBLEM WITH MONEY

Money is the most obvious reward. No one ever says he or she wouldn't like more money. It's also easy to administer. The award can be added right into the next payroll check. But money has some drawbacks as an effective reward in a recognition plan:

- *Money is too easily confused with compensation.* It looks the same and is administered the same way. When the reward and recognition program becomes a means to make up for perceived shortfalls in compensation or bonus, the message becomes confused.

- *Money can become an entitlement.* Someone who makes the production target every month begins to count on the extra cash. It then feels "taken away" when the program stops or the target is raised.

- *Money disappears.* For most people, the money is put into the wallet and used for general expenses and bills.

- *Finally, money leaves nothing memorable or tangible to reinforce what went well.* Few people go out and buy something special to remind themselves of the recognition.

On the other hand, it is difficult for most managers to know their teams well enough to choose a nonmonetary reward that will be appreciated and meaningful. Most of us have a hard enough time choosing gifts for our friends and relatives, much less for the people with whom we work.

Provide People with a Choice

One way to avoid putting your managers in the position of guessing what people would like for rewards is to use one of the many incentive plan vendors. These third-party companies can help develop a "catalog" of rewards that plan participants can choose from. The catalog is customized to the needs of the business and can include general merchandise, company logo merchandise, as well as local gift certificates and memberships. The catalog can even include things like time off. Typically, participants are given "points" for achieving goals, demonstrating behaviors, special achievements, etc. The number of points, who can award them, and when they are given become part of the program guidelines unique to each organization.

Another advantage of this approach is that even though the points have an underlying monetary value (and ultimate cost to the company), the connection is not explicit, which therefore delinks the whole process from compensation and money.

Merchandise/tangible rewards work best when combined with other types of recognition, such as thank-yous, certificates, public acknowledgement of achievements, and celebrations. In this way the key messages are reinforced verbally and the person receives a tangible, valuable reminder of the achievement.

Such a system, however, shouldn't preclude managers and management from buying something when appropriate. Often a small reminder for the desktop—a team picture, small plaque, or coffee cup with the name of the project—can be a continual reminder for the person, and for others who see it, of what was achieved.

SUGGESTED DESIGN APPROACH

The previous discussion suggests the following approach to designing a reward and recognition program: Create a formal, time-bound "program" that focuses attention on one key message for the near term. At the same time, embed recognition into the culture and management skill set for the long term.

1. CREATE A PROGRAM

A program is what most people think of when they hear of rewards and recognition. The benefits of a having a program include:

- Programs are highly visible and attract attention. They often have a theme that can link to other initiatives, communication opportunities, and events.

- Programs are fun. They lighten the work environment and can break down barriers between departments or between employees and managers, provided they are not competitive.

- By being time sensitive, programs create a sense of urgency, particularly when they are linked to an overall business goal that has a similar time frame.

- Programs usually combine tangible rewards with public recognition. Messages can be communicated widely and consistently across the organization.

- The formal and typically centralized aspect of programs ensures a measure of equity across units. The "rules of the game" are clear and the criteria for participation are documented. Less is left to manager discretion, which reduces charges of favoritism.

Stopping at this point in the design has significant disadvantages, however. Creating a program doesn't necessarily impact either employees' or managers' behaviors for the long term. When the program is over, people revert to the old way of doing things. Programs are often too much about "do this" and you'll "get that" in the short term.

2. BUILD MANAGEMENT AWARENESS AND SKILLS

To make real change, recognition has to be embedded into your new organizational culture—the way people operate day to day. To complement the "program," managers will need to be educated about the variety of recognition options available, how to give recognition skillfully, and how to determine what people will find meaningful.

Managers who are not good at giving feedback or coaching their staffs will probably not be comfortable with recognition either. Awareness and some basic skills can be built into other training programs. Modeling by senior management, however, is the most effective method for embedding recognition into the culture.

What is recognized and rewarded may change as business objectives change. As progress is achieved, the bar will be raised. However, what remains is the awareness of the power of recognition to improve both performance and the skills for delivering it. The benefits of relying on managers to deliver recognition to their own teams include:

- Managers have wide discretion regarding how to reward their people and how to customize recognition to the needs of individuals on a team.

- The emphasis is more on the intangible rewards that impact the quality of the work environment.

- The forms of recognition are flexible and can evolve as needs change.

- This type of recognition can also be easily demonstrated peer to peer. As employees see their managers recognizing others, they will be more comfortable give recognition to their peers as well.

By combining a recognition program with an emphasis on building management awareness and skills, you can realize the benefits of both approaches.

DESIGN CHECKLIST

There are some items to keep in mind when designing a reward and recognition program.

- *Make everyone eligible.* If everyone is not eligible for the program, carefully consider why particular groups are excluded (temps, certain levels, certain job groups). Make the program as inclusive as possible within the defined business unit.

- *Reward both high performers and those who are making progress.* Create a variety of opportunities that reflect all dimensions of recognition. Avoid making people feel that they don't have a chance to qualify in any area.

- *Create a goal-based, noncompetitive system.* Employee-of-the-month awards and contests, though well intentioned, create winners and losers. Only a few people can get the prize. Everyone else becomes aware that he or she lost. Goal-based programs allow everyone who meets a target to win. (Of course, if everyone does, the target is probably set too low.)

■ *Ensure a mix of timing for rewards.* Some opportunities should be at set intervals (e.g., end of the month), particularly those tied to measures. Other types of recognition, such as for behaviors, should be delivered on the spot or as soon as possible after it is observed. Having a mix of timing keeps the interest level high and makes recognition an ongoing event.

■ *Build in recognition for all levels, including peer to peer and employee to manager.* Top-down programs, where only managers have the ability to nominate people for recognition, may create the perception that this is another management "program of the month." Encouraging peer-to-peer recognition, particularly across departments that are interdependent, puts more ownership in the hands of employees. Include the opportunity for employees to recognize supervisors and managers—it reinforces the importance of management behaviors in any change process.

■ *Make the plan easy to administer.* Finally, the easier the plan is to administer, the more successful it will be. Try to avoid complex nomination or approval processes. Put more energy into gathering feedback and evaluation and making any necessary ongoing changes. The problem is rarely that people give too much recognition or abuse the program. More often, programs are underpublicized and not utilized enough.

Use Tool 5-5 as you design your program.

SUMMARY

This chapter highlighted some of the design issues that need to be taken into consideration when constructing measurement and reward systems. Desired behaviors reflect the vision and values of the company and underlie the organization's culture. By making the behaviors explicit, through vision storytelling and by translating the values into actions, everyone in the organization gains a common frame of reference. Performance measurement, compensation, and reward and recognition programs can be designed to encourage and motivate people to demonstrate the desired behaviors and to flexibly adapt to change when new organizational goals and outcomes need to be achieved.

Chapter Six examines options for people practices and human resources management systems to select, assess, and develop the right people for the organization.

NOTES

1. E. E. Lawler, *Rewarding Excellence* (San Francisco: Jossey-Bass, 2000), pp. 10–11.

2. R. S. Kaplan and D. P. Norton, "The Balanced Scorecard—Measures That Drive Performance," *Harvard Business Review,* January/February 1992, pp. 71–79.

3. R. Simons and A. Davila, "How High Is Your Return on Management?" *Harvard Business Review,* January/February 1998, pp. 71–80.

4. R. Alsop, "Harris Interactive Survey Indicates Fragility of Corporate Reputations," *The Wall Street Journal,* February 7, 2001.

5. E. R. Silverman, "Once Upon a Time," *Human Resource Executive,* June 4, 1999, pp. 48–50.

6. L. R. Gomez-Mejia and D. B. Balkin, *Compensation, Organizational Strategy and Firm Performance* (Cincinnati: South-Western, 1992), p. 57.

7. "1998 Hewitt Variable Compensation Measurement Database," cited in "Variable Compensation Plans Increasing and Improving, but Still Delivering Mixed Results" (1998), www.comsoptions.com/solutions/hewitt.

8. R. Johnson, "Employers Now Vie to Hire Moms With Young Children," *The Wall Street Journal,* September 19, 2000, p. B1.

9. "2000 World at Work Survey," cited in "Compensation Trends for the Year 2001" (2000), www.aon.com/inteligence/issues.

10. E. Lawler, *Strategic Pay: Aligning Organization Strategies and Pay Systems* (San Francisco: Jossey-Bass, 1990), p. 129.

Tool 5-1. Metrics: key questions to consider.

Purpose:	Use the questions in this tool to think through the design of your measurement systems.
This tool is for:	Leadership Team.

	Notes
Breadth Do your metrics have an appropriate balance of financial and operational performance categories? If they are too focused on financial indicators, what operational areas might you include?	
Criticality Have you narrowed your performance indicators to the critical few?	
Are your metrics weighted according to their importance? Does the weighting reflect your strategy and design assumptions?	
Are your metrics based on data you can collect with accuracy and reliability? What systems do you need to build to ensure that the data you gather are reliable?	
Time Orientation Do your measurement systems have leading as well as lagging indicators?	
Consequences Do measures appropriately focus employee behavior? List three measures you use now.	1. _____ 2. _____ 3. _____
What unintended consequences could result from how the measures influence behaviors? How can you balance them through the use of other measures?	
Alignment What process have you used to align measures up and down the organization and between units?	
Targets How are targets set: against internal baselines or against industry benchmarks? Are they attainable yet require people to stretch to reach them?	

Tool 5-2. Vision storytelling.

Purpose:	The act of storytelling reinforces the intention of the vision in language that has relevance to everyday experience. Use this tool to help connect actions and behaviors to the vision. It can be used in group settings, at a leadership offsite, or at team meetings to clarify and share each person's understanding of the vision and the behaviors that support it.
This tool is for:	Leadership Team, Employees.

Set-Up

- Use this tool with a group of eight or more people.

- Distribute copies of the organization's vision to the group.

- Divide participants into small groups of no more than four people each.

Individual Work

Describe an incident that illustrates when you or a colleague exemplified the vision. Think of successes over the past year. Draw upon memories of times that made you proud to be part of this organization. Imagine you are telling this story to someone newly hired and you want to convey the impact that this organization can have.

A. What was the situation, the problem to be solved?

_____

_____

B. What did you or your colleague specifically do that made a difference?

_____

_____

C. What is the lesson that others can learn from this story?

_____

_____

Small Group Discussion

- Each person shares his or her story with the other people in the group.

- After everyone has shared his or her story, the small groups generate a list of the seven to ten key behaviors that made a difference in the outcomes of their stories and illustrate the vision in action. The behaviors are posted on a flipchart.

As a Large Group

- Each small group shares its list of behaviors.

- The lists are refined and consolidated.

- Depending on the size of the group and the amount of time available, people can share some of the stories with the whole group that exemplify the vision.

- The outcome is a set of behaviors that supports the vision. The exercise also reinforces what people are already doing right to support the organization's new direction. The act of sharing stories gives life and texture to behavioral norms.

Tool 5-3. Turning values into behaviors.

Purpose:	Use this tool to create a set of behaviors that exemplifies the organization's values.
This tool is for:	Leadership Team, Employees.

Setup

- Use this tool with a group of eight or more people.
- Distribute copies of the organization's values to the group.
- Divide participants into small groups of no more than four people each.

Individual Work

- Look at the value your group is assigned and answer the following question:

    What does this value mean to you?

    _____

    _____

    _____

Small Group Discussion

1. Discuss your responses with your group and develop a group answer to what the value means.

2. Using this common definition of the value, identify what actions an employee could do to exemplify this value:

    – In front of clients?

    – With colleagues?

    – With his or her team (if this is a manager group)?

3. For each value, identify what expected and exceptional behaviors would look like. Use the table to format your group's response on a flipchart.

(continues)

Tool 5-3 (Continued).

Organizational Value: _____

	Behavior in Front of Clients	Behavior in Front of Colleagues
Expected		
Exceptional		
Expected		
Exceptional		
Expected		
Exceptional		
Expected		
Exceptional		
Expected		
Exceptional		
Expected		
Exceptional		
Expected		
Exceptional		
Expected		
Exceptional		

Tool 5-4. Compensation systems: key questions to consider.

Purpose:	Use the questions in this tool to think through the design of your compensation system.
This tool is for:	Leadership Team.

	Notes

1. What are people paid for in your organization?
  ▪ Time?
  ▪ Performance?
  ▪ Skills and knowledge?	

2. How clear do you believe people are about what their compensation represents?
  ▪ Reward for past performance?
  ▪ Motivation for future performance?
  ▪ Retention?	

3. How aware are people of the value of their individual total compensation—salary, bonuses, stock, benefits, and other rewards combined? How is this communicated to the employees?	
4. How well does your performance management and compensation system differentiate performance? How do you ensure that high performers are rewarded substantially more than average and low performers?	
5. In what areas of the organization might skill- or knowledge-based pay be appropriate?	
6. To what extent does your compensation system distinguish between team versus individual contributions?	
7. Do people have control over the variables that affect their compensation? Be specific.	
8. Are payouts based on objective measures of performance and contribution?	

Tool 5-5. Reward and recognition design checklist.

Purpose:	Use the questions as a checklist when designing a reward and recognition program.
This tool is for:	Leadership Team.

1. Is everyone eligible?	❏
2. Are high performers rewarded as well as those who are making progress?	❏
3. Is the reward system goal based and noncompetitive?	❏
4. Have we ensured a mix of timing for rewards?	❏
5. Have we built in recognition for all levels including peer to peer and employee to manager?	❏
6. Is the plan easy to administer?	❏

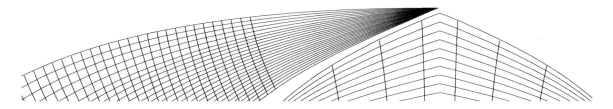

CHAPTER SIX

PEOPLE PRACTICES

People practices are the collective human resources (HR) systems and policies of the organization. They include selection and staffing, performance feedback and management, training, development, and careers. Up to this point in this book, we have discussed how to align the organization's structure, processes, and metric and rewards to the strategy. People practices are the final point on the star model (Figure 6-1). However, this is not to imply that the consideration of people comes last in the design process. Staffing the organization is an issue that will arise as soon as any structural changes are contemplated. In fact, getting the right senior team in place may be one of your first priorities and a key factor in the success of the design and implementation process.

A challenge in designing dynamic organizations is to create systems that will attract, develop, and retain people whose individual and collective capabilities can support the current direction and yet who are flexible enough to be refocused and redeployed when that direction changes. We made the point in the preface of this book that having the right people won't compensate for the lack of other essential organizational elements. Their talent will be wasted if the structure, processes, and metrics dissipate their energy and create barriers to their collective effectiveness. On the other hand, no matter how well designed, no business can realize its goals without the right people in place—people with the right mind-set, skills, and ability to grow and learn with the organization.

In Chapter Two we looked at how each strategic focus—product, operations, customer—leads to different processes, measures, and culture (refer back

Figure 6-1. Star model.

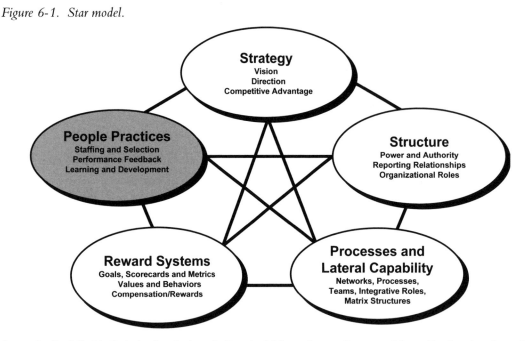

Source: Jay R. Galbraith, *Designing Organizations: An Executive Briefing on Strategy, Structure, and Process* (San Francisco: Jossey-Bass, 1995).

to Figure 2-2). Different strategies also imply that different types of people will succeed in the organization. Every business wants to hire smart, experienced, and hard-working people. But such generalizations don't differentiate enough among candidates to identify who is likely to make the critical contributions to help your business achieve competitive advantage.

Reconfigurable organizations are able to adapt quickly to a dynamic marketplace that requires shifts in the strategic focus of the business. As the organizational definition of success changes, so will the skills, knowledge, and behaviors required. Any system or process you design, therefore, must be capable of responding quickly to changes in the direction of the business without sacrificing the integrity of the system itself. The goal is not to be continually changing your organization's HR systems, but to create aligned systems that contribute to organizational flexibility and responsiveness.

Figure 6-2 illustrates how each HR system can support a reconfigurable organization design. *Assessment and selection* processes ensure the right people are hired, not only for the work that must be done today, but for the future as well. Different organizations require different skill sets, but all reconfigurable organizations need learning-agile people willing to accept that their assignments will change and priorities be reordered. *Performance feedback* mechanisms not only provide the basis for compensation, rewards, and recognition, but they provide employees with the information they need to take control of their own learning and development. Many companies are supplementing supervisor-

Figure 6-2. An integrated model of people practices.

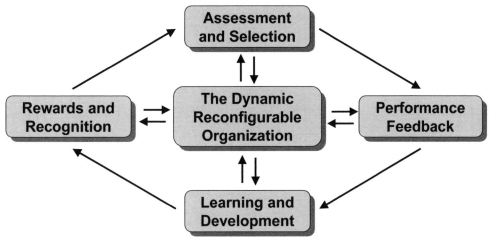

centered feedback with the use of peer and upward feedback to give a fuller and more actionable picture of performance and to reflect the importance of the work occurring through the lateral organization. *Learning and development* and the management of knowledge have become key enablers for the organization. Learning also has become the new currency used in the employee contract. A promise of job security is replaced with the opportunity for developing skills and knowledge that will be valued within the organization and in the external talent marketplace. *Rewards and recognition* are the link between the metrics that define organizational success and individual contribution.

Compensation systems that reward high performance, as discussed in Chapter Five, help attract and retain the right people to the organization. Dynamic, reconfigurable organizations are characterized by people practices that support learning and the development of strategically important capabilities.

This chapter is not a comprehensive review of all the decisions that need to be made in the design of HR systems. There are many important decisions to be made regarding sourcing, recruiting, and hiring; orientation, assimilation, training, development, and career paths; goal setting and performance appraisal; and HR policies in the areas of employee relations, diversity, and work environment—to list just a few. Rather, this chapter highlights the areas that are most likely to create the behaviors and mind-sets that support reconfigurability. The chapter has four sections:

- *Staffing the New Organization* presents principles and tools to guide the process of placing people into new roles and positions.

- *Assessing for Learning Aptitude* presents a way to select for learning-agile candidates.

- *Performance Feedback* reviews the ways in which multidirectional feedback can support building lateral capability.

- *From Training to Learning* provides a checklist of the best practices that many organizations are utilizing to create a learning organization.

STAFFING THE NEW ORGANIZATION

The most immediate concern of the employees in an organization going through a redesign is, "Where am I going to end up?" Until this question is answered, there will be a high degree of uncertainty and anxiety in the organization that can distract people from their work and lower productivity. We recommend that leaders announce as soon as possible the *process* they will be using for placing people in new positions, even if the structure and roles are still in the design phase. Letting people know how decisions will be made will minimize the rumors that can build during a design process.

PRINCIPLES

When staffing the new organization there are some key principles to keep in mind.

- *Fill senior positions first.* Gaps on the executive team or any changes that are contemplated due to new roles or required skills should be dealt with as soon as possible in the design process. This way the new executive team can contribute to the overall design and take responsibility for designing and staffing their own organizations as a new, aligned executive team.

- *Conduct the staffing process quickly.* It will take some time before you are ready to staff. You will need to fully design the new structure and roles and develop profiles of what the successful candidate should look like. However, once the staffing process is under way, it should be completed as quickly as possible and announcements made. In this way people will know where they stand and can begin planning the transition to their new roles.

- *Balance risk.* You might be tempted to reduce risk for the new organization by placing people only in roles where they can fully perform to the new requirements. It is unlikely, however, that you'll have the right profiles available in your current organization or even obtainable through hiring. You'll need to take some risks by placing people in roles for which they are not fully ready. Don't shy away from putting some people in positions that require growth and development if they have demonstrated potential and learning aptitude. Just be sure that if an assignment will be a stretch for a person, their skill or experience deficits are counterbalanced by someone else (a manager, team member, or colleague) who has strength in those areas. After making your initial staffing plan, revisit the balance of skills across locations, units, and teams and make adjustments to create strong working groups.

■ *Make the process transparent.* The more people understand how decisions will be made, the more likely they will accept the decisions and move forward. An open process, where the criteria and position requirements are clearly stated, will also help avoid any legal challenges based on adverse impact. Given that placing people in new positions is such a sensitive topic with intense personal impact, the staffing process itself should mirror the organization's values and new way of operating.

INFORMATION TO CONSIDER

A range of information can be used to assess your current staff members against new role requirements. Much of this will be built upon the work you did in Chapter Three on defining and clarifying organizational roles. That work can be used as the basis to create job specifications. Some of the tools you can use to assess people for new roles include:

■ *Assessment Interview.* An assessment interview is an approximately two- to three-hour in-depth interview structured to allow people to discuss past work accomplishments and how they approach different types of situations. The interviewer listens for patterns, not only of results but of how work is approached. An assessment interview also assesses learning aptitude. For each competency area required by the new role, the persons are asked to describe a time when they used or demonstrated the competency, the challenges they faced, and what they learned and applied from the experience. This is often a critical component of the assessment process, because new roles frequently re-quire people to learn a significant number of new skills quickly.

An assessment interview can be conducted by an internal or external inter-viewer. The advantages of external assessors when making staffing decisions (as opposed to a purely developmental assessment) include:

—Time saved and a condensed staffing process timeline

—Consistency across interviewers

—Objectivity and elimination of bias based on past experience

■ *Knowledge and Skills Audit.* An assessment interview focuses on accom-plishments and competencies, not necessarily skills and knowledge. If technical knowledge is important or difficult to obtain, then ideally an objective assess-ment should be made of each person's skill level as well.

■ *Past Performance Reviews.* If past performance data is robust and reliable, it can be a valuable source of information. However, since they were conducted against different role requirements and standards, performance reviews, even if positive, may have limited value.

■ *Mobility.* If the organization has multiple locations, ability and willingness to relocate will be a factor in placement decisions.

BENEFITS OF A STRUCTURED PROCESS

Although any restructuring process that results in people being let go—either through the elimination of jobs or as a result of changed skill requirements—is painful for all involved, using a structured process can provide a number of benefits for your organization:

■ *Decisions Based on Common Criteria, Not Horse Trading.* When staffing decisions are made without criteria, an executive team can easily get into conflicts over choice candidates. A more forceful player may prevail in assembling talent that would be better placed elsewhere in the organization. A facilitated decision-making meeting with agreed-upon ground rules ensures that decisions are made for the good of the organization. Although members will champion certain candidates based on their own experience working with a person, and heated debate will certainly precede a number of decisions, the outcome will be agreements that everyone can live with.

■ *Strengthened Executive Team.* The process allows the executive team to engage what can be an emotional, contentious topic as a unified group. No simulated decision can serve as a better "team-building" exercise. The executive team builds skills in assessment and selection that can be applied in future recruiting and staffing. More important, they build the skill of working as a true team, able to rise above their individual concerns to make decisions for the whole organization utilizing their collective knowledge.

■ *Information on Skill and Knowledge Gaps.* A list of development needs is compiled as an outcome of the assessment process. This can serve as the basis for individual development-planning discussions between individuals placed in new roles and their managers. In addition, by looking at all the assessments, the executive team can identify gaps that are common across the organization. This minineeds assessment can point out areas where training or other broad-based development may have high impact.

■ *Increased Internal Mobility.* Once the executive team has reviewed all of the talent in the organization, it is more likely that an internal candidate will be considered when a promotion or developmental assignment becomes available. Often internal candidates are not considered for positions outside their own business unit because they are not visible to other senior managers. Many organizations are beginning to conduct yearly talent inventories to make executives aware of up-and-coming high performers who may be ready for their next move.

■ *A Plan and Process for Recruiting.* The tools used for internal staffing can be modified for assessing external candidates to fill empty positions. The benefit is that the same standards are being applied externally and internally, and that all interviewers are using the same decision-making criteria.

■ *Minimized Adverse Impact or Legal Action.* The openness of the process helps to avoid legal challenges. Of course, any staffing process should take place with the guidance of the organization's employment specialists to provide advice on legal issues.

■ *An Energized, Focused Group of Employees.* One of the determinants of employee commitment is a person's satisfaction with the competence of co-workers. Knowing that one's colleagues have the skills to do the work, especially in team settings, gives a person confidence that the organization cares about the quality of work and wants to enable people to perform at their best.

An example of how one company staffed a redesigned HR function will illustrate how these principles can be put into practice as well as present the tools that you can use when planning to staff your own organization. This case emphasizes how an open, structured staffing process can provide a firm foundation at a critical point in the design and begin to accelerate the implementation process. With a little imagination, the process can be modified to fit a variety of situations. The objective is to build organizational capability and tools that can be reused when the organization needs to be reconfigured again or new roles need to be crafted and staffed.

CASE STUDY

AgroLife is a large and well-established insurance company. It sells life, disability, home, auto, dental, annuities, and other products to both individuals and businesses under a number of brand names. It has more than 20,000 employees located in sales offices and operations centers across the United States. Through its long and stable history, AgroLife had been legally structured as a mutual company. Under mutual ownership, shares are held by policyholders rather than traded in the open market, as is the case with a public company. The repeal of major sections of the depression-era Glass-Steagall laws, which had kept banking, insurance, and securities businesses separate, spurred a number of insurance companies to consider converting to public companies in the late 1990s. Once public, they would have access to capital through the equity markets, which would allow them to grow and diversify through mergers or acquisitions.

As AgroLife began to prepare itself to go public, Wall Street analysts made clear that the company would have to make some major changes if its stock was to perform well. Although the company had a well-known brand, an extensive distribution network, and a solid mix of products, it would be held back by what the analysts termed a ''mutual culture.'' The company's focus on stability and the lack of external scrutiny under mutual ownership had resulted in low productivity, high expenses, and a low tolerance for risk and change. Advancement was largely based on seniority. Beyond technical training, development was minimal. Many employees had worked at AgroLife their whole careers, with little feedback or few consequences for their performance. The company's image in the employment marketplace was as an unexciting, stodgy company providing few advancement opportunities. Although its sales positions continued to be attractive, AgroLife had trouble competing with dot-coms and other financial service companies for technology, marketing, and product development talent.

The chairman of AgroLife decided to use demutualization as a catalyst for transforming the organization. Managing for performance would become an enterprise-wide theme and a way to change the culture from one of complacency to one of urgency and high performance. Central to this effort would be HR. However, the HR function would first need to transform itself from the company's personnel department to a business partner prepared to lead this change. A new director of HR was hired, who reported directly to the chairman. She set about redesigning her organization.

HR at AgroLife had been structured into six regional offices, each supporting a range of businesses and locations in that region. Many of the HR staff had started their career at AgroLife in entry-level administrative positions and had moved into HR with little or no HR training or background. Many had never worked anywhere else or had never seen a different model of HR. Much of their time was devoted to transaction processing—new hires, payroll issues, benefit changes—and handling employee concerns. The regional staff had little direct connection with or in-depth knowledge of the businesses they supported. Difficult problems were referred to specialized compensation, benefits, and employee relations units at company headquarters. Given the low skill level in the organization, the new HR director decided to involve only her executive team in the redesign. Most of these people had strong skills and experience.

The design process was accomplished over a period of two months and resulted in a vision of a new organization ready to lead AgroLife forward. The HR function's strategy would be to "add value by building and maintaining the enterprise's organizational capabilities." A particular focus would be creating new performance management and compensation systems that would differentiate and reward high performers. HR would have to help the line managers identify new performance metrics and coach them on making hard decisions regarding the people in their units. Building a new performance culture required a completely new role for HR and a new set of skills for the HR staff. To guide the executive team, five design criteria were identified. The new organization would need:

- Clear accountability in roles and responsibilities

- Knowledgeable staff able to respond to specific business unit strategies

- Common policies, procedures, and processes where appropriate to leverage best practices and provide consistency

- The ability to meet service expectations cost effectively

- The ability to flexibly adapt to changes in the business and advances in technology

The executive team's design featured a customer-oriented structure and new organizational roles.

1. The regional structure was replaced with a customer structure. Each AgroLife line of business was given a dedicated team of HR professionals (Figure 6-3). Business managers now had a single point of contact for all their HR issues.

2. HR was expanded from six locations to twenty in order to support the larger operational sites that would benefit from on-site HR staff.

3. Two new roles were defined: generalist and senior generalist. Performance expectations in these roles were set high. Although the business managers were not ready to utilize HR as a full partner, the new roles anticipated the skills HR staff would need to build credibility and contribute to the business. These included being able to diagnose issues, develop solutions, and coach and influence line managers in a wide range of HR topics.

4. A new HR service center was established along with intranet-based self-service technology to handle all transaction processing. This would pro-

Figure 6-3. AgroLife HR structure.

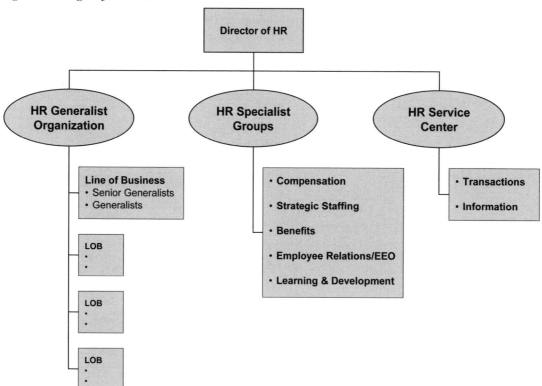

vide HR generalists with significantly more time to pursue value-added work and build relationships with line managers.

5. Specialized units for employee relations, benefits, compensation, and strategic staffing remained at headquarters. Their focus shifted from front-line problem solving to policy, program development, and building the skills of HR generalists in the field.

With a vision in place of the how the organization would operate, and the new structure and roles defined, the next challenge facing the HR director was how to redeploy her existing staff into the new generalist roles supporting the businesses. The new structure anticipated seventy-five positions, of which approximately sixty were generalist positions and fifteen were senior generalist positions. This was an increase from the fifty-seven people currently in the regional structure. She and her executive team wanted a process that would work for placing existing staff as well as for assessing external hires. They decided to assess each existing staff member against the new role requirements using:

■ *Assessment Interviews.* For AgroLife, the interview protocol was constructed around the competencies required by the generalist and senior generalist roles, including client service, process management, people management, teamwork and partnership, influence, and analysis and problem solving. The AgroLife HR executive team decided to have five external assessors skilled in talent assessment and familiar with the requirements of progressive HR organizations conduct two-hour assessment interviews with each person in order to save time and ensure objectivity.

■ *Knowledge and Skills Self-Audit.* Given the broad range of HR knowledge required by the generalist roles, it would have been an expensive process for AgroLife to assess individual competence. In addition, the executive team determined that gaps in knowledge could be filled through training and development, and it was more important to focus the assessment process on underlying competencies and capabilities. Therefore, the skill assessment was administered as a self-audit. Each person rated himself or herself on a scale of one to five for over seventy knowledge areas, grouped under the topics of employment law, employee relations, compensation, benefits, HR management, change management, recruiting, career management, training, and technology. This information was mainly used as the basis for creating development plans for those that were placed in new positions.

■ *Past Performance Reviews.* Since the role expectations had changed so radically for AgroLife HR, and since performance expectations had been so low in the past, performance review results were used only as a secondary factor in decision making.

■ *Mobility Data.* The AgroLife HR organization structure established HR offices in fourteen new locations around the United States. Staffing decisions considered each individual's willingness to relocate.

An overview of the process, the role profiles, assessment interview questions, and knowledge and skill self-audit, were distributed to all fifty-seven people two weeks before the interviews were to take place. The intent was to provide as much information to the staff as possible to ensure that there would be no surprises during the interview and to alleviate anxiety about the staffing process. The goal was to allow each person to have an equal opportunity to describe his or her skills and experience in the best light possible.

The interviews were held over a three-week period. After the interviews were completed, the external assessment team summarized the recommendations for each person in a standard format. In addition to a placement recommendation, each form provided the interviewer's rationale for the recommendation, the suggested development actions, a summary of accomplishments, and a listing of strengths and development needs based upon the interviewer's assessment. This information, together with the self-audit results, past performance reviews, and mobility were compiled into a binder for each member of the executive team. Figure 6-4 shows how the form was organized, including instructions to the assessors.

As soon as the data was compiled, a two-day facilitated decision-making meeting was scheduled for the executive team. During this meeting, each internal candidate was reviewed and a determination made. Only thirty-seven of the fifty-seven existing staff were offered positions in the new organization. The remaining twenty were transitioned out, either immediately or as they finished project work. Many were able to find positions elsewhere in the organization where they could use their transaction and administrative skills. Following the meeting, the executive team immediately flew to each of the regional centers to speak with each person individually, face-to-face, and to discuss the results of the staffing process.

It was obviously a difficult decision for the executive team to let go 35 percent of the AgroLife HR organization, especially since many of them were hard-working, long-tenured employees who had performed adequately under the old, lower expectations. The openness of the process, however, made it easier on everyone. As one person who was let go at AgroLife commented, "By the end of the process I knew I wasn't right for the new job. I wasn't happy, but at least there were no surprises."

Use Tool 6-1 as a checklist when planning your own staffing process.

ASSESSING FOR LEARNING APTITUDE

Learning aptitude is a measure of a person's desire and aptitude to draw meaning from past experiences, and to utilize these lessons creatively to master new challenges.[1] A new organization design requires more than new skills. It also requires that people learn new roles, build new relationships, acquire new knowledge, and apply all of this learning to new situations. Even then, learning will be required as the work continues to change in response to shifts in business

Figure 6-4. Assessment summary sheet.

INTERVIEWEE: _____

DATE OF INTERVIEW: _____

INTERVIEWER: _____

Performance Review Rating _____

Mobility

CURRENT LOCATION: _____

WILLING TO RELOCATE TO: _____

_____

_____

_____

Summary of HR Knowledge and Skills

AREAS OF STRENGTH	AREAS OF ABILITY	AREAS OF WEAKNESS

Recommendation for Placement from Assessment Interview

Based upon the accomplishment interview results, the placement recommendation is as follows:

	GENERALIST	SENIOR GENERALIST
Poor fit for position		
Is a stretch for this position		
Is a solid fit for this position		
Is a solid fit for this position and has potential to take on a bigger job in the future		

(continues)

Figure 6-4. (Continued).

Rationale

Support your recommendation made on the previous page. This should be a holistic assessment that includes the evidence of skills, motivation, traits, and experience that you heard during the interview. Include strengths; weaknesses and risks (particularly if rated a "stretch"); basis for "potential" rating, if applicable (e.g., evidence of learning aptitude); situations this person is particularly suited for or not suited for (e.g., needs a strong boss, would be good at handling sensitive employee relations issues).

Accomplishments

Scope of current job and accomplishments. Repeat for at least one previous job.

Strengths	**Development Needs/Risks**

Development Actions

Development needs and suggested actions (if you can, indicate how difficult you believe the development needs would be to overcome).

strategy, markets, customers, competition, and technology. In the case of AgroLife, the ability to discern the current staff's aptitude for learning was a critical part of the assessment process because many people's current transaction-processing skills and knowledge would be irrelevant for the new HR roles.

Companies need people with learning aptitude who:

- Fit the organization, not only the job.
- Bring an ability to learn, in addition to current knowledge.
- Have organizational savvy, not just technical knowledge.

A change in the organization structure provides an opportunity to bring new people into the organization to help lead it forward; people who possess the mind-sets, skills, and characteristics needed by the new organization. Many existing employees will be able to make the transition with some support, but some will be neither willing nor able to make the personal changes required to meet the expectations of the new organization.

How do you sort those who have learning aptitude from those who don't? People high in learning aptitude tend to display agility in four areas:

1. *Mental*: They think through problems from a fresh point of view and are comfortable with complexity, ambiguity, and explaining their thinking to others.

2. *People*: They know themselves well, are open to personal change, and treat others constructively; they understand how the politics of organizations and systems work.

3. *Change*: They are curious, have a passion for ideas, and like to experiment; they are resilient under the pressures of change.

4. *Results*: They get results under tough conditions, inspire others to perform, and are willing to challenge the status quo.

Learning-agile people share some characteristics no matter what type of job they are in (Figure 6-5). They see the gaps between their own behaviors and desired results and are able to look at their own experiences and assess what needs to change. Many organizations use competencies as a basis for identifying the general skills, knowledge, and ability that one needs to succeed. Learning is the "superordinate" competency, the one that enables a person to fully develop all others.

Knowledge-intensive businesses are particularly dependent on their ability to identify and hire people who have high learning aptitude. In the late 1990s, Ernst & Young Consulting Services found that the types of skills and knowledge that customers required of consultants were changing rapidly. Many of the firm's clients were installing complex enterprisewide information technology

Figure 6-5. Characteristics of learning-agile people.

- Seek learning opportunities.

- Speak in specifics with examples, rather than vaguely "talking about" a topic.

- Can identify and appreciate the complexity of situations.

- Have a broad range of interests.

- Can make comparisons and see connections.

- Are curious and have a broad range of interests.

- Are good listeners and can read other people well.

- Are candid and self-aware.

- Are willing to admit mistakes.

- Are aware of impact on others.

- Focus on problem solving.

- Like to master things.

- View learning as "end."

systems, such as SAP, Oracle, and PeopleSoft. These projects represented significant growth opportunities for the firm and required cutting-edge technical knowledge as well as client, consulting, and project management skills. The firm had also taken on a portfolio of Y2K business—projects to ensure that its client's legacy computer systems would not crash as the calendar changed from 1999 to 2000. These projects required a different set of skills and were of a limited duration. Given the difficulty in predicting the mix of work after 2000, the firm was eager to hire people who were willing and able to learn new skills and would provide a more flexible pool of talent to draw upon in a very dynamic market. As a result, the ability to learn from experience was embedded into Ernst & Young's recruiting and selection process to ensure that new hires met this requirement.

How do you assess for learning aptitude? An assessment for learning aptitude can be incorporated into any behavioral interview. A person is asked to describe a particular situation that relates to a desired competency (e.g., planning, decision making, customer relations). For each situation, the person is asked four questions:

1. How did you approach it?
2. Why did you do it that way?

3. What did you learn from this experience?

4. Can you give me some examples of how you applied what you learned in this situation to another situation?

Listen for evidence that the person:

- Grasped a learning dilemma.

- Can tell how and why they did something.

- Learned something new.

- Can articulate what they learned.

- Has applied what they learned to a new situation.

From these interviews, evidence of learning barriers and behaviors emerge and form a basis for comparison between candidates. Indicators are shown in Figure 6-6.

Figure 6-6. Learning barriers and behaviors.

Learning Barriers	Learning Behaviors
Uses abstractions to talk about experiences.	Describes specific situations with detail.
Gives inappropriate or evasive responses.	Provides frank and appropriate disclosure.
Presents situation from one point of view.	Demonstrates multiple ways to view a situation.
Accepts situation at face value.	Articulates patterns of similarity and difference.
Connects ideas in a rigid, logical order.	Connects ideas in unexpected logical patterns.
Describes only personal strengths.	Discusses strengths and specific weaknesses or mistakes.
Takes actions that have unforeseen negative consequences.	Anticipates and intends impact and consequences of actions.
Presents self as expert; "knows it all."	Presents self as learner; shows interest in gaining knowledge.
Generalizes about learnings.	Uses examples to illustrate how learning has been applied.

   The example below is from a transcript with Tom, a general manager for a personal computer manufacturer. Tom is in charge of all operations for one European country. Previously he had been a marketing director. This is his first general manager job with a full scope of responsibility. As part of a restructuring, he is being considered for a broader management position. The excerpt is taken from the portion of the interview that focuses on how Tom manages control issues.

   Interviewer: Tell me about a time when things got out of control.

   Tom: Unfortunately, although our products are the latest technology, some of the assembly machines are pretty old. They've been retrofitted. In the course of two months Station Five and Station Six broke down. The plant manager made some quick purchases that ended up costing us $10 million. And with my lack of experience in manufacturing it didn't click in my head, that if these machines are down now, and we're buying stuff from the outside, how much are we losing? What's the impact on our profits going to be and can we restructure these costs some better way, maybe leasing rather than buying so somehow the costs would be shared regionally not just by my unit?

   I didn't get right away what this was going to cost us. If we would have picked up on that as it happened we wouldn't have had that adverse effect on our P&L. Of course, no one else in my organization mentioned how it was going to impact the bottom line, but I can only blame myself for that really. I didn't know to ask the right questions.

   Interviewer: What did you learn from this experience?

   Tom: I really blame myself, even though the plant manager knows also that in the future he needs to address these issues a lot quicker. It was a learning experience for everybody involved. Now we put together a report where we look at variances that each plant runs monthly. And we do it regardless if it's positive or negative. So we'll pick up a mistake in the booking which we didn't do last year. Last year we said, "Well, it's a nice positive credit variance. Why worry about it?" And then also I've told my people that if we have a problem, they are expected to share that problem with me today, it's our problem. If you share it with me tomorrow, it's your problem. I think people understand that I'm willing to shoulder all of these mistakes, but only if we've discussed them up front right away. If you try to fix it and keep it to yourself, well then you sort it out yourself.

   From this excerpt, some evidence of learning aptitude is evident in Tom. He describes the incident in detail, he is frank about his failure, and he can articulate how he set up systems to prevent similar incidents in the future. He also articulates how the incident had multifaceted implications. Not only did he personally lack the knowledge to make a well-informed decision, he needed to create an organizational culture that encouraged others to speak up and identify issues.

Assessing for learning aptitude feeds not only into the hiring and selection process, but into the development process after a person takes a new position. The new hires can be coached on how to use this information to build and reinforce their own propensity for learning.

PERFORMANCE FEEDBACK

Performance feedback systems monitor performance and inform each person how well he or she is doing against expectations. Performance feedback is one aspect of a broader performance management system that includes goal setting, performance measurement, and performance appraisal. Organizations that truly believe that people provide competitive advantage know that they have to connect the strategic business imperatives to individual employee performance. As shown in Figure 6-7, performance metrics translate the strategy into required individual and team behaviors and standards. In Chapter Five we discussed how the organization's reward system can motivate and reinforce the right behaviors. Performance feedback is the final element in this equation. It lets people know how they are doing so that they can make corrections.

Traditional performance feedback systems depend upon yearly goal setting and performance-appraisal meetings between an employee and his or her manager. No matter how well constructed, traditional systems will have limitations. This is especially true if you have redesigned your organization to configure

Figure 6-7. The link between strategy and performance feedback.

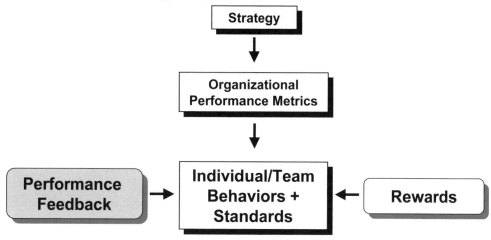

work around changing projects and processes, if you extensively utilize teams, and if you use managers as facilitators, advisers, and coaches rather than simply as supervisors of work. Traditional top-down systems depend largely on the view of one person—the boss. In a flexible and dynamic organization, the boss may have the least-informed view of an individual's performance for a number of reasons.

■ *Use of Teams.* As work becomes more cross-functional, customer-oriented, and process-oriented, lateral rather than vertical relationships tend to define performance. The basic unit of work configuration becomes a team, requiring a high degree of interdependence among members to get the work done. If one person doesn't deliver, someone else has to pick up the slack. Although the quality of performance of individual team members will be apparent to the team, it may not always be apparent to a manager, who only sees the integrated output of the team.

■ *Increased Management Span of Attention.* When organizations flatten and remove management layers, the span of management control and attention increases. Managers who oversee the work of people scattered among multiple locations have less opportunity to observe how the work is getting done.

■ *Multiple Bosses.* It is increasingly common for people to have more than one boss during the course of a year, because they either work on multiple project teams or are part of a matrix structure. Each of the project teams may have different leaders. In some cases, a peer in one situation may be a project leader in another. An employee may end up having limited direct contact with his or her formal manager.

■ *New Role for Management.* Perhaps the largest trend driving the emergence of new performance management systems is the rethinking of the role of supervisors and managers in the organization. The traditional hierarchical pyramid implies that managers supervise and control the work of those below them in the hierarchy. In organizations that have successfully empowered and enabled their front-line workers, the manager becomes a facilitator and boundary manager who supports the workers, rather than the other way around. For example, such a manager might be focused on securing resources for the group, developing their skills, and helping them interact and resolve differences with other groups. In this scenario, having the group evaluate the manager can be more important than the manager's evaluation of the group.

The increasingly broad range of performance indicators—not all of which are quantifiable with hard data—requires the use of new forms of performance feedback, particularly at the management level. As you design your organization, you may want to consider three types of performance feedback that can supplement your existing systems and provide multidirectional views of performance:

1. *Peer and Team Evaluation*: Peer appraisal gathers input from a person's colleagues who are at or about the same level. The peers work and interact together but may not share responsibility for outcomes. Team appraisal is essentially the same except that the peers are on a formal team and do have shared responsibility for their work products. In both these systems, input on performance is gathered from the peers of the person being evaluated on the assumption that colleagues have the best sense of how people approach their work, the results they achieve, and how well they work with others. If the organization is completely team-based, the majority of performance feedback may take this form. In other organizations, input from peers and team members may supplement a traditional supervisor-oriented appraisal. Peer and team evaluation systems reinforce the organizational message that collaboration and integration are important. Introducing peer and team evaluation systems, however, presents some challenges:

Getting honest feedback. Peers may be less than eager to play the role of judge. Even when kept completely confidential, peers tend to rate each other highly. People don't want to undermine positive working relationships or hurt other people's promotion or pay opportunities, possibly in the hope that others will do the same for them.

Individual performance not always adding up to team performance. Peer appraisal provides valuable insights into individual performance, but may not reflect the complex group dynamics that influence how well the team as a whole performs.

Linking feedback to rewards. If compensation and reward systems are built around performance measures, than peer and team feedback can be designed to serve as a source of input for these decisions. Linking feedback to rewards will certainly heighten the attention and interest given to the feedback process. On the other hand, people tend to be more honest and critical if they know that the results will only be used for developmental purposes.

2. *Cross-Evaluation.* In a cross-evaluation system, an individual receives feedback from others in a position to assess job performance strictly as it relates to meeting customer needs. Whereas peer and team evaluation systems tend to collect feedback from people who reside in the same business unit, cross-evaluation systems are often composed of people in different parts of the larger organization. Cross-evaluation differs from peer evaluation in that peer evaluation focuses on teamwork whereas cross-evaluation deals with business results and is linked to customer indicators. Typically, participants come from func-

tions that are highly dependent on one another for accomplishing a process or producing a customer deliverable. Feedback is focused on how an individual's job skills and behavior impact the ability of others to perform.

For example, in a functional organization a cross-evaluation system could be used to assess the new business development process. Participants might include members from sales, marketing, strategic planning, and product development. Each person would identify the relevant standards of performance (timeliness, quality, etc.) needed from each other person in order for them to collectively produce a successful customer bid. The work you did to identify role interdependencies in Chapter Three can be helpful in determining mutual expectations in a cross-evaluation system.

Cross-evaluation is a powerful way to promote collaboration between business units and functions. The ongoing communication built by the cross-evaluation process is as important an outcome as the actual ratings themselves. Cross-evaluation systems are particularly useful in strengthening horizontal links in a matrixed environment. Setting up a process whereby a group of individuals with common goals provide each other with periodic feedback builds a safe environment for people to share information and ideas and to begin collaborating through a legitimized, business-focused mechanism.

The focus on business results is critical. Many senior executives, who have the most to benefit from tools that help them negotiate complex matrix systems, are resistant to spending time on activities that seem soft and not directly linked to business results. While the design of such systems presents the same challenges as peer and team evaluation systems, cross-evaluation is focused more on a particular process or customer outcome and the standards are determined up front, thereby making it easier to identify and collect honest and critical feedback.[2] Performance feedback used in this way helps the organization build lateral capability by linking parts of the organization that may not be grouped together in the vertical structure.

3. *Upward and 360° Feedback.* Upward feedback tells managers how they are perceived by people in the work groups they manage, and 360° feedback adds in peer, boss, customer, or other perspectives. Organizations that emphasize the importance of learning and development find that upward feedback is one of the best tools for making managers aware of the gap between how well they *believe* they manage their people and what they *actually* do in day-to-day practice. Many managers believe that they delegate effectively, that they coach and support their people, and that they give frequent feedback—when in fact they don't. The fact that data is gathered confidentially allows subordinates to express observations about their managers more honestly than they would feel comfortable doing face-to-face. If this awareness is backed up by a plan for

development, then upward and 360° feedback can be an effective way for building the organization's management capabilities.

FROM TRAINING TO LEARNING

If the organization redesign is in response to a fundamental change in direction, employees at all levels will have to "retool" their skill sets. One of the most significant trends in the 1990s has been the effort by many companies to transform themselves into "learning organizations." It began with Peter Senge's belief that organizations that learn by tapping into individual and team potential and through systems thinking will have a competitive advantage.[3] Just as an individual's learning aptitude can contribute to success in a dynamic world that requires capacity to deal with unanticipated problems and opportunities, building learning capability into the organization should provide similar benefits.

As a result of this thinking, many organizations have reconceptualized their training functions. These companies have transformed departments that had focused solely on delivering skill-based courses into "learning and development" functions closely tied to broader organizational development activities. Figure 6-8 summarizes the changes organizations that focus on learning have been making. The new employment contract also means a new learning contract. In exchange for providing the opportunity and support for skill development and rewards for learning, employers expect employees to invest in their own development and help build the competence of others in the organization.

A paradox is that as organizations have put a greater emphasis on learning, there are fewer opportunities to attend traditional programs. In many businesses, the pressure to meet short-term performance targets and lean staffing mean that employees may never get around to attending elective and sometimes even so-called required training programs. It is important to leverage other activities for their learning potential. Many of the network-building practices we discussed in Chapter Four also support learning, such as job rotation and communities of practice. Technology is being widely used to enable distance learning and self-instruction.

SUMMARY

In this chapter we have looked at the final point of the star model, People Practices, to identify what types of HR systems can contribute to a reconfigurable organization. The chapter used the case example of AgroLife HR to illustrate a process for placing people into the new organizational structure. It also highlighted three pivotal practices that support the selection, performance, and

Figure 6-8. From training to learning.

Traditional Training Perspective		Learning Organization Perspective
Developing one's own expertise *A focus on building personal skills*	**to**	Leveraging others' expertise *Creating networks, identifying information sources, and collaborating to leverage complementary skills*
Training by external experts *One-way information flow from consultants or professional trainers*	**to**	Emphasis on sharing internal knowledge *Manager and others modeling and teaching new skills and behaviors; transferring success between areas*
Information acquired for the long term *Learning in isolation from the current business issues; accumulation of information for future use*	**to**	Just-in-time *Emphasis on access to information and knowledge rather than individual acquisition*
Work <u>or</u> learning *Training and education separate from work*	**to**	Work <u>and</u> learning *Action learning to solve real business issues; application of skills and knowledge on the job*
Single distribution channel *Training and development departments*	**to**	Multiple distribution channels *Training plus managers, technology, self-study, peer and team learning*
Program focused *Learning as an event*	**to**	Continuing process *Learning as ongoing reflection, interpretation, and sharing of knowledge*

development of the right talent for the organization. These practices begin with selecting people who have the aptitude to embrace and apply learning gained from new experiences and challenges. They include providing feedback from multiple sources to reflect the importance of peer interactions and the changing role of managers. Finally, broadening the concept of training to encompass learning and development is another practice that sustains the organization's ability to respond to change.

This chapter leads into the final chapter of this book—Implementation—which focuses on managing the transition from design to reality.

NOTES

1. See also E. V. Velsor and V. A. Guthrie, "Enhancing the Ability to Learn From Experience" in *Handbook of Leadership Development,* C. McCauley, R. S. Moxley, and E. V. Velsor, ed. (San Francisco and Greensboro: Jossey-Bass and Center for Creative Leadership, 1998).

2. For a fuller discussion of the challenges of peer feedback and cross-evaluation see M. A. Pieperl, "Getting 360 Feedback Right," *Harvard Business Review,* January 2001, pp. 142–147.

3. P. M. Senge, *The Fifth Discipline: The Art and Practice of the Learning Organization* (New York: Doubleday, 1990).

Tool 6-1. Staffing the new organization.

| **Purpose**: | Use this tool as a checklist when planning your own staffing process. |
| **This tool is for**: | Executive Team. |

	Staffing Process Checklist	
		Notes
Senior positions are filled first.	❑	
The process for staffing is communicated to the organization as soon as possible to minimize rumors and anxiety.	❑	
New roles, expectations, and standards are clearly defined and communicated.	❑	
The process is transparent and mirrors the organization's values.	❑	
The sources of data (interviews, performance appraisal, self-assessment, etc.) and the weight assigned to each are identified and agreed upon by the executive team.	❑	
The executive team has established clear criteria for decision making.	❑	
The process includes assessment for learning aptitude.	❑	
Placements are made based on individual capability and potential for learning, and to create groups and teams with complementary skills.	❑	
Development plans are created for all people placed or hired into new roles.	❑	

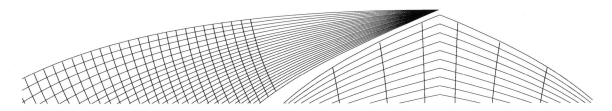

CHAPTER SEVEN

IMPLEMENTATION

Implementation is the process of putting all your good intentions to work. You have worked through the star model to determine the strategic design framework, designed the structure and the lateral organization, developed metrics to measure performance, and identified the people practices that will ensure that resources are effectively deployed against your new strategy and design. Now it's time to put all of this planning into meaningful action for every member of your organization. As your first phase of work is ending, an entire new phase of work is starting. Implementation introduces the unpredictable human element into your organizational design.

The focus of this book has been on organization design. The brief attention given to implementation is not an indication of our view of the relative importance of the two topics. Throughout this book, we've stressed that although some design options are more appropriate to a given situation than others, the process of fully developing the details is what makes the difference between a great idea on paper and a successful plan in reality. There is little correlation between a particular structure and the overall satisfaction of people who work in that structure. Usually, when there *is* disappointment with the new strategy and structure, it is usually a result of *how* the strategy and structure were implemented as opposed to dissatisfaction with the structure itself. Regardless of what type of organization you are trying to build, an implementation plan that is only partly executed guarantees lack of anticipated results.

This chapter emphasizes three components of implementation that when attended to will significantly smooth the transition to your new organization design.

- *Planning* helps you define a systematic transition between where you are and where you want to be.

- *Managing Skepticism* helps you anticipate common responses to change and provides tactics for acknowledging and addressing legitimate concerns as well as unfounded fears.

- *Assimilating into the Organization* provides a framework for assisting everyone in the organization in getting comfortable with new configurations, roles, and expectations.

PLANNING

Planning is the up-front work you do to map and manage the implementation process. It encompasses both the organizational changes and the individual transitions that are part of your organization design. As you've done your design work, you have already done a significant amount of planning. As you completed the tools in this book, you have been making conscious decisions that will impact the implementation process. In addition, the governance structure you set up to assist in developing the design details can carry you through the implementation phase.

There are several key components in the planning process, each of which is discussed below:

- Pacing

- Sequencing

- Piloting

- Communicating

- Sustaining momentum

- Feedback loops

PACING

The complexity of the design issues as well as the size of the gap between where your organization is today and where you would like it to be will impact how long the design and implementation process will take. Assuming a strategy is in place, the time frames in Figure 7-1 can serve as a guide. To some, these time frames will seem impossibly long. You may be thinking, "I don't have

Figure 7-1. Time frame (actual not elapsed) for design and implementation.

Phase	Time frame
I. Design Framework/Current State Assessment	1 to 1.5 months
II. Design Work	1 to 3 months
III. Development of Design Details	2 to 3 months
Total Design and Development	***4 to 7.5 months***
IV. Full Implementation	Additional 3 to 9 months

that much time to put everything in place." Others who have experienced redesigns may have the opposite reaction and think, "Those numbers are crazy. It takes at least two years to get a major reorganization up and running."

This is the dilemma of organizational change. Most change efforts fail because they aren't given the sustained attention, commitment, and time to take hold before the next change comes along. On the other hand, it will be true for many organizations that within two years after the initial design work is completed, external conditions will have changed substantially and may require another design modification.

There are no hard-and-fast rules regarding how long the design and implementation process will take. A major determinant is how much time, money, energy, and resources can be dedicated to the design and development work while maintaining the day-to-day operation of the business. Figure 7-2

Figure 7-2. Speed of implementation.

If you go too slow . . .		If you go too fast . . .
You lose momentum—the process doesn't seem important enough and gets lost in the day-to-day priorities.	← →	You leave people behind—they don't understand why the change is happening and they resist it.
Change feels like a Band-Aid being pulled off slowly—employees just want to get it over with.	← →	Too many unanswered questions are left to the implementation stage—people waste energy sorting out internal confusion.
The competitive environment will change before you have realized the benefits of the redesign.	← →	You defocus the organization from day-to-day work and your fundamental business suffers.

highlights some implications of going too slow or too fast. When planning the timing of your implementation, consider the following general guidelines:

■ *Not everyone has to be comfortable before you begin.* Although it is important that you have communicated the new design and strategy before you put it into action, it is not always necessary to wait until everyone is fully comfortable with it. If you wait too long to begin implementation, it will likely exacerbate those feelings of discomfort. When people experience the change firsthand, they will quickly discover that the change is probably not anywhere near as difficult as they had imagined it would be.

■ *Expect twelve to eighteen months before seeing solid results.* This is a realistic amount of time to spend before you can really expect to fully realize performance improvements. This range is based on the experience of numerous organizations that have undergone similar transitions. In order to sustain momentum during this time, set visible, significant milestones so that you can chart your progress and experience success along the way.

■ *Manage your own expectations for progress.* Give the design some time to work and for people to adjust before you expect results and full performance. Although you would never deliberately try to set people up for failure, that is often the unanticipated consequence of "raising the bar" too quickly without giving people the opportunity to meet new expectations. Don't make the mistake of thinking you can simply replace people who don't perform at the expected level. This will only slow down your implementation process because new employees have to be brought up to speed.

SEQUENCING

Implementation is not a onetime event—it is an iterative process that involves a series of changes that occur over time. In developing a sequence for implementation, bear in mind that some things must occur before others. For example, if you haven't defined the key behaviors that are required from your workforce, you can't hold people accountable for them. If you haven't determined the skills people need to fulfill their new roles, you can't plan training and development programs to provide those skills. As you consider the sequencing of the implementation process, keep the following points in mind:

■ *Start with high-visibility changes.* People will be skeptical that there is a real leadership commitment to change. Changing the performance measurement and reward systems signal in a very personal way that the organizational change is real. Even if the compensation system won't be changed quickly, introducing new measures and some visible rewards and recognition will help give momentum to the change.

■ *Implement in overlapping waves.* Don't assume that you need to wait to introduce the next phase of your implementation process until the previous one is firmly embedded in the organization. Energy will be lost if people sense that you are waiting for everything to be perfect before moving ahead with the next change.

■ *Avoid patchwork changes.* As you go forward, there will be changes to the design as well as the implementation plan. These will probably be made for good reason as you get feedback from the system and reality intrudes on your well-laid plans. When alterations are necessary, avoid making hasty changes without considering overall implications. The organization is a complex system. A change in one area has impact on others. As issues arise, address them as new design issues. Get the right people in the room to identify the root cause of the problem, integrate the change into the overall plan, and work through which other parts of the system will need to be adjusted accordingly.

■ *Celebrate achievements as they happen.* Reward small steps in the implementation process—not only when the work gets done but also when there is evidence of positive impact of the design on your workforce and your customers. Celebrate accomplishments along the way.

PILOTING

You may choose to pilot certain aspects of the design before implementing them fully across the whole organization. A pilot is a "test run" within a contained arena (e.g., a department, a location, or a product line) that lets you see how your plans work in action and then make modifications. Piloting offers the advantages of:

■ Testing the design in areas that are likely to be successful and can be used as models

■ Focusing resources, training, and attention effectively

■ Building internal knowledge and competence that can be transferred

■ Gaining feedback from employees and customers

■ Learning from experience before organizationwide rollout

Piloting may allow for faster implementation with less disruption to the larger business. You can begin to implement the design without the risk of imposing untested changes on an entire organization.

COMMUNICATING

The importance of a good communication plan cannot be underestimated. Nothing will demotivate a workforce more quickly than the feeling that they are being "kept in the dark" as change gets under way. Remember that the people in your organization will need to go through a process similar to the one the leadership team completed. They will need to understand the rationale for the change, the options that were considered, and how a redesign has benefits that outweigh the current state. As you and your leadership team create a communication plan for your workforce, keep the following tips in mind:

- *Create excitement around the future.* Be as complete as you can in painting a picture of the future for your workforce. The more you tell employees, the more they will commit to the process and embrace your vision of the future. Involve people in creating scenarios of how the change will benefit them personally.

- *Give the context.* Everyone will first focus on the new structure and where he or she will sit on the organization chart. Don't stop with the structure. When you explain the changes mentally divide your time the following way:

    30 percent on the urgent business case for change (external realities, markets, competitors, changes in the strategy—why the status quo is not sustainable)

    20 percent on how the organization needs to change (the new organizational capabilities that need to be created)

    30 percent on the roles and behaviors (how new expectations will impact and benefit people individually)

    20 percent on organization charts, new reporting relationships, and new assignments (include options that were considered and why they were rejected)[1]

- *Repeat yourself.* You've been thinking about this for months. Consider how long it took you to get comfortable with the scope of what needed to change. Don't expect everyone to go along the first few times you communicate. Repeat yourself, provide opportunities for follow-up, and communicate using a variety of methodologies. People who haven't been involved in the design will have trouble absorbing all the information in one sitting.

- *Provide regular progress updates.* Unless your organization is small, most people won't be involved directly in the implementation planning and execution. Even those who are may not know what other groups are doing. Create a mechanism for providing regular status reports on the implementation. Some organizations designate a work group expressly to focus on communication. These groups often use the vehicle of a bimonthly newsletter to highlight successes and communicate the progress on each front of the implementation.

- *Communicate up as well as down.* If your organization is nested within a larger one, keep your senior management well informed. It's important to maintain their support throughout the implementation process because you may be called upon to justify the time and resources you will expend during the change effort.

SUSTAINING MOMENTUM

Making the transition to the new organization will require a tremendous amount of time and energy. While it is occurring, you will still need to manage the day-to-day operations of the business. You would not have embarked on the redesign if the risk of maintaining the status quo didn't outweigh the risks of change. However, as you transition roles and processes, there is risk that the change effort will lose momentum. Another risk is that if the redesign involves a new line of business, those who are left attending to business as usual will feel demoralized. Some things you can do to sustain the change momentum while still keeping your business running include:

- *Use your governance structure.* You put the steering committee and work groups in place to carry the design work forward. Have them continue with the implementation. This ensures that attention is given to the change and that it is not overwhelmed by the demands of the day-to-day work. Since the steering committee works closely with the leadership and executive teams, it is also a mechanism to ensure that the redesign and implementation is not diverting attention from customers or ongoing business needs.

- *Keep the executive team involved.* Designing the organization is fun. Implementing the design is hard work. You'll be tempted to delegate responsibility down and move on to other business issues once the major design decisions have been made. However, you and your executive team need to remain involved because there are still many decisions and trade-offs to make. You'll need to hold people accountable for progress and to ensure that they have the resources they need to keep the work moving forward. If the organization's leadership disengages at the implementation, all your design efforts can be derailed.

- *Incorporate the change plan into your business plan.* A common mistake leaders make is to create a detailed implementation plan that is separate from their business plan. This sends a message to the organization as well as to the leader's boss that the two are not integrated and that perhaps the redesign is not as important as other business initiatives. The danger is that if either the redesign or the business hits a rough patch, the redesign can get scrapped and the budget cut. By incorporating it into the business plan, it is less likely to be seen as something separate from the work of the organization and will remain the business priority that it is.

FEEDBACK LOOPS

Feedback is the process by which you can gain valuable insight into what is and isn't working, how people feel about the process, and how the implementation is proceeding. Creating feedback loops should be an essential component of the planning process. Don't wait until something is going wrong to reach out and get information, and don't count on people coming forward to raise problems proactively. As you proceed through the transition, keep your finger on the pulse of the organization to determine:

- Requirements for more and different types of communication about the change

- Elements of the design that require modification

- Gaps in planning or coordination among work groups

- Interpersonal or group process issues that are hampering the progress of the work groups

- Unanticipated events or consequences of decisions

- Resistance or morale issues

Feedback will allow you to be proactive rather than reacting to situations that may already be beyond your control.

Feedback should be gathered through a mix of formal and informal methods. At some point you may want to conduct interviews, focus groups, and surveys (e.g., climate, employee satisfaction, or customer satisfaction surveys) to gather formal feedback. These can be structured similarly to the current state assessment, but this time focusing on people's understanding and concerns regarding:

- Extent to which current and future priorities are in conflict

- Particular elements of the new business model and organization design

- Steps and milestones in the implement plan

- Adequacy of information, systems, and technology to accomplish new goals

- Openness of lines of communication up, down, and laterally

- Clarity and effectiveness of decision-making processes

- What is "falling through the cracks"—work that needs to get done but isn't

- Feedback from customers regarding their perception of the new practices and behaviors

More informally, you can hold regular breakfasts with groups of employees to hear how people are coping with the changes, whether new processes are supporting the change, and how they feel about the new direction. An intranet site dedicated to the change, which encourages questions and feedback, can also be helpful. The mechanism you choose should fit your organization's culture and situation. In order for any feedback loop to work, however, there must be commitment by the members of the executive and leadership teams to listen to and address concerns without creating any fear of retribution. The feedback mechanisms created to support the change process can provide an opportunity for the organization's leadership to create a new environment of openness if there wasn't one before.

MANAGING SKEPTICISM

The resistance encountered from those who are either unwilling or unable to follow the organization's leadership into the change is probably the single largest unplanned-for event that occurs in implementing new structures and processes. Very often, when people are resistant to change, it is easy to dismiss them by saying, "They're just afraid of change." This is almost always *not* the case. When people need to change from point A to point B, it is not point B that they are resisting. They are resisting the messy process of getting *from* point A *to* point B.

Leaving behind the familiar for the unknown is never easy for anyone. In addition, it is healthy for people to be skeptical. Many organizations certainly have a history of less than successful change initiatives. It should be expected that people will hold back their support until they are convinced that the change is warranted and in the right direction, but that there is commitment from the organization's leadership to see it through.

No matter how well you plan to implement your new organization design, you will almost certainly encounter doubt and skepticism at some point during the implementation process. Helping people to understand the desired future state and the process for achieving it may lessen resistance. But don't make the mistake of thinking you *won't* encounter it—because you will. How you learn to recognize it, address it, and manage it throughout the transition will be a critical factor in the success of your implementation process.

Much work has been done on identifying common reactions to change.[2] The more you are able to recognize these reactions, the greater the likelihood that you will be able to acknowledge and address them. Some of the reactions you may encounter are listed below, along with the actions you can take to respond to them.

■ *People feel they are losing power or control.* Lack of participation or involvement in decisions creates feelings of defensiveness and territoriality. This manifests itself in petty behavior, grasping for control of *any* process, and resisting other's ideas.

—Create opportunities for involvement in both the decision-making and planning process.

—Provide as many choices as possible for people to have control over how their work will change.

—Continually reinforce the "greater good" that is at the root of the organization redesign when individual needs threaten to take precedence over the desires of other areas.

■ *People feel uncertain about the change.* When people lack information on the purpose, rationale, and key steps involved in the change, they are more likely to resist it. People may also not take initiative because they are uncertain as to how to proceed or to whom they should go for decisions. The tactics discussed in the Communicating section of this chapter can help address this, along with some additional strategies.

—Share the rationale, purpose, and vision of the future state. Provide clear and consistent communication about the change.

—Provide milestones for assessing the success of the change. Help people understand the steps involved in reaching the goal.

—Consistently and visibly demonstrate leadership commitment to the change. Model the new norms that will be required on an ongoing basis.

—Ensure that everyone is working from the same set of assumptions.

—Acknowledge and reward initiative when it is demonstrated.

—Clearly define where decision-making power and authority lie.

■ *People are uncomfortable with what is going to be different.* They resist change because it forces them to challenge the assumptions, norms, and behaviors upon which their daily routine is based.

—Be clear and honest about what will change but also emphasize what works well and will stay the same.

—Don't fall into the trap of believing that "everything should change" as a means to support "what must change."

—Support familiar routines that will maintain a link between the old and the new.

■ *People are forced to confront the fact that the way they have been doing things is "wrong."* Change is often positioned as a way of eliminating "bad habits," thereby making people feel ashamed of or embarrassed by past accomplishments. People may be concerned that they will be unable to succeed in the new environment if new competencies and skills are required.

—Position the change in its context. The old way wasn't necessarily bad; it's just not appropriate for the current situation.

—Help people to envision how new behaviors and practices will benefit them and not only the business.

—Provide ample training and support for the new competencies required for success in the new organization.

—Create an atmosphere where people can ask questions about how things should or will be done.

—Give everyone the opportunity to learn in an environment that, at least initially, rewards effort as well as results.

■ *People are concerned that the change will mean more work for them.* People simply may not want to have to sacrifice even more personal or family time to do more for the organization.

—Understand that some people will require flexibility to schedule their lives or other work projects around the change. Sensitivity to this impact, built by maintaining open communication, will increase the likelihood that people will embrace the change when the time is right.

—Support people through the change either through recognition and rewards programs or through other means. Acknowledge the difficulty of making change happen.

—Adjust expectations for timing on other projects to accommodate the extra work associated with implementation.

—Visibly demonstrate your own commitment to the change. If people are working late to get the job done, be there with them to show your support.

■ *People are resistant because the threat to their power, influence, job security, or comfort level is real.*

—If proposed changes will impact people's power or job status, acknowledge that it will happen and address it as quickly as possible. Even in situations where the news is bad, people will usually feel relieved to know what is happening rather than continue to wonder and suspect the worst.

—Avoid making false promises or operating under false pretenses. If there are going to be layoffs or significant changes, address them honestly and directly.

—Give people a chance to "mourn" those aspects of the change process that involve loss. Provide opportunities for people to do this together, because it will increase the opportunities for team building.

ASSIMILATING INTO THE ORGANIZATION

Assimilation is the process by which people acculturate to one another and to the organization as a whole. Assimilating people into the organization is a critical part of the implementation process. The assimilation process usually applies to new hires, but after a redesign everyone will be "new" to the organization, no matter how long they worked in the old organization. Organization redesign means new roles, new expectations, and new ways of operating, not just new configurations. Without the proper support from the organization as they adjust to new roles, new responsibilities, new decision-making structures, and especially new relationships, people in the organization can find themselves:

- Frustrated by a lack of information and information-gathering networks

- Lacking a clear sense of how to build coalitions to get things done

- Uncertain about which aspects of their knowledge and experience apply in the new context

One element of assimilation into the new organization is the formation of new relationships built on new behavioral norms and around new work activities. Even if you won't be using cross-business teams as we defined them in Chapter Four, people will be working together in groups of various configurations. Getting these groups functioning effectively will speed the implementation process. Figure 7-3 summarizes the characteristics of groups that work effectively.

During their life cycle, groups go through five stages of development: exploring, testing, harmonizing, individuating, and performing. Only at the performing stage will the group exhibit all the characteristics of an effective group. In addition, groups move back and forth among these stages at varying times. When new group members are introduced, they may fall back to the exploring stage. Figure 7-4 describes each stage in detail, highlights the typical

Figure 7-3. Effective groups.

Characteristic	Evidence
The group has clear goals and understands its purpose.	• People know what they are striving toward and share the group's goals. • People feel that they are part of an interdependent group rather than being isolated individuals. • People have an explicit understanding of how things will be accomplished.
The group engages in collective decision making when appropriate.	• People share assumptions as a means to understand others' viewpoints. • People maximize relationships; consensus is used whenever possible to reach decisions. • Decisions are supported and enacted by the group as a whole. • Everyone shows commitment to creating results.
The group uses a shared problem-solving process.	• There is an agreed-upon problem-solving process and the group adheres to it.
All members participate actively.	• Everyone takes responsibility for achieving the group's goals. • Members feel safe to participate and are not afraid of being "shot down." • The group makes full use of its available resources.
Open, honest communication is a basis for working together.	• People share ideas and information freely and listen actively to one another.
Group members have high trust among the group and aren't afraid to take risks.	• The group is innovative and takes risks. • Group members tolerate and learn from mistakes.
Contention is used to surface differences in perspective.	• Differences of opinion are encouraged. • Conflict is dealt with openly.
The group uses frequent self-assessment.	• The group periodically examines how well it is doing and what progress has been made toward stated goals. • Adjustments are made based on group assessment.

feelings and behaviors that can be observed, and how you might intervene when the group is demonstrating such behaviors. Awareness of these typical stages can help you and the leadership team support the formation of new networks, relationships, and effective groups.

In addition to people working in new group and team configurations, your senior-level hires will also need assimilation support.[3] The arrival of a new manager adds to the instability caused by the transition to the organization design. New managers come with their own set of assumptions and will largely

(text continues on page 268)

Figure 7-4. Stages of group and team development.

	Major Issues	Typical Behaviors	Typical Feelings	Facilitative Support	Resolution
Stage 1: Exploring	During this stage, the issue is identity. Group members may question their identity within the group as well as the identity of the group. They may be wondering: ■ What will this group be like? ■ How will I fit in? ■ What are we really going to be doing? ■ What are my goals? ■ What are the group's goals?	In new group situations, members react in a variety of ways. They may: ■ Sit back and take a "wait and see" attitude. ■ Seek information and clarification to get their questions answered. ■ Seek support from the leader or other members. ■ Try to make light of the situation by joking and "horsing around."	Members also respond emotionally to this new situation. They may feel: ■ Tense or anxious ■ Insecure or skeptical ■ Curious or anticipatory	■ Support group to clarify its goals, roles, and responsibilities. ■ Establish group ground rules. ■ Be supportive and legitimize anxiety. ■ Emphasize noticeable strengths. ■ Note incremental development steps and accomplishments.	As the group continues to work together, answers to its initial questions begin to emerge. A sense of group begins to develop, and its goals and direction become clearer to its members. The unfamiliar becomes familiar, and members begin to feel more comfortable with each other, and less anxious or insecure.
Stage 2: Testing	As the group starts to feel more "at home," members may begin to flex their muscle a bit, to see how far they can go in this new atmosphere. Frequently this involves some sort of challenge to authority, usually toward the leader, but it may also be directed toward other members.	Members try on new behaviors including: ■ Challenging group process, goals, and objectives ■ Giving information and opinions more than seeking them ■ Participating more than before ■ Acting rebellious	While security usually increases, the increased challenge and conflict can result in feelings of: ■ Frustration ■ Resistance ■ Hostility	■ Encourage expression of differences, and clarification of issues. ■ Acknowledge differences and issues (without taking sides). ■ Continue to encourage participation. ■ Probe for reasons behind statements. ■ Be candid. ■ Raise some of the difficult issues.	Over time, the group establishes limits and boundaries for its members. The role of the leader in the group is more widely shared as members practice new skills and behaviors and take on a variety of roles.
Stage 3: Harmonizing	Once the group has established limits and begins to share the leadership role, members typically seek to put conflict and rebellion behind them, and enter a stage of harmony. However, they are often so intent on avoiding any conflicts in this stage that they tend to deny or ignore differences within the group on important issues.	At this point, you may see: ■ Eagerness to agree ■ Strong mutual support of the group ■ Striving toward quick consensus on issues ■ Burying of negative feelings	Feelings during this stage include: ■ Euphoria ■ Warmth ■ Security ■ Acceptance	■ Probe for and confront differences. ■ Stress the value of alternative points of view. ■ Note that interdependence does not mean identical thinking. ■ Use a structured problem-solving process to surface contention.	The harmonizing process often passes quickly as group members come to realize that glossed-over differences are important and need to be dealt with.

	Major Issues	Typical Behaviors	Typical Feelings	Facilitative Support	Resolution
Stage 4: Individuating	After a period of very close "groupiness" and submerged differences, many group members naturally react by re-asserting themselves and their individual opinions. This often leads to strong conflict within the group.	You may see members: • Entering into personality clashes that interfere with the group's direction • Forming subgroups that seek to take over the leadership role and/or fight over the group's direction • Rejecting the group or some of its members • Giving personalized or destructive feedback	It can be an uncomfortable period in the group, and members may feel alienated, negative, hopeless, and impatient.	• Focus on indicators of progress. • Use effective conflict management techniques. • Encourage open discussion of feelings. • Act as a "bridge." • Help the group clarify and define its mission and goals.	Despite the discomfort, group members usually learn to handle their conflicts constructively while this process is going on. They come to accept differences within the group and to value the results of working out these differences in a positive way. Group members arrive at realistic procedures for working together.
Stage 5: Performing	This last stage represents the group at its most effective level. There is a balance of task functions and maintenance functions to achieve goals.	Members will: • Achieve and maintain momentum. • Give constructive and appropriate feedback. • Accept responsibility for the success of their group.	Members also feel a sense of well-being and accomplishment and become comfortable, secure, and proud of their group.	• Support what else may be possible for the group. • Recognize the capacity for self-regulation and intervention skills already present in the group. • Support distributive leadership.	The group continues in this stage until changes such as new members, change in leadership, reorganization, or new concerns move the group to an earlier stage of development.

be unaware of the strengths and weaknesses of the teams they will be managing, nor of the teams of which they will be members, such as leadership teams and project teams.

These new senior people were hired because they already have demonstrated the skills, behaviors, and mind-sets you hope to instill throughout the organization. By definition and by design, new leaders often don't "fit" in—especially if they've been hired to lead a change effort based on their experience with how your organization *wants* to operate in the future. The turmoil of the implementation process and the resistance that is likely to manifest itself against the change can create significant barriers to the success of these new hires. Without an intervention focused on surfacing these issues and expectations, it can take months for the group and the manager to learn about one another and develop mutual confidence and trust. This is valuable time that is lost, which will impede the group's progress toward goals.

In fact, many new senior hires leave their new organizations before they've been able to implement significant change or have had the impact others hoped they would have. It's virtually impossible for a new leader to succeed within a reasonable amount of time without a structured assimilation process that facilitates communication, network building, and information gathering, as well as provides coaching and support to help manage interpersonal resistance. If the new leader does get discouraged and leaves, it will cause even more disruption and delay for your redesign.

During this critical stage, you can help new managers and leaders assimilate by:

■ *Planning Facilitated Team Assimilation Meetings.* These meetings provide a vehicle for the leader to share expectations and commit to how the leader and the team will work together. Team members learn about the new person and share their understanding of the strategy and goals for the future.

■ *Providing a Structured Assimilation Plan.* Formally introduce the new leaders to different parts of the organization so that they can meet the key players and develop a network among their peers. Provide new people with opportunities to meet those with whom they must interface. To ensure consistency and to help them assimilate, those people with whom the new leader is to meet should be coached in advance on the information they are expected to provide.

■ *Appointing a "Mentor" or "Assimilation Coach."* Choose a mentor who is outside their immediate peer group to whom new leaders can go with questions or for guidance. The mentor should be someone with a broad view of the organization, with an intimate understanding of the work the person will be expected to do, and who has a solid understanding of the strategy, culture, norms, and history of the organization. The mentor and the new leader should schedule regular sessions so that communication lines stay open and regular guidance is provided.

An assimilation coach is an external consultant with expertise in helping new leaders manage the specific personal and professional issues that arise during the assimilation period. They can contact an internal mentor by providing objective feedback, assisting with organizational and cultural assessments, and facilitating the initial meetings between the new leader and his or her team. A focus on assimilation ensures that individual needs are recognized and attended to during implementation, and it also speeds the transition process. Use Tool 7-1 to guide your implementation planning.

NOTES

1. O. Gadiesh and S. Oliver, "Designing for Implementability," in *The Organization of the Future*, Frances Hesselbein and Marshall Goldsmiths, eds. (San Francisco: Jossey-Bass, 2000).

2. See R. M. Kanter, "Managing the Human Side of Change," *Management Review,* April 1985, pp. 52–56.

3. For more on assimilation, see D. Downey, with T. March and A. Berkman, *Assimilating New Leaders: The Key to Executive Retention* (New York: AMACOM, 2001), pp. 101–112.

Tool 7-1. Implementation checklist.

Purpose:	Use this tool as a checklist when planning implementation of your new organization design.
This tool is for:	Leadership Team, Steering Committee.

Planning

❑ You have developed a realistic time frame for implementation with milestones.

❑ A governance structure with well-defined roles is in place to support ongoing momentum and coordinate implementation planning and execution.

❑ The implementation plan has been incorporated into your business plan.

❑ The implementation time frame accounts for current business initiatives, funding, resource availability, and other constraints.

❑ The implementation plan incorporates a logical sequence of events so that each activity builds upon prior work.

❑ Sequencing is structured so that high-visibility changes happen early and demonstrate leadership commitment to the change effort.

❑ A plan for celebrating and rewarding achievements as they occur is in place.

❑ Leadership expectations are consistent with the organization and people's ability to change.

❑ Pilot sites, if used, are chosen to provide a realistic test of the design.

Communication and Feedback

❑ There is a communication plan regarding the redesign and implementation including rationale, impact, expectations, and milestones.

❑ A variety of mechanisms are in place (work group, newsletter, Internet site, etc.) to regularly communicate the progress of the implementation to the entire organization as well as other stakeholders (senior management, customers, partners, etc.).

❑ Feedback loops are in place to ensure that employee concerns and issues are surfaced and addressed by leadership during the implementation.

❑ The organization's leadership is aware that resistance, skepticism, and doubt are normal and messages to acknowledge and address concerns are incorporated into communication plans.

Assimilation

❑ There is a plan to assist new groups and teams to assimilate and speed their effectiveness.

❑ The organization's leadership understands the characteristics of effective groups and has the skills to intervene and assist them.

❑ A structured process is in place to assimilate new leaders into the organization and support their successful entry into the organization.

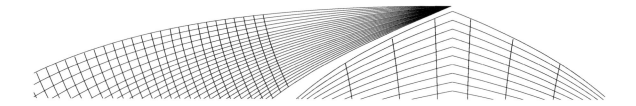

CONCLUSION

This book has provided a guide for designing a dynamic organization—an organization that can be easily and proactively reconfigured to take advantage of market opportunities and that views organization design as a competitive advantage. If you are using this book in whole or in part as you are redesigning your own organization, you have deepened your own organization design competency.

Although the future is unpredictable, we can be sure there will continue to be change. Leaders who know how to complement sound strategies with the right organizational structures and capabilities will hold the key to developing the flexibility, coordination, and nimbleness that organizations of all sizes require in today's environment. Leaders who understand how integral performance measurement, rewards, and other human resource systems are to the success of their design decisions will be able to realize the power of an aligned organization. Finally, leaders who help their organizations develop collective competence in asking the right questions, making informed decisions, and implementing with attention to both the needs of the business and the individual will be successful in building the dynamic organizations of the future.

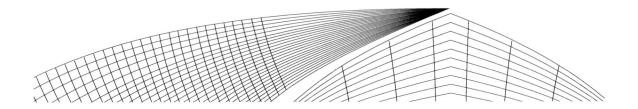

GLOSSARY OF TERMS

Assessment and selection   The processes that ensure that the right people are hired, not only for the work that must be done today, but also for the future.

Assimilation   A process in which new hires acculturate to an organization and in which both the individual and the organization are transformed by the process.

Communities of practice   Formalized networks of employees that encourage people with common organizational interests to learn and share knowledge.

Cross-evaluation   A type of evaluation in which individuals receive feedback from other functions (that are highly dependent on one another for accomplishing a process) regarding their job performance as it relates to meeting customer needs.

Current state assessment   An analysis that defines the gap between the desired future state and where the organization is today, and that provides a snapshot of the strengths and weaknesses of the organization at a point in time.

Customer structure   A structure organized around major market segments, such as client groups, industries, or population groups.

Design criteria   The organizational capabilities that the business needs to have in order to achieve its strategy.

Design phase   The phase that identifies those changes in the organization that need to be made to align the organization to the strategy.

272

Development phase   The phase in which elements of the design are fleshed out and refined.

Distributed structure   A structure in which a headquarters activity is placed in a field location based on local competence.

Feedback loops   A process by which the organization's leadership gains valuable insight into what is and isn't working, how people feel about the process, and how the implementation is proceeding.

Front-back hybrid structure   A structure that combines elements of both the product and the customer structures in order to provide the benefits of both.

Functional structure   A structure organized around major activity groups, such as operations, research and development, marketing, finance, and human resources.

Geographic structure   A structure organized around physical locations, such as states, countries, or regions.

Governance structure   A set of roles and processes put into place in order to ensure that design and implementation plans are moved forward, activities are coordinated, and the change process is not overwhelmed by current business demands.

Implementation phase   The phase in which the entire organization is involved as the new design is rolled out and put into practice.

Implementation planning   The up-front work required to map and manage the implementation process.

Integrative roles   Managerial, coordinator, or boundary-spanning positions charged with orchestrating work across units, using influence rather than formal authority.

Lateral capability   The ability to build, manage, and reconfigure various coordinating mechanisms to achieve strategic goals.

Lateral organization   All the coordinating mechanisms (networks, processes, roles, teams, and reporting relationships) that augment the structure to create a complete structural design.

Lateral processes   The business and management processes that move decisions and information through the organization in a formalized flow.

Learning aptitude   A measure of a person's desire and ability to draw meaning from past experiences and to utilize these lessons creatively to master new challenges.

Limits   Boundaries that determine what is and what is not part of the design process.

Matrix structures   A system of dual reporting relationships put into place in order to ensure that people focus simultaneously on two or more organizational forces (functional, customer, product, or geographic).

Networks   The interpersonal relationships and communities of practice that underlie all other types of lateral capability and that serve to coordinate work informally.

Organizational capabilities   The skills, processes, technologies, and human abilities that create competitive advantage.

Organizational role   A distinct organizational component defined by a unique outcome and set of responsibilities, such as a business unit, a function, or a type of job.

Organization design   The deliberate process of configuring structures, processes, reward systems, and people practices and policies to create an effective organization capable of achieving the business strategy.

Organization structure   The formal manner by which people and work are grouped into defined units.

Pay for performance   A philosophy of compensation that rewards people for their results and contributions rather than their time and effort.

People practices   The collective human resources systems and policies of the organization, including selection and staffing, performance feedback and management, training, development, careers, and rewards and recognition.

Performance drivers   The components of performance that, if changed positively or negatively, impact outcomes. These are sometimes called *leading indicators*.

Performance feedback   Mechanisms that provide employees with the information they need in order to understand their own performance and take control of their own learning and development. They are often used as the basis for compensation, rewards, and recognition.

Product structure   A structure organized around product divisions, with each division having its own functional structure to support its product(s).

Reconfigurable organization   An organization that can modify itself to respond quickly and flexibly to changes in the environment.

Reward systems   Pay and recognition systems that define expected behaviors and increase the likelihood that people will demonstrate those behaviors.

Role outcome   An end state or expected result to be achieved by the role within some defined time period.

Role responsibilities   The tasks to be performed that will close the gap between the current state of the work and the desired end states.

Rotational assignments An organizational strategy for building lateral capability by moving people through the organization at defined intervals, to broaden skills, to promote and reinforce best practices and knowledge transfer, and to embed an enterprisewide perspective.

Skill-based pay or knowledge-based pay A philosophy of compensation that values the skills and/or knowledge a person is able to contribute to the organization.

Success indicators Descriptors of the desired future state in terms of the business *outcomes* to be achieved.

Teams Groups of people brought together across business and organizational structures to work interdependently and share collective responsibility for outcomes.

Total compensation A view of compensation based on a combination of salary, cash payments, and benefits received by an employee.

Value proposition An organization's unique combination of qualities that the strategy attempts to exploit.

Variable compensation Compensation comprising performance-based awards that have to be reearned each year, and that don't permanently increase base salaries.

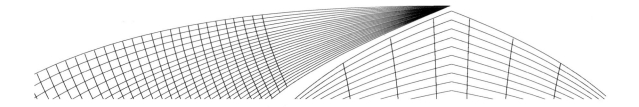

BIBLIOGRAPHY

Alsop, R. "Harris Interactive Survey Indicates Fragility of Corporate Reputations." *The Wall Street Journal,* February 7, 2001.

Anderson, R. E. "Matrix Redux." *Business Horizons,* November/December 1994, pp. 6–10.

Atkinson, A. A., J. H. Waterhouse, and R. B. Wells. "A Stakeholder Approach to Strategic Performance Measurement." *Sloan Management Review* 38.3 (1997), pp. 25–37.

Banner, D. K. and T. E. Gagne. *Designing Effective Organizations: Traditional and Transformational Views.* Newbury Park, Calif.: Sage, 1995.

Bartlett, C. A. and S. Ghoshal, "Matrix Management: Not a Structure, a Frame of Mind." *Harvard Business Review,* July/August 1990, pp. 139–145.

Beckhard, R. and R. T. Harris. *Organizational Transitions: Managing Complex Change.* Reading, Mass.: Addison-Wesley, 1977.

Boem, R. and C. Phipps. "Flatness Forays." *McKinsey Quarterly* 3 (1996), pp. 129–143.

Brown, J. S. "Unfreezing the Corporate Mind." *Fast Company,* June 16, 1998.

Brown, M. G. "Metrics for the .coms." *Perform Magazine,* Summer 2000, http://www.pbviews.com/magazine/.

Brown, S. and K. Eisenhardt. *Competing on the Edge: Strategy as Structured Chaos*. Boston: Harvard Business School Press, 1998.

Burrows, P. "The Radical: Carly Fiorina's Bold Management Experiment at HP." *Business Week*, February 19, 2001, pp. 70–80.

Cummings, T. G. and E. F. Huse. *Organization Development and Change*, 4th ed. St. Paul, Minn.: West Publishing, 1985.

Davis, M. R. and D. A. Weckler. *A Practical Guide to Organization Design*. Menlo Park, Calif.: Crisp Publications, 1996.

Davis, S. M. and P. R. Lawrence. "The Matrix Diamond." *Wharton Magazine* 2.2 (1978), pp. 19–27.

———. "Problems of Matrix Organizations." *Harvard Business Review*, May/June 1978, pp. 131–139.

Deeprose, D. *How to Recognize and Reward Employees*. New York: AMACOM, 1994.

Downey, D., T. March, and A. Berkman. *Assimilating New Leaders: The Key to Executive Retention*. New York: AMACOM, 2001, pp. 101–112.

Earl, M. J. and I. A. Scott. "What Is a Chief Knowledge Officer?" *Sloan Management Review*, Winter 1999, pp. 29–38.

Eccles, R. G. "The Performance Measurement Manifesto." *Harvard Business Review*, January/February 1991, pp. 131–137.

Galbraith, J. R. *Competing With Flexible Lateral Organizations,* 2nd ed. Reading, Mass: Addison-Wesley, 1994.

———. *Designing the Global Corporation*. San Francisco: Jossey-Bass, 2000.

———. "Designing the Innovating Organization." *Organization Dynamics,* 1982, 19(3): 4–25.

———. *Designing Organizations: An Executive Briefing on Strategy, Structure and Process*. San Francisco: Jossey-Bass, 1995.

———. *Organization Design*. Reading, Mass.: Addison-Wesley, 1977.

Galbraith, J. R. and E. Lawler, eds. *The Future of Organizations*. San Francisco: Jossey-Bass, 1993.

Gomez-Mejia, L. R. and D.B. Balkin. *Compensation, Organizational Strategy and Firm Performance*. Cincinnati: South-Western, 1992.

Gordon, J. "Feeding the Monster: Cambridge Technology Was So Obsessed With Growth That It Forgot How to Build a Business." *Forbes*, September 2000, pp. 70–71.

Graham, W., D. Osgood, and J. Karren. "A Real-Life Community of Practice." *Training and Development*, May 1998.

Hackman, J. R. and G. R. Oldham. *Work Redesign.* Reading, Mass.: Addison-Wesley, 1980.

Hagel, J. III, "Fallacies in Organizing for Performance." *McKinsey Quarterly* 2 (1994), pp. 97–106.

Hamel, G. and C. K. Prahalad. *Competing for the Future.* Boston: Harvard Business School Press, 1994.

Hass, N. "The House the Bloomberg Built." *Fast Company,* premier issue, November 1995, p. 97.

Hesselbein, F. and M. Goldsmiths, eds. *The Organization of the Future.* San Francisco: Jossey-Bass, 2000.

Hiam, A. *Motivating and Rewarding Employees.* Holbrook, Mass.: Adams Media, 1999.

Hunsaker, P. and C. W. Cook. *Managing Organizational Behavior.* Reading, Mass.: Addison-Wesley, 1986.

Johansen, R., David Sibbert, Suzyn Benson, Alexia Martin, Robert Mittman, and Paul Saffo. *Leading Business Teams: How Teams Can Use Technology and Group Process Tools to Enhance Performance.* Reading, Mass.: Addison-Wesley, 1991.

Johnson, R. "Employers Now Vie to Hire Moms with Young Children." *The Wall Street Journal,* September 19, 2000.

Kanter, R. M. "Managing the Human Side of Change." *Management Review,* April 1985, pp. 52–56.

Kaplan, R. S. and D. P. Norton. "The Balanced Scorecard—Measures That Drive Performance." *Harvard Business Review,* January/February 1992, pp. 71–79.

———. "Putting the Balanced Scorecard to Work." *Harvard Business Review,* September/October 1993, pp. 134–147.

———. "Using the Balanced Scorecard as a Strategic Management System." *Harvard Business Review,* January/February 1996, pp. 75–85.

Katzenbach, J. R. and D. K. Smith. "The Discipline of Teams." *Harvard Business Review,* March/April 1993, pp. 111–119.

Keidel, R. W. "Rethinking Organizational Design." *Academy of Management Executive* 8, 4 (1994), pp. 12–28.

Kerr, S. "Ultimate Rewards: What Really Motivates People to Achieve." Boston, Mass.: Harvard Business Review Press, 1997.

Klubnik, J. *Rewarding and Recognizing Employees.* New York: McGraw-Hill, 1995.

Knight, C. "From Business Strategy to Balanced Scorecard." *Perform Magazine,* Spring 1999, http://www.pbviews.com/magazine/articles/business_strategy.html.

Lawler, E. *Rewarding Excellence.* San Francisco: Jossey-Bass, 2000.

————. *Strategic Pay: Aligning Organization Strategies and Pay Systems.* San Francisco: Jossey-Bass, 1990.

Lewin, R. *Complexity: Life at the Edge of Chaos,* 2nd ed. Chicago: University of Chicago Press, 2000.

Majchrzak, A. and Q. Wang. "Breaking the Functional Mind-Set in Process Organizations." *Harvard Business Review,* September/October 1996, pp. 93–99.

McCauley, C., R. S. Moxley, and E. V. Velsor, eds. *Handbook of Leadership Development.* San Francisco and Greensboro, N.C.: Jossey-Bass and Center for Creative Leadership, 1998.

Mintzberg, H. *The Structuring of Organizations: A Synthesis of the Research.* Englewood Cliffs, N.J.: Prentice Hall, 1979.

Mohrman, S. A. and A. M. Mohrman. *Designing and Leading Team-Based Organizations: A Workbook for Organizational Self-Design.* San Francisco: Jossey-Bass, 1997.

Mohrman, S. A., J. R. Galbraith, and E. Lawler, eds. *Tomorrow's Organization: Crafting Winning Capabilities in a Dynamic World.* San Francisco: Jossey-Bass, 1998.

Mohrman, S. A., S. G. Cohen, and A. M. Mohrman. *Designing Team-Based Organizations: New Forms for Knowledge Work.* San Francisco: Jossey-Bass, 1995.

Morrison, E. W. and C. C. Phelps. "Taking Charge at Work: Extrarole Efforts to Initiate Workplace Change." *Academy of Management Journal* 42, 44 (1999), pp. 403–419.

Nadler, D. A. and M. L. Tushman. *Competing by Design: The Power of Organizational Architecture.* New York: Oxford University Press, 1997.

Pieperl, M. A. "Getting 360 Feedback Right." *Harvard Business Review,* January 2001, pp. 142–147.

Prahalad, C. K. and G. Hamel. "The Core Competence of the Organization." *Harvard Business Review,* May/June 1990, pp. 79–90.

Raimy, E. "Community Zest." *Human Resource Executive,* August 2000, pp. 34–38.

Senge, P. M. *The Fifth Discipline: The Art and Practice of the Learning Organization.* New York: Doubleday, 1990.

Silverman, E. R. "Once Upon a Time." *Human Resource Executive,* June 4, 1999.

Simons, R. "How New Top Managers Use Control Systems as Levers of Strategic Renewal." *Strategic Management Journal* 15 (1994), pp. 169–189.

———. *Levers of Control.* Boston: Harvard Business School Press, 1995.

Simons, R. and A. Davila. "How High Is Your Return on Management?" *Harvard Business Review,* January/February 1998, pp. 71–80.

Smith, D. and J. Katzenbach. *The Wisdom of Teams.* Boston: Harvard Business School Press, 1992.

Stacey, R. D. *Managing the Unknowable: Strategic Boundaries Between Order and Chaos in Organizations.* San Francisco: Jossey-Bass, 1992.

Sunoo, B. K. "Redesign for a Better Work Environment." *Workforce* 79, 2 (2000), pp. 38–46.

Tam, P. "Pixar Bets It Can Boost Output to One Movie Feature a Year." *The Wall Street Journal,* February 15, 2001.

Thompson, J. D. *Organizations in Action.* New York: McGraw-Hill, 1967.

Treacy, M. and F. Wiersema. *The Discipline of Market Leaders: Choose Your Customers, Narrow Your Focus, Dominate Your Market.* Reading, Mass.: Addison-Wesley, 1995.

Wheatley, M. *Leadership and the New Science Revised: Discovering Order in a Chaotic World.* San Francisco: Berrett-Koehler, 1999.

Wilson, T. B. *Rewards That Drive High Performance.* New York: AMACOM, 1999.

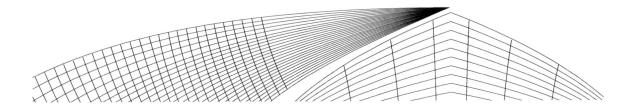

INDEX

ABACUS system, 174
ABB, *see* Asea Brown Boveri
AgroLife (case study), 233–240
alignment, role, 83–84
Amazon.com, 27–28, 63–65, 96
Andersen Consulting, 145–146
annual meetings, 147–148
Apple Computers, 143
Asea Brown Boveri (ABB), 172–174
assessment interviews, 231
assimilation, 264–269
assumptions, 32, 54
AT&T, 72

balanced scorecard, 192–195
Baldrige award, 27
Bankers Trust, 9
banking industry, 9
Barnes and Noble, 96
Barnevik, Percy, 173
behavior(s)
    and recognition, 213
    and rewards, 199, 201–202
Bloomberg, Michael, 144–145

BMW, 143–144
boundary-spanning roles, 166–168
Bridgestone/Firestone, 200
business development, 152
business incentive plans, 206
business plans, 259–260
business strategies, 7

call centers, 197
Cambridge Technology Partners (CTP), *x*
Capital Bank Corporation (case study)
    determining design framework at, 22–23,
        44–45
    lateral capability at, 134–135, 174, 176
    structure of, 58–59, 80, 81
CARE International, 150
change
    in business strategy, 8–9
    levers of, *ix*
    managing skepticism about, 261–264
    in organization, 9
    pace of, *ix,* 31
    readiness for, in reconfigurable organizations,
        6–7

chaos theory, *x*
Citibank, 172
Citigroup, 67–68, 149
CNN, 28
coaches, 268–269
co-location, 143–145
communal space, 144
communicating, 257–259
communities of practice, 145–147, 249
compensation, 202–212
   of business units, 209–210
   designing systems for, 210–212
   pay for performance, 205–207
   skill-based, 207–208
   of teams, 209–210
   tool for assessment of, 225
   total, 203–204
   variable, 204–205
complexity (of organizational structure), 97–98
conflict, in lateral organizations, 14
consultants, 35
coordinator roles, 166
core strategy, 28, 30
CRM (customer relationship management) systems, 150
cross-business teams, 156–158
cross-evaluation, 247–248
cross-selling, 76
CTP (Cambridge Technology Partners), *x*
culture, organizational, 98–99
current state assessment, 32–43
   analysis of data from, 43
   benefits of, 32
   consultants for administering, 35
   documents for, 32–33
   methodology for, 35–37
   questions to ask in, 37–42
   sources of data for, 33–35
   tool for planning of, 55
customer-centric companies, 27–28
customer relationship management (CRM) systems, 150
customer service, as lateral process, 152
customer structure, 72–74
customization, 73

DaimlerChrysler, 73
decision making, 140–141, 161

design, organization, *see* organization design
design criteria
   and strategy, 25–30
   and structure, 93
   tool for determination of, 51–52
Designing the Organization phase, 11, 60, 61
design process, 9–12
   Designing the Organization phase of, 11
   Determining the Design Framework phase of, 10–11
   Developing the Details phase of, 11
   Implementing the New Design phase of, 12
Determining the Design Framework phase, 10–11, 24–25
Deutsche Bank, 9
Developing the Details phase, 11
distributed structure, 94–95
distribution channels, 96–97
divergence, 71
divisions, launching new, 8
Dominos Pizza, 197–198
Dow-Corning, 149
drivers (balanced scorecard), 194

e-commerce, 167
economies of scale, 65, 71
employees, 233
   participation by, 13
   in reconfigurable organizations, 6
   see also staffing
Employer Services, 153
Ernst & Young, 27, 167, 241, 242
executive teams, *xiv,* 92–93, 116, 232, 259
"extrarole" behavior, 165

Federal Express, 200
feedback, 260–261
feedback, performance, 245–249
financial function, as lateral process, 152
flexibility
   in lateral organizations, 140
   in reconfigurable organizations, 6
focus groups, 36–37
Ford Foundation, 146
framework, design, 22–57
   assumptions about, 32

case study involving, 22–23, 44–45
current state assessment for, 32–43
and design criteria, 25–30
limits on, 30–32
phases of, 24–25
free riding, 209–210
front-back hybrid structure, 74–79
advantages of, 76–77, 79
challenges of, 77, 79
examples of, 78
functional structure, 63–67

gain-sharing plans, 206
General Motors (GM), 8
geographic structure, 67–69
Glass-Steagall Act, 9
GM (General Motors), 8
governance structure, 114–120
definition of, 114
executive team as element of, 116
implementation teams as element of, 119–120
leader as element of, 116
leadership team as element of, 116–117
process manager as element of, 118–119
purpose of, 114–115
sponsor as element of, 115, 116
steering committee as element of, 118
and sustaining momentum, 259
tool for determining, 133
work groups as element of, 117–118
groups
effectiveness of, 16–17
focus, 36–37
work, _xiv–xv,_ 117–118, 156
growth, effects of, 8

Hackman, Richard, on groups, 16–17
Harris Interactive, 200
Hewlett-Packard (HP), 27, 28, 78
high-priority issues, determination of, 56–57
HP, _see_ Hewlett-Packard
human resources (HR), 4, 64, 94, 168

implementation, 253–270
assimilating into the organization as component of, 264–269

checklist for, 270
definition of, 253
managing skepticism as component of, 261–264
planning as component of, 254–261
implementation teams, 119–120
implementing the New Design phase, 12
incentive plans, 206–207
information technology (IT), 144–146, 150
integration, in reconfigurable organizations, 6
integrative roles, 165–169, 168–169
interfaces, 86–88, 126–127
Internet, 167
interviews, 36, 231
issue teams, 156
IT, _see_ information technology

job rotation, 249
Jobs, Steve, 143
Johnson Controls, 73
Johnson & Johnson, 27, 200

knowledge-based pay, 207
knowledge management, 5, 167
knowledge sharing, 65

lateral capability, 4, 134–188
advantages of building, 139–140
case study involving, 134–135, 174, 176
and decision making, 140–141
definition of, 136
integrating mechanisms for building, 175, 186–188
integrative roles as type of, 165–169
lateral processes as type of, 151–156, 182–183
matrix structures as type of, 169–174
need for, 138–139
networks as type of, 141–151, 179–181
potential challenges to building, 140
teams as type of, 156–165, 184–185
tool for building, 186–188
lateral processes, 151–156, 182–183
leader(s), _xiv_
and governance structure, 116
managers vs., 1
leadership
and organizational roles, 90–93

leadership (*continued*)
    in reconfigurable organizations, 5
    styles of, 162
leadership teams, *xiv,* 116–117
learning
    in reconfigurable organizations, 6
    training vs., 249, 250
learning aptitude, 238, 241–245
legal issues, 233
limits, 30–32, 53
long-term incentive plans, 206–207
LotusNotes, 150

management
    as lateral process, 152
    layers of, 90–91
manager(s)
    expanded roles for, 165–166, 246
    leaders vs., 1
    new, 8
mapping (of structure), 99–100
Marriott, 72, 73
matrix structures, 169–174
    managing in, 172–174
    relationships in, 169–172
Matsushita, 27
McDonald's, 27, 149
meeting rooms, tools for, 145
meetings
    annual, 147–148
    off-site, 102, 106–112, 131–132
mentors, 268–269
MetLife, 26
metrics, 191–199
    alignment of, 198
    breadth of, 192–195
    consequences of, 197–198
    criticality of, 195–196
    targets for, 198–199
    time orientation of, 196–197
    tool for assessment of, 221
Microsoft Exchange, 150
Mies van der Rohe, Ludwig, 23
modeling, of new relationships, 14
momentum, sustaining, 259–260
money, as reward, 215–217

multiple bosses, 246

networks, 141–151
    and annual meetings/retreats, 147–148
    and co-location, 143–145
    and communities of practice, 145–147
    fostering of, 142–143
    importance of, 142
    and rotational assignments, 148–150
    and technology, 150
    tool for building, 179–181
    and training programs, 148

off-site meetings, 102, 106–112, 131–132
operations, as lateral process, 152
operations-focused companies, 27
Oracle, 242
organizational capabilities, 25
organizational structure, *see* structure(s)
organization design
    assessing reasons for changing, 20
    components of, 2–3
    definition of, 2
    framework for, *see* framework, design
    participative approach to, 12–17
    people practices as element of, 4
    process as element of, 3–4
    process of, 9–12
    responsibility for, 1
    reward system as element of, 4
    strategy as element of, 3
    structure as element of, 3
    triggers for, 8–9
organization(s)
    changes within, 9
    definition of, *xi*
    reconfigurable, 4–8
    size of, 78–79
outcomes, 84–86
overall contribution, recognition/rewards for, 215
overlay structures, 62

pacing, 254–256
PalmPilot, 26–27
Panasonic, 27

participation, 12–17
    benefits of, 14
    conditions for successful, 15–17
    forms of, 13–14
    inappropriate, 14–15
    levels of, 13
    tools for determining need for, 21
past performance reviews, 231
pay for performance, 205–207
peer evaluation, 247
people management, as lateral process, 152
people practice(s), 227–252
    assessment of learning aptitude as, 238,
        241–245
    case study involving, 233–240
    integrated model of, 228–229
    and learning, 249, 250
    performance feedback as, 245–249
    staffing of new organization as, 230–233
PeopleSoft, 242
performance categories (balanced scorecard),
        193
performance feedback, 245–249
performance incentives, 209
performance indicators (balanced scorecard),
        194–195
performance problems, 9
piloting, 257
Pixar, 143
planning (for implementation), 254–261
    communicating as component of, 257–259
    feedback as component of, 260–261
    pacing as component of, 254–256
    piloting as component of, 257
    sequencing as component of, 256–257
    sustaining momentum as component of,
        259–260
power relationships, 60, 93–95, 262–264
PriceWaterhouseCoopers, ix, 28
process, 3–4, see also design process
process managers, 118–119
product development cycle, 70
product-focused companies, 26–27
product structure, 69–72
project management, 167

qualitative surveys, 37
quantitative surveys, 37

recognition
    design approach to, 217–219
    dimensions of, 213–215
    meaningfulness of, 215–217
    rewards vs., 212–213
    see also rewards/reward systems
reconfigurable organizations, 4–8, 18–19
recruitment, 233
relationships, and customer structure, 73–74
representatives, 15, 16
representative sampling, 33, 34
responsibilities, 84–86, 128
retreats, annual, 147–148
rewards/reward systems, 4, 189–226
    allocation of, 210
    compensation as component of, 202–212,
        225
    and definition of success, 189, 190
    desired values/behaviors as component of,
        199–202, 222–224
    meaningfulness of, 215–217
    metrics as component of, 191–199, 221
    reward/recognition programs as component
        of, 212–219, 226
    tool for assessment of, 226
risk management, as lateral process, 152
roles, organizational, 81–93
    alignment of, 83–84
    case study involving, 100–110, 112–114
    clarification of, 87, 89–90, 128
    definition of, 81
    and functional perspectives, 83
    identifying/defining, 84–86, 124–125
    interface between, 86–88, 126–127
    and leadership, 90–93
    levels of, 82–83
    off-site meeting for determining, 102, 106–
        112, 131–132
rotational assignments, 148–150

SAP, 242
Saturn (automobile), 8
Selectron, 27
sequencing, 256–257
Shell Oil, 149–150
size, organizational, 78–79

skepticism, managing, 261–264
skill-based pay, 207–208, 209
social time, structured, 147–148
Sony, 27
span of control, 91
special achievement, recognition/rewards for, 215
specialization, 65
sponsors, 115, 116
staffing, 230–233
standardization, 65
star model, 2–3
start-ups, 8
steering committees, 118
strategic focus, confirmation of, 49–50
strategy, 3, 8–9
structure(s), 3, 58–133
    assessment of current, 121–122
    "best," 60
    case study involving, 58–59, 80, 81
    complexity of, 97–98
    customer, 72–74
    definition of, 60
    and design criteria, 93
    design of new, 123
    and distribution channels, 96–97
    and flow of work, 96
    front-back hybrid, 74–79
    functional, 63–67
    geographic, 67–69
    governance, 114–120, 133
    mapping of, 99–100
    matrix, 169–174
    and organizational culture, 98–99
    and organizational roles, 81–93
    overlay, 62
    and power relationships, 60, 93–95
    product, 69–72
    and size of the organization, 78–79
    steps for determination of, 60
    and testing of design, 93–99, 129–130
success
    defining, 189, 190
    identifying indicators of, 25–26, 47–48
    of teams, 160, 162
surveys, 37

team evaluation systems, 247
team(s), 156–165
    assessing readiness of, 184–185
    cross-business, 156–158
    executive, xiv, 92–93, 116, 232, 259
    implementation, 119–120
    issue, 156
    leadership, xiv, 116–117
    management of, 160, 161
    rewarding of, 209–210
    success of, 160, 162
    types of, 158–160
    work groups as, 156
technology, as lateral process, 152
telecommunications companies, 27
Tennyson, Alfred Lord, on loving, 211
testing (of design), 93–99, 129–130
Textron, 167
360° feedback, 248–249
time constraints, 139–140
total compensation, 203–204
training
    learning vs., 249, 250
    and networking, 148
Tylenol, 200

UNOPS, 100–110, 112–114
UPS, 200
upward feedback, 248–249

value proposition, 26–30
value(s)
    added, 76
    and recognition, 213
    and rewards, 199–202
variable compensation, 204–205
vendors, leverage with, 65
vision, 199
vision storytelling, 200–201, 222–224

Web sites, 196–197
work groups, xiv–xv, 117–118, 156
World Bank, 147

Xerox, 146